# Understanding Patent Law:
# A Beginner's Guide

*by*

**Linda A. Tancs**

Oceana's Legal Almanac Series:
*Law for the Layperson*

**Oceana**®
NEW YORK

# OXFORD

## UNIVERSITY PRESS

*Oxford University Press, Inc., publishes works that further Oxford University's objective of excellence in research, scholarship, and education.*

Copyright © 2010 by Linda A. Tancs
Published by Oxford University Press, Inc.
198 Madison Avenue, New York, New York 10016

Library of Congress Cataloging-in-Publication Data

Tancs, Linda A.
  Understanding patent law : a beginner's guide / by Linda A. Tancs.
    p. cm. — (Oceana's legal almanac series : law for the layperson)
  Includes bibliographical references.
  ISBN 978-0-19-973023-0 ((hardback) : alk. paper)
  1. Patent laws and legislation—United States.  I. Title.
  KF3114.85.T36 2010
  346.7304'86—dc22                                            2010000390

**Note to Readers:**
This publication is designed to provide accurate and authoritative information in regard to the subject matter covered. It is based upon sources believed to be accurate and reliable and is intended to be current as of the time it was written. It is sold with the understanding that the publisher is not engaged in rendering legal, accounting, or other professional services. If legal advice or other expert assistance is required, the services of a competent professional person should be sought. Also, to confirm that the information has not been affected or changed by recent developments, traditional legal research techniques should be used, including checking primary sources where appropriate.

*(Based on the Declaration of Principles jointly adopted by a Committee of the American Bar Association and a Committee of Publishers and Associations.)*

You may order this or any other Oxford University Press publication by visiting the Oxford University Press website at www.oup.com

For my father Tibor, the consummate inventor

-and-

In gratitude to my husband Barry for his constant
support and encouragement

# Table of Contents

CHAPTER 3:
INTERNATIONAL CONSIDERATIONS

# ABOUT THE AUTHOR

**LINDA A. TANCS** has extensive experience as a transactional attorney in both corporate and private practice, concentrating in intellectual property, entertainment, information technology, e-commerce and general business matters. Ms. Tancs holds a Juris Doctor degree, with honors, from Seton Hall University School of Law in Newark, New Jersey. She is admitted to practice in several jurisdictions in the United States as well as internationally.

Ms. Tancs managed the worldwide trademark portfolio of leading industrial and consumer products companies and regularly counseled in-house attorneys, executives and small business owners on all aspects of intellectual property acquisition and enforcement. She won first place for a meritorious paper on copyright law submitted in ASCAP's Nathan Burkan Memorial Competition at Seton Hall Law School. Ms. Tancs is the author of *Understanding Trademark Law: A Beginner's Guide*, and *Understanding Copyright Law: A Beginner's Guide*, other legal almanacs in the series.

Ms. Tancs has held leadership positions in bar associations, taught legal courses at two colleges and has authored several articles for legal periodicals and general interest magazines. She operates her own consulting practice in the field of brand identification and management and offers dispute resolution services in the nature of mediation for complex commercial matters, including intellectual property disputes. She is also certified as a coach in the fields of personal, executive and organizational coaching by New York University and works with both lawyers and nonlawyers to meet their personal and professional goals.

# INTRODUCTION

This text explores the mechanics of the patent application process. A patent is a limited monopoly granted to a patent owner, allowing the owner to exclude others from making, using, offering for sale, selling or importing the invention covered by the patent for a period of time. An inventor seeking patent protection in the U.S. must file an application with the United States Patent and Trademark Office (PTO). In fiscal year 2008, the PTO received 456,321 utility patent applications. Patent protection can be obtained under the laws of many other nations as well. This book will emphasize the process for filing a utility patent application with the PTO.

The reader will be introduced to the nature and function of intellectual property law as it relates to patents. Intellectual property law is an evolving body of law that seeks to create a fair balance between the privilege to enter markets and compete and the privilege to realize the full value of one's own goods and services without unfair competition. Through this book, the reader will gain an understanding of: the types of property that may be patented; how to protect and use patented property; how to complete a patent application; pre- and post-issuance procedures; how to monetize patents; and infringement issues.

The appendices, together with the bibliography and recommended reading, provide readers of this Almanac with relevant statutes and other information to further the reader's knowledge of the matters discussed in this book. The glossary contains a summary of key terms defined throughout the book.

The information presented in this book is intended for general information purposes only and does not constitute the provision of legal services or advice. If such services or advice are required, the assistance of an appropriate professional should be sought.

# CHAPTER 1:
# THE NATURE AND FUNCTION
# OF A PATENT

## THE HISTORY OF PATENTS

Article 1, Section 8, Clause 8 of the United States Constitution authorizes Congress to "secur(e) for limited Times to . . . Inventors . . . the exclusive Right to their . . . Discoveries." Pursuant to its constitutional authority, Congress passed the first patent law in 1790, a simple act of no more than seven sections granting a limited monopoly of 14 years to the claims of an invention deemed a useful art and providing for remedies in the event of infringement. Since then, federal patent law has undergone many revisions, including an increase in the term for patent protection. In particular, the patent act was significantly amended in 1952, including providing a framework for patentability requiring a showing of novelty, utility and nonobviousness (to be discussed further below in the section entitled **What is a Patent?**). The 1952 act (effective as of January 1, 1953) is codified in title 35 of the United States Code, which provides the law governing patents (the Patent Act). Another material amendment to the Patent Act occurred in 1999 with the enactment of the American Inventors Protection Act. Among its significant provisions, this amendment provided for the publication of certain United States patent applications following a term of secrecy and set forth a public forum for complaints against invention promotion companies.

This Almanac will focus on the provisions of the Patent Act in effect as of this writing, and section references provided in this book will relate to that act unless otherwise specified.

Appendix 1 provides the text of the original patent law enacted in 1790.

Appendix 2 provides excerpts from the American Inventors Protection Act of 1999.

**WHAT IS A PATENT?**

A patent can be defined both in terms of its function and its nature. A patent functions as a property right, giving its owner the right for a term of years to *exclude* others from commercializing the patented invention throughout the United States. This principle of exclusion, found in section 154 of the Patent Act, expressly grants the patent holder (also known as the patentee) the right to exclude others from making, using, offering for sale, or selling the invention or importing it into the United States. Notably, the holder of a patent right does not possess an affirmative right to manufacture, use or sell its own invention. In fact, a common misconception regarding patent ownership is that a patentee acquires the absolute right to commercialize its own invention. Many considerations, however, underlie the need for statutory language lacking an affirmative right. For instance, chapter 18 of the Patent Act provides for the potential disposition of patent rights for inventions secured with federal assistance. In other instances, a state or federal law (particularly those addressing public health or safety) may preclude a patentee from using an invention in the field of interest governing its application. Also, in some cases a new and useful improvement of an existing process or article (although found patentable on its face) may violate the rights of the holder of a patent on the original process or article or perhaps violate the rights of some other party. Such earlier rights are likely to be uncovered during a freedom to operate search conducted prior to product launch (or sooner). This and other searches related to patents are discussed further in chapter 2 in the section entitled **Conducting Patent Searches**.

A patent is also definable by its nature—that is, to be patentable, an invention must possess the characteristics of usefulness, novelty and nonobviousness. The requirement that an invention or discovery be useful is specifically delineated in section 101 of the Patent Act. Moreover, according to United States Supreme Court decisions, a useful invention is one with a specific and substantial utility. Also, usefulness has been deemed to include a requirement that the invention perform in accordance with its intended purpose. Inherent in this requirement is that the invention be capable of being reduced to practice; in other words, it must be sufficiently described to allow one who is skilled in the art of the invention to practice it.

The requirement of novelty has its origins in both sections 101 and 102 of the Patent Act. A novel invention is one that is new; hence, section 101 provides that, subject to certain conditions (particularly those set out in section 102), an invention that is new is patentable. Section 102 provides examples of scenarios that will defeat a claim of novelty, thereby impairing patentability. For example, section 102(a) provides that an invention is not novel if it has been patented or described in a publication anywhere in the world or known or used by others in the United States. Section 102(e) further provides that an invention is not novel if it has been described in a pending patent application that has been published. Publication of pending applications will be discussed further in chapter 2 in the section entitled **Publication**. Another event defeating novelty is found in section 102(g), which provides that a senior inventor is entitled to a patent over the first person to file an application covering the invention, provided that the senior inventor exercised reasonable diligence to perfect the invention. This statutory provision embraces the principle in the United States that the first to invent is entitled to priority over the first to file, unlike other nations where a first-to-file system is in place. However, under various legislative proposals (most recently the Patent Reform Act of 2009), U.S. patent law would be harmonized with foreign patent practice by amending the current law to provide for a first-to-file patent system. The procedure in the United States for resolving a dispute among a senior inventor and a junior filer is known as an interference proceeding, which will be discussed in chapter 2 in the section entitled **Interferences**.

In addition to the utility and novelty requirements for patentability, the nonobviousness requirement means that an obvious invention cannot be patented—in other words, some level of inventiveness must exist with respect to the claimed patentable matter. According to section 103 of the Patent Act, if the claimed subject matter of the patent would be "obvious" to a hypothetical person "having ordinary skill in the art" related to the patent when compared with the prior art, then the invention is not patentable. Prior art refers to any information related to the field or scope of an invention that has been previously disclosed to the public, including issued patents and publications. A person having ordinary skill in the art (popularly referred to by the acronym PHOSITA), is one having average skills and knowledge in a certain technical field.

Over many years, the test established by the courts for determining nonobviousness required a showing whether a teaching, suggestion or motivation to combine the teachings in the prior art can be found in the prior art, the nature of the problem, or in the knowledge of one skilled in the art. The courts' reliance on this test, known as the TSM test, was challenged in 2007 in a significant United States Supreme Court decision, *KSR Int'l Co. v. Teleflex, Inc.* In this decision, the Court declared that the TSM test is only one means of inquiry in determining nonobviousness. Notwithstanding the elements of that test, the Court stated that an invention that combines known prior art elements in a familiar manner or one that is obvious to try is likely to be obvious and unpatentable. Conversely, an invention combining familiar prior art elements in a manner that is fruitful and that leads to unexpected results would likely be nonobvious and therefore capable of being patentable. As a result of this case, patent examiners must routinely consider whether known work in one field may prompt predictable variations of it in the same or different field from the perspective of one skilled in the art.

Even if an invention meets the tests of being new, useful and nonobvious, it must not be barred from patentability under any of the exclusionary scenarios set out in section 102 of the Patent Act in subsections (b), (c), or (d). These scenarios, each referred to as a statutory bar against patentability, refer to events occurring after the invention has taken place but before the filing of an application. Under subsection (b), an inventor will be precluded from obtaining a patent on an invention that: (i) has already been patented somewhere in the world more than one year before the present application; or (ii) has been described or disclosed in a publication more than one year before the present application; or (iii) is in public use or on sale for more than one year before the present application. Similarly, subsection (d) precludes an inventor from obtaining a patent in the United States on an invention subject to foreign rights if those rights were acquired more than 12 months before the filing of a U.S. application. The effect of subsections (b) and (d) is to provide inventors with a one-year grace period in which to file an application after disclosing the invention in some manner. Finally, subsection (c) provides that a patent will not issue for an invention that has been abandoned.

Given the high standard of scrutiny accorded inventions as set forth above, not all works are capable of patent protection in the first instance. Unpatentable subject matter includes printed material such as a business form, products of nature (i.e., a naturally occurring substance), natural phenomena, and a mere idea or suggestion. As to the latter point, although ideas form the basis of patent protection, the idea or suggestion underlying an invention must be sufficiently described to allow one who is skilled in the art of the invention to practice it.

Provided an invention is eligible for protection and the patentability requirements are met, several kinds of articles qualify for protection under federal law. These articles include designs, certain plants, and inventions encompassing a process, machine, manufacture, composition of matter or any improvement of the foregoing. The word *process* is defined in section 100 as a process, act or method, including industrial or technical processes. The term *composition of matter* relates to chemical compositions and may include mixtures of ingredients as well as new chemical compounds.

Appendix 3 contains definitions and conditions for patentability.

## NOTICE OF PATENT

Section 287(a) of the Patent Act provides a patentee with the option of placing a notice of patent on an invention for which a patent has issued, providing constructive notice of patent rights to potential infringers. Such a notice consists of the use of the word *Patent* or the abbreviation *Pat.,* together with the number of the patent as issued by the PTO. The notice should be placed on the invention (if practicable) or on its packaging. Notwithstanding the optional nature of this provision (known as the patent marking statute), most patentees elect to put a patent notice on their works. This is not surprising, considering that the failure to provide the notice can result in economic harm to the patentee seeking redress for infringement. In fact, the statute provides that the patentee may not recover damages from an infringer unless the infringer was duly notified of the infringement and continued to infringe after the notice. Therefore, a later placed notice will preclude the collection of damages for events taking place prior to the notice.

Sometimes a form of notice, such as "Patent Pending," is used in conjunction with an invention. This notice merely indicates that a patent application has been filed in connection with one or more of the features of the invention. Such an advisory may deter activity that could be potentially infringing should a third party believe that a patent may ultimately issue. In no event, however, should a patent applicant use the word *Patent* to imply that a patent has been granted, nor should the notice "Patent Pending" or "Patent Applied For" be used when an application has not been filed. Under section 292, such markings are fraudulent and susceptible to fines.

Appendix 4 contains the notice requirements and penalties set out in sections 287 and 292 of the Patent Act.

## DURATION OF PATENTS

Patent duration is measured from the date of the patent's grant, or issuance. Once the patent term expires, the invention is available to everyone. For utility and plant patent applications filed after June 8, 1995, patents are granted for a term beginning with the date of the grant and ending 20 years from the date of filing, provided that the applicable maintenance fees in the case of utility patents (to be discussed further in chapter 2 in the section entitled **Maintenance**) are paid over the life of the patent. Design patents, on the other hand, are valid for a term of 14 years from the date of the grant and, like plant patents, are not subject to maintenance fees. Utility, plant and design patents will be discussed in more detail in chapter 2 in the section entitled **Types of Patent Applications Generally**.

Notwithstanding the basic patent terms for utility and plant patents, patents in force on June 8, 1995 and patents issued thereafter on applications filed prior to June 8, 1995 automatically have a term that is the greater of the 20-year term discussed above or 17 years from the patent grant. The patent term was amended in 1995 as a result of U.S. adherence to the World Trade Organization's Agreement on Trade-Related Aspects of Intellectual Property Rights (TRIPS), which provides that the term of protection available for patents shall not end before the expiration of a period of 20 years counted from the filing date. TRIPS and other international aspects of patents will be discussed further in chapter 3.

In some cases, patents may be issued for terms longer than 20 years. For instance, section 155 provides for the extension of patent terms for pharmaceuticals subject to Food and Drug Administration regulatory approval before commercialization, a process that can easily encompass most of the patent term. Section 154(b) also lists a series of events that may lead to patent term extension or adjustment. Specifically, utility and plant patents which issue from original applications filed between June 8, 1995 and May 28, 2000 may be eligible for patent term extension as a result of delays due to interference proceedings, secrecy orders, or successful appellate review. In addition to the above events, patents based on applications filed on or after May 29, 2000 may be eligible for patent term adjustment based on the failure of the PTO to take certain actions within 14 months following the filing of an application, such as the transmittal of a notice of rejection or other communication related to the application, or the failure of the PTO to issue a patent within three years of the actual filing date of the application. Any term adjustment will be reduced by the time period during which an applicant failed to engage in reasonable efforts to conclude prosecution of the application. An exhaustive list of activities constituting failure to engage in reasonable efforts to conclude prosecution of an application is set forth in the Code of Federal Regulations (CFR), the federal rules implementing patent practice and procedure.

Appendix 5 sets out the statutory provisions concerning duration of patents and pertinent regulations in the CFR.

## PATENTS AND TRADE SECRETS

A trade secret is, as the name implies, business information that is secret—that is, it is not generally known to the public, thereby giving its owner a competitive advantage. An example of a trade secret is the formula for Coca-Cola® beverages, which has never been patented. Unlike patents, trade secrets have no specific duration after which they are dedicated to public use. Instead, a trade secret may be preserved in perpetuity so long as the information is kept secret and remains economically valuable to its owner. Furthermore, unlike patents, trade secrets are defined by state law; therefore, the basic elements of what constitutes a trade secret will vary from state to state. In an effort to conform the laws of various states related to trade secrets, a model law known as the Uniform Trade Secrets Act (UTSA) was crafted by a panel of legal professionals and scholars; a majority of the states has adopted its provisions in determining trade secret rights.

Given the possibility that a formula, device, or process may not meet the threshold of patentability, trade secret protection is often employed as an alternative means of maintaining property rights over valuable information. Conversely, a highly patentable system may have greater value to its owner if maintained perpetually as a trade secret by keeping certain safeguards in place, such as by imposing confidentiality obligations on those with a need to know the secret information. Of course, at times trade secrets are misappropriated by employees, former employees, or others. Similar to patent infringement cases, an aggrieved trade secret owner may seek an injunction against the offending party or pursue damages. The misappropriation of trade secrets may also be a criminal offense under state law. Furthermore, with the enactment of the Economic Espionage Act of 1996, trade secret theft is brought under the ambit of federal law, imposing severe criminal penalties for the unlawful appropriation of confidential business information by either a foreign or domestic entity.

Appendix 6 contains the text of the Uniform Trade Secrets Act as well as a list of states that have adopted its terms.

Appendix 7 contains the text of the Economic Espionage Act of 1996.

# CHAPTER 2:
# THE APPLICATION PROCESS

## ABOUT THE UNITED STATES PATENT AND TRADEMARK OFFICE

As indicated in the introduction to this Almanac, inventors seeking protection under the Patent Act for their inventions must file a patent application with the PTO. The PTO, established over 200 years ago, is an agency of the United States Department of Commerce located in Alexandria, Virginia. Its staff examines applications for both patents and trademarks. Among its activities, the PTO administers the federal laws governing trademarks and patents and advises the Secretary of Commerce, the President, and the administration on intellectual property protection and trade.

## TYPES OF PATENT APPLICATIONS GENERALLY

In the first instance, a patent claimant must decide upon two things: (i) the nature of the patent application to be filed; and (ii) if permitted, whether the application will be provisional or nonprovisional. The Patent Act provides for three types of patents: plant, design, and utility patents. Plant patents are addressed in section 161 of the Patent Act, which provides for the patentability of a new and distinct variety of an asexually reproducing plant. Section 161 further states that the basic conditions for patentability (e.g., novelty and nonobviousness) equally apply to plant patents. However, the plant patent provisions set forth an additional requirement of distinctness. The legislative history pertaining to the plant patent statute specifies that a plant may be distinct in terms of such characteristics as its form, color, odor, soil conditions, immunity, productivity, storability, or flavor. Moreover, similar to a patent grant for a process or machine, a plant patent gives the patentee the right to exclude others from commercializing the invention—that is, from asexually reproducing the plant and from using, offering for sale, selling, or importing the reproduced plant, or any of its parts, throughout the United States. Notably, the statute does not provide patent protection for sexually reproduced plants (i.e., those grown from seeds). Patent-like protection for those plant products is provided by the Plant Variety Protection Act of 1970. Similar to plant patents, inventions subject to design patents must be novel and nonobvious. In addition, section 171 covering design patents requires that the invention be ornamental; in other words, patentability of the article lies in its unique appearance rather than in its functionality.

A utility patent generally covers inventions related to a process, machine, manufacture, composition of matter, or any improvement of the foregoing. Of all the types of utility patents, a species of process patent known as the business method has gained widespread attention since a landmark case in 1998 known as *State Street Bank & Trust Co. v. Signature Financial Group, Inc.* In that case, an appellate court declared that the business method at issue—an aspect of running a business—is patentable so long as the method produces a useful result. As a result of this decision, methodologies of varying nature such as online dating services, cash management account systems, airline seat upgrades, home shopping through the Internet, and a method for lifting a box have been patented. However, amid the explosion of business method patent grants in industries as diverse as information technology, financial services, and sales and marketing, the fate of this species of patent is imperiled as a result of a current appellate case known as *In re Bilski,* which held that a business method comprising a process for anticipating risk in commodities trading was not patentable because it was not tied to a machine or transformative beyond the manipulation of an abstract idea. As a result of this decision, the earlier patentability for such a process under the *State Street* decision was invalidated. As of this writing, the U.S. Supreme Court will review *In re Bilski* in the coming months, the outcome of which could affect an entire class of process patents.

In addition to the nature of the application, in some instances an applicant may elect to file a preliminary application to secure an early filing date and thereby preserve rights in an invention, particularly if an inventor is pursuing further research and development to determine the invention's potential for commercialization. Such an application, in force since June 8, 1995, is known as a provisional patent application (PPA). The PPA system was preceded by the PTO's Disclosure Document Program, which remained in force from 1969 until February 1, 2007. Similar to the PPA system, the Disclosure Document Program provided inventors with the opportunity to file basic initial evidence of an invention to establish its conception without the need to file claims. The program did not, however, provide a filing date for any such submission; instead, it merely provided inventors with evidence of conception prior to a filing date. With the enactment of the PPA system and its benefits as to a priority filing date pending the subsequent filing of a nonprovisional application, the usefulness of the Disclosure Document Program was largely superseded.

Both plant and utility applications may be filed provisionally; design patent applications are not allowed on a provisional basis. Unlike a nonprovisional application, a PPA need not include information disclosures in the nature of prior art, a claim, or an inventor's oath or declaration (all of which will be discussed in greater detail below). However, a properly completed PPA must include the filing fee and a cover sheet that (i) identifies the submission as provisional and includes information related to the inventors and a correspondence address; (ii) states the title of the invention; and (iii) attaches a full written description of the invention and any drawings necessary to understand it. Submissions received without a full description of the invention and necessary drawings will be denied a filing date. As the purpose of a PPA is to eliminate the lengthier requirements of a nonprovisional application so that inventors can obtain early filing dates, careful observance of the filing requirements for a PPA is paramount.

A properly filed PPA will remain in effect for 12 months following its filing date, and applicants are entitled to use the phrase "Patent Pending" even though a PPA is not reviewed on the merits by an examiner at the PTO. Prior to its expiration, a nonprovisional application disclosing the same invention must be filed so that the applicant retains the priority of the filing date accorded to the PPA. A PPA that is not converted to a nonprovisional application during the 12-month pendency period cannot be revived.

Appendix 8 contains the statutory references regarding plant and design patents.

Appendix 9 contains a sample data transmittal sheet for a nonprovisional plant patent application.

Appendix 10 contains a sample data transmittal sheet for a design patent application.

Appendix 11 contains statutory and regulatory references to the provisional application process.

Appendix 12 contains a sample cover sheet for a provisional utility application.

## CONDUCTING PATENT SEARCHES

Before submitting a patent application to the PTO, applicants generally undertake a search (independently or through the use of a firm specializing in patent searches) to determine the scope of protection that is likely to be afforded an invention. For example, a search may yield information relative to one or more aspects of the claimed invention that may be subject to challenge by the holder of a patent on an earlier, broader invention. Patent searches may likewise be initiated at other points in the patenting process, such as after issuance of a patent but prior to product launch. In any case, a diligent search serves two important purposes: (i) it provides the applicant with critical information to make an informed investment decision on the commercial viability and defensibility of the claimed invention; and (ii) it facilitates the patent candidate's duty of disclosure to the PTO. As to the latter point, section 1.56 of the CFR sets forth the applicant's duty to disclose information material to patentability. Among other things, the rule makes clear that the duty is a continuing one and does not end with the filing of an application. Therefore, any material (such as prior art found during a search) coming to the attention of an applicant that may affect the patentability of the invention in whole or in part must be yielded to the PTO for examination. This duty of candor and good faith in dealing with the PTO likewise extends to the applicant's attorneys, agents, and assigns. Depending on the needs of the patent applicant, a search may be initiated on one or more of the following issues: (i) patentability; (ii) infringement; (iii) validity; or (iv) freedom to operate. Each of these search types will be discussed below.

### The Patentability Search

A patentability search (also called a novelty or prior art search) is conducted at the earliest instance in the life of an invention to determine whether its scope is taught by the prior art. In other words, the search determines the invention's novelty or nonobviousness. If such a search is conducted by a third party, then a brief invention disclosure is made to the searching firm or agent for purposes of searching all issued and published U.S. and foreign patents within the subject area, both unexpired and expired, together with non-patent literature. A disclosure should be adequate enough to provide the searcher with a sense of the patent classifications that need to be searched to uncover relevant prior art. Patent classifications can be accessed at http://www.uspto.gov/web/patents/classification. Depending on the technology, a searcher may review the claims of patents as well. The results of a patentability search will usually be provided in the form of a search report enclosing documentation of central or peripheral interest, together with an explanation of the patent classification areas searched.

### The Infringement Search

Unlike a patentability search, an infringement search is conducted by focusing on the patent's claims. Those claims are analyzed in relation to all unexpired (in-force) patents, and a determination is then made whether the invention infringes one or more other patents. Like a patentability search, an infringement search can be useful in the early stages of the patenting process, particularly in determining whether the patent claims can or have been properly designed around potentially problematic claims.

### The Validity Search

Similar to an infringement search, a validity search focuses on claims. However, the claims being searched are those relating to a patent sought to be invalidated. Therefore, patents, technical publications, and/or any other available written materials that may be relevant to the patented invention are searched and analyzed to determine whether the patent should have issued in the first place. A validity study may therefore assist in averting infringement claims or mitigating damages as discussed in Chapter 5 in the section entitled **Defenses**.

### The Freedom to Operate Search

As the term implies, a freedom to operate search is undertaken to determine whether an inventor or a designee will ultimately have the right to use an invention. As indicated in Chapter 1, an issued patent only gives the patentee the right to exclude others from commercializing the invention. A freedom to operate search, therefore, may provide an inventor with more detail whether the invention can be actually marketed without fear of infringing an earlier patent. For this reason, such a search is typically conducted prior to the launch of a product. In addition to reviewing claims of unexpired patents, the parameters of this search also include data on expired patents to better understand what matter has already been dedicated to the public domain for anyone's use.

## SEARCH FACILITIES

### Patent and Trademark Depository Libraries

Throughout the United States qualified libraries serving as Patent and Trademark Depository Libraries (PTDLs) house patent collections. A list of libraries and other information related to the PTDL system can be found at http://www.uspto.gov/web/offices/ac/ido/ptdl/ index.html.

### Public Search Facility

The public records room of the PTO contains data on patents from 1790 to the current week of issue in a variety of media, such as microfilm, print, and online access using the PTO's full text and image database. These records also include patent assignments. The facility is open to the public on weekdays (excluding public holidays) and is located at 600 Dulany Street, Alexandria, Virginia 22314.

### Electronic Searching

In addition to local and national reference libraries, electronic resources provide remote access for searches. For example, once a U.S. patent application has been published, bibliographic data is available to the public on the PTO's Patent Application Information Retrieval System (PAIR), located at http://portal.uspto.gov/external/portal/pair; copies of documentation can be ordered on payment of the applicable fee. Published applications or issued patents may be searched via PAIR under various control numbers assigned to an application by the PTO, such as its application number, patent number, publication number, or an international number for international, or PCT, applications. PCT applications will be discussed in greater detail in Chapter 3 in the section entitled **Patent Cooperation Treaty**. Another version of PAIR, known as private PAIR, is available to those who have filed patent applications and wish to check the ongoing status of an application. Access to private PAIR is limited to a registered patent attorney or agent, an inventor, or a person granted limited recognition who possesses a customer number and a digital certificate to secure the transmission of an application to the PTO. Customer numbers and digital certificates will be discussed in more detail in the section below entitled **A General Overview of the Patent Application Process.** In addition to U.S. patent data, the PTO also provides links to foreign databases of high interest to filers. In particular, the European patent database can be accessed at http://ep.espacenet.com.

### Professional Services

Because it could be quite timely for a filer to conduct any or all of the above searches, applicants often rely on companies specializing in the production of search reports to compile the data set forth above or engage the services of an attorney to compile or analyze the information. Typically, an attorney will offer a prospective applicant a written legal opinion whether the matter uncovered during a search is valid or enforceable against the desired patent and address such other matters as may be required depending on the nature of the search conducted.

## DOCUMENTING AN INVENTION

In many cases, an inventor may opt to document work that is potentially patentable or may be directed to do so by an employer. Such recording of an invention is often embodied in what is commonly referred to as an inventor's notebook. In the event of a challenge regarding the timing or nature of the conception of an invention (particularly with respect to an interference proceeding), a comprehensively compiled notebook may have tremendous evidentiary value. Therefore, it should be kept in a safe place. Although there are no specific rules or requirements regarding notebooks, the best notebook is one that records all concepts, experiments, results, drawings, and other information related to the invention both consistently and concisely. For example, inventors should number each page of the notebook consecutively and ensure that no pages are removed. Another guideline is to document all dates related to the invention—from its conception to reduction to practice (e.g., the making of a prototype)—because dates illustrate diligence in the pursuit of the invention. Also, all drawings should be numbered, and any corollary documents should be pasted whenever possible into the notebook under the appropriate date. Under no circumstances should material be erased; any errors should be corrected by striking a line through the material and initialing any changes. Furthermore, the inventor's signature should accompany each dated entry. With respect to material evidencing how to make and use the invention and the best mode of practicing it, these entries should also be witnessed by the signature of two non-inventors having no interest in the outcome of the invention. Finally, each entry should be legible and rendered in permanent ink.

## A GENERAL OVERVIEW OF THE PATENT APPLICATION PROCESS

To obtain a patent, an inventor must file an application with the PTO that discloses a single invention in sufficiently detailed terms to permit one skilled in the art to make and use it. The inventor must also disclose the "best mode" (discussed below in the section entitled **Detailed Description of the Invention**) then contemplated for practicing the invention. Because the preparation of a patent application and the conduct of proceedings at the PTO to obtain a patent require extensive knowledge of patent law and procedure, many applicants generally retain the services of a patent attorney or patent agent. Unlike an attorney, a patent agent is not licensed to practice law but is nonetheless qualified through technical expertise to represent an inventor in the prosecution of a patent application at the PTO. Agents, however, cannot represent an applicant in litigation or in the preparation of documents unrelated to the prosecution of the application (e.g., licensing contracts) if such activity would be considered the unauthorized practice of law in the agent's jurisdiction. Both patent attorneys and agents pass a rigorous examination known as the patent bar examination to obtain credentials to represent applicants before the PTO. Representation, however, is not required; a knowledgeable applicant may successfully prosecute his or her own application. For those wishing to secure the services of a patent expert, the PTO maintains a directory of registered patent attorneys and agents at https://oedci.uspto.gov/OEDCI/.

The PTO encourages applicants to file eligible applications and subsequent documents electronically using EFS-Web, the PTO's electronic filing center, which is located at http://www.uspto.gov/ebc/index.html. The advantages of filing with EFS-Web include faster processing time given the ability to upload required subject matter for a patent application directly to the PTO, instant confirmation of filings, and the ability to retrieve information within hours using private PAIR. However, as noted above, new users desiring private PAIR capabilities must first become registered e-filers by obtaining a customer number and a digital certificate; a guide to becoming a registered e-filer is found at http://www.uspto.gov/ebc/portal/infocustomernumber.htm. Unregistered filers will not have access to private PAIR but may still file electronically. Among other things, EFS-Web accepts applications for provisional and nonprovisional utility patents. As of this writing, a number of documents are not permitted for filing with EFS-Web, including assignments, plant patent applications, maintenance fees and papers involving matters being contested before the Board of Patent Appeals and Interferences, a tribunal within the PTO that hears appeals of adverse decisions of patent examiners and retains jurisdiction over interference proceedings. Applications and other documents outside the EFS-Web filing parameters can be mailed to the PTO.

For ease of reference, following are five general milestones in the process of applying for a patent:

1. Upon receipt by the PTO, the application will receive a filing date (if the Initial Processing Branch determines that the application contains the minimum filing requirements as discussed below in the section entitled **Elements of a Patent Application**) as well as a serial number that should be used in all correspondence with the PTO. If found in

compliance, the application is then forwarded to an examining group, where it is classified and assigned to a patent examiner in the appropriate Technology Center; a list of Technology Centers is located at http://www. uspto.gov/web/info/pat-tech.htm.

Applications are generally examined in order of their submission. However, in some cases applications may be examined out of order under certain conditions. For instance, applicants over the age of 65 or with health conditions may request an accelerated examination under section 1.102 of the CFR. Another method of fast-track examination exists under the PTO's new accelerated examination procedure (excluding existing reasons for acceleration under section 1.102), in effect since August 25, 2006, which provides for a goal of completing examination of a patent application within 12 months following its filing provided that the petition, corresponding application, and all corollary documents are filed via EFS-Web and further provided that the application meets the requirements of the program. The guidelines for the program are available at http://www.uspto.gov/web/patents/accelerated/ ae_guidelines_120607.doc. In either case, accelerated examination is useful for qualified applicants considering that the time between the filing of an application and the first communication with an examiner may be three years or more as of this writing.

Furthermore, under the Patent Prosecution Highway (PPH) program, an applicant receiving a ruling from a first office of filing that at least one claim in an application is patentable may request that a second office of filing fast track the examination of corresponding claims. The PTO has arrangements with many filing offices around the world in connection with the PPH program; further information is located at http:// www.uspto.gov/web/patents/pph/index.html.

Recently, the PTO has considered instituting a deferred examination procedure whereby an application will only be reviewed at the request of the applicant. Such a procedure could be beneficial to applicants seeking more time to conduct research and development concerning the viability of an invention, the results of which may prompt an inventor to move forward with an application by requesting its examination or else abandon it. As of this writing, the PTO has closed another round of public comment on the proposed procedure. Implementation of the rule will have the practical effect of producing another means of examining applications out of order and, for those applications deferred, reducing backlog in examination in the short term.

2. An examiner's review of the application for compliance with the Patent Act includes checking for compliance with formalities and

comparing the claimed subject matter with the prior art. In many instances, an examiner may reject one or more claims in the application for a number of reasons. In such a case, the examiner will then issue an official communication known as an office action (discussed later in the section entitled **Office Actions**), detailing the rejection and addressing the substantive matters which affect patentability. An office action may also contain suggestions by the examiner regarding amendments to the application.

3. Depending on the circumstances, a patent application may be published in the PTO's text and image database after 18 months. Previously, patent applications were maintained in strictest confidence until the patent issued. However, with the enactment of the American Inventors Protection Act, publication of U.S. patent applications is required for those that have also been filed abroad, thus harmonizing U.S. law with the laws of other nations that have long required publication. Under the act, publication will occur 18 months after the earliest filing date, and the applicant will receive a notice of publication from the PTO. Nonetheless, an applicant may make a request not to publish in the application data sheet accompanying an application (discussed below in the section entitled **Application Data Sheet**) based on a certification that the application has not and will not be the subject of an application filed in another country or under a multilateral international agreement requiring publication after 18 months.

4. If the claimed subject matter is found to be patentable in the first instance or any objections to it are resolved (including the successful disposition of an interference proceeding), then the application will be "allowed" and instructions will be provided to the applicant for completing the process to permit issuance of a patent. The issuance of a patent will be discussed in more detail in the section below entitled **Issuance of a Patent**.

5. All issued patents are published in the electronic edition of the PTO's *Official Gazette* for patents, known as eOG:P. A searchable database of *Gazette* entries is located at http://www.uspto.gov/web/patents/patog/. Otherwise, an annual subscription can be made for a CD-ROM version. Patents are searchable by patent number, classification, a range of classes, patent type, and patentee name or geographic location. The eOG:P also contains information on expired and reinstated patents, patents reexamined or reissued, certificates of correction, and PTO notices.

Appendix 13 contains a form for requesting accelerated examination of an application based on the petitioner's age.

Appendix 14 contains a petition to proceed with an application under the PTO's accelerated examination program.

## ELEMENTS OF A PATENT APPLICATION

This Almanac will focus on the procedure for applying via mail for a nonprovisional utility patent although the information provided herein can also be used as a general guide for filing electronically. The Patent Act and CFR address utility patent laws and regulations, respectively. Moreover, the Manual of Patent Examining Procedure (MPEP), a manual published by the PTO to guide examiners in the examination of patent applications, is instructive in addressing best practices in the filing of an application.

At a minimum, section 111 of the Patent Act provides that an initial application must consist of the following elements: (i) a specification, including a claim; (ii) drawings, when necessary; (iii) an oath or declaration; and (iv) the prescribed filing, search, and examination fees. Further, section 1.53(b) of the CFR provides that an application's filing date shall be the date on which a specification, at least one claim, and a drawing (where necessary) are submitted. Therefore, an oath or declaration and payment of the fee are not required for purposes of assigning a filing date and may be submitted at a later time on payment of an additional surcharge. Moreover, section 1.77 of the CFR provides for an arrangement of documents in a patent application in the following order: (i) a utility patent application transmittal form or a transmittal letter; (ii) a fee transmittal form and appropriate fees; (iii) application data sheet (if submitted); (iv) the specification (with at least one claim); (v) drawings (when necessary); and (vi) an executed oath or declaration.

This chapter will address the elements of an application that are required (in the order set out in section 1.77 of the CFR) as well as those that may be voluntarily made a part of the application package. The elements to be discussed, then, are as follows:

(1) the transmittal form;

(2) the fees;

(3) the application data sheet (if used);

(4) the specification;

(5) drawings, if any;

(6) an executed oath or declaration;

(7) models or specimens, if needed;

(8) a power of attorney, if required;

(9) a right of priority, if any; and

(10) a receipt for documents.

Appendix 15 sets forth statutory and regulatory provisions concerning the content and order of an application, including paper size, margins, and other structural requirements.

### The Transmittal Form

A transmittal form or letter expedites the processing of a new application with the PTO by identifying the name of the applicant, the type of application, the title of the invention, the contents of the application, and any accompanying enclosures. Applicants should be sure to include a correspondence address in whatever form of transmittal is used. As set forth in section 1.33 of the CFR, the PTO will transmit all official communications related to the application to the party indicated in the correspondence address. If the applicant chooses to retain counsel for the filing process, then the correspondence address will be the attorney's address. Moreover, each further communication with the PTO (once an application number has been assigned) should be accompanied by a transmittal form or letter. Section 1.5 of the CFR provides that such subsequent communications include at least the application number and the filing date assigned to the application. This rule is particularly important to observe in those instances wherein certain elements of an application (such as the oath or declaration and filing fees referred to above) will not be transmitted in the same package as other elements as contemplated by section 1.54 of the CFR. Communications not in compliance with the rule will be returned to the applicant where a return address is available.

Appendix 16 contains the PTO's nonprovisional utility application transmittal form.

Appendix 17 contains a transmittal form for subsequent communications with the PTO following filing.

Appendix 18 sets forth regulatory references to the filing process.

### Fees

A current fee schedule for PTO filings and methods of payment is located at http://www.uspto.gov/main/howtofees.htm. Current filing fees are also posted in section 1.16 of the CFR and section 41 of the Patent Act and are discussed in section 607 of the MPEP. At the filing stage, the fee comprises a basic filing fee, search fee, examination fee, and application size fee and is dependent upon such factors as the number of sheets of paper in the specification and drawings and the number and type of claims presented. If the applicant qualifies as a small entity pursuant to section 1.27 of the CFR (e.g., an independent inventor, a small business, or a nonprofit organization), then the filing fees are reduced by half if the small entity status is claimed and the invention is not otherwise assignable to an entity that does not qualify for the reduction, such as a non-qualifying employer of the inventor entitled to take ownership of the invention. Other post-filing fees are due for patents that are allowed for issuance. Those fees will be discussed later in this Almanac as applicable.

Appendix 19 contains the PTO's fee transmittal form.

Appendix 20 provides information on fees, including requirements for the small entity fee reduction as set out in the CFR.

### Application Data Sheet

Section 1.76 of the CFR sets out the requirements for an application data sheet, a voluntary yet useful submission made in the course of filing a patent application. If the PTO's prescribed form is not used, then any submission purporting to be an application data sheet must so state and also must contain the applicable contents using each of the following headings: (i) applicant information; (ii) correspondence information; (iii) application information; (iv) representative information; (v) domestic priority information; (vi) foreign priority information; and (vii) assignee information, if any. The information sought in the PTO-prescribed form (found in Appendix 21 as indicated below) is fairly self-explanatory; however, certain provisions benefit from further clarification. For instance, the secrecy order provision relates to matters that are national security classified and therefore is unlikely to be invoked in many instances. Second, the early publication provision allows applicants to make a request that an application eligible for publication be published earlier than the standard time frame of 18 months following the earliest filed application. Third, domestic priority information relates to any other U.S. application from which a benefit is being claimed, such as an earlier filed PPA. Likewise, foreign priority relates to any foreign application previously filed from which a benefit is being claimed. Last, assignee information relates to any entity to which the right, title and interest in the application is being transferred, such as an inventor's employer. Assignments will be discussed further below in the section entitled **Assignments**.

Information provided in an application data sheet may be changed prior to the allowance of an application by providing a form labeled "Supplemental Application Data Sheet" and using the same headings as the original sheet with changes clearly marked. In some instances, changes may be required in a format other than a supplemental application data sheet. Two such instances, changes in inventorship and correspondence changes, will be addressed in the sections below entitled **Inventorship Changes** and **Change of Correspondence Address**, respectively.

Appendix 21 contains the PTO's Application Data Sheet.

Appendix 22 sets forth the regulatory requirements concerning an application data sheet.

### Specification

The specification, discussed in section 112 of the Patent Act, is the principal part of an application. In general terms, the specification must be sufficiently detailed so that one skilled in the art of the invention can make and use it—in other words, the inventor must make an enabling disclosure. Another general requirement of the specification is that the inventor set forth the best mode for carrying out the invention. Best mode will be discussed in greater detail in the section below entitled **Detailed Description of the Invention**. A third general requirement of the specification is that it ends with at least one claim, broadly defined as a characteristic of the invention purported to be useful, novel, and nonobvious. Claims will be discussed below in the section entitled **Claims**.

In addition to the general statutory requirements applicable to a specification, section 1.77(b) of the CFR lists with particularity the elements comprising a patent specification. Those elements, and the order in which they should appear in the specification (as upper case headings), are as follows: (i) the title of the invention; (ii) a cross-reference to related applications, if any; (iii) a statement regarding federally sponsored research or development, if applicable; (iv) the names of the parties to a joint research agreement; (v) a reference to a sequence listing, table, or a computer program on CD; (vi) the background of the invention; (vii) a brief summary of the invention; (viii) a brief description of the drawings; (ix) a detailed description of the invention; (x) the claim(s); and (xi) an abstract of the disclosure. Each of these elements will be discussed below.

Appendix 23 sets forth statutory and regulatory references to the specification.

### Title of the Invention

Section 1.72(a) of the CFR specifies that the title of the invention should be short, specific, and no greater than 500 characters in length. Section 606 of the MPEP further provides that words such as *new, improved, improvement of, improvement in, a, an,* and *the* are not considered part of the title of an invention. Such words, if used, will be deleted when the PTO enters the title into the Office's computer records and when any patent issues. Furthermore, if a title is not sufficiently descriptive of the invention, an examiner may require that the title be amended to better indicate the nature of the invention.

Appendix 24 sets forth excerpts from the CFR and MPEP relating to the title of an invention.

### Cross-Reference to Related Application

In some cases, cross-references to related applications may be appropriate. For instance, a nonprovisional application may be related to and claim priority from a prior provisional application. In other cases, an application may state a claim for the benefit of a prior-filed nonprovisional or international application. Cross-references may be recited in the application data sheet as well, in which event these references need not be repeated in the specification. In any event, the applicant in a later-filed application will likely seek priority based on the earlier filed references. Priority will be discussed in more detail below in the section entitled **Right of Priority**.

### Statement Regarding Federally Sponsored Research or Development

In some cases, an invention may be made with Government support and the Government may retain certain rights in the invention. In such an event, the applicant is required to make a statement to that effect pursuant to section 202(c)(6) of the Patent Act.

### Names of the Parties to a Joint Research Agreement

Section 103(c)(3) of the Patent Act defines a joint research agreement as a written agreement between two or more persons engaged in cooperative research. Pursuant to section 103, joint research agreements are required to be in writing and disclosed so that later inventive work by any one of the cooperative researchers is not impaired by way of obviousness if prior art is found that arises from the earlier collaboration. This exclusion related to obviousness was enacted in 2004 as a result of passage of the Cooperative Research and Technology Enhancement (CREATE) Act, intended to foster, among other things, development and collaboration among public and private entities.

Appendix 25 contains section 103(c) of the Patent Act, constituting the CREATE Act.

### Reference to a Sequence Listing, Table, or Computer Program on CD

Certain gene sequences, tables, or computer programs may be listed as an appendix via a compact disc (CD). In some cases, information presented in a CD will be excluded from the application size filing fee calculation.

Appendix 26 contains guidelines from the CFR concerning the submission of eligible materials via compact disc.

### Background of the Invention

Section 608.01(c) of the MPEP states that the background of the invention portion of the specification comprises two elements: (i) the field, or subject matter, of the claimed invention; and (ii) an indication of the state of the prior art, including information disclosures. With respect to the latter requirement, sections 1.97 and 1.98 of the CFR set forth the timing for filing of information disclosures and the content of such disclosures, respectively. Generally, information disclosures encompass relevant U.S. patents, foreign patents, and non-patent literature that may bear on the patentability of the subject invention. Information disclosure statements may be filed as an accompanying document as indicated on the PTO's transmittal form referenced above in Appendix 16.

Appendix 27 contains references in the MPEP and CFR to the background of the invention portion of the specification.

Appendix 28 contains the PTO's information disclosure statement forms.

### Brief Summary of the Invention

Section 1.73 of the CFR and section 608.01(d) of the MPEP provide guidance on the nature of the summary of the invention. Generally, the summary should state the object, or general idea, of the invention. It should also explain the invention's operation and precise nature as opposed to stating generalities that could apply to numerous inventions.

Appendix 29 sets forth the guidelines from the CFR and MPEP concerning a summary of the invention.

### Brief Description of Drawings

Section 1.74 of the CFR states that the specification should include a brief description of the views of the drawings, if any. For instance, the applicant should indicate whether a drawing represents a side view, detail view, sectional view, or other representation. Drawings will be discussed in greater detail in the section below entitled **Drawings**.

### Detailed Description of the Invention

The detailed description of the invention is sometimes referred to as the "Detailed Description of the Preferred Embodiment" or "Detailed Description of the Best Mode and Preferred Embodiment." Indeed, section 1.71(b) of the CFR states that the description must contain an explanation of the preferred embodiment of the process, machine, manufacture, composition of matter, or improvement invented as well as the best mode of carrying out the invention. As explained in section 608.01(h) of the MPEP, the best mode is not necessarily indicative of a production specimen. Although subjective in nature, the best mode disclosure must at least be complete or else the application will fail. Moreover, a failure to disclose the best mode known at the time of the invention may lead to invalidation of an issued patent. An examiner will generally assume that an inventor has disclosed the best mode unless evidence to the contrary is presented.

Appendix 30 contains references from the CFR and MPEP concerning the best mode requirement.

### Claims

The requirement of at least one claim is grounded in section 112 of the Patent Act and further delineated in section 1.75 of the CFR. Although not specifically defined in the act, a claim is characterized as one that particularly points out and distinctly claims the subject matter that the applicant regards as the invention. No specific maximum number of claims is set by law as of this writing. However, in 2007 the PTO had finalized a rule known as the 25/5 rule, limiting the number of claims that may be presented in an application to 25, including up to 5 independent claims. Due to widespread opposition, the proposed rule was never implemented and has now been withdrawn.

A claim may be written in independent, dependent, or multiple dependent form. As the name suggests, an independent claim is one that is capable of standing alone and is the broadest statement of the invention. A dependent claim, on the other hand, relates back to a previous claim and is therefore narrower than an independent claim. Regardless of the form of claim described, the MPEP instructs that each claim must be precise, clear, correct, and unambiguous. Indeed, the claims form the most significant portion of the specification; in any action for infringement, the scope of the plaintiff's claims will be analyzed to determine the defendant's liability. Therefore, proper claims drafting is paramount.

Appendix 31 contains statutory, regulatory, and MPEP references regarding claims.

### Abstract of the Disclosure

Section 1.72(b) of the CFR sets forth that the purpose of the abstract is to enable the PTO and the public to quickly discern the gist of the invention. Accordingly, the rules provide that the abstract should not exceed 150 words. Further guidelines for the preparation of an abstract are provided in the MPEP.

Appendix 32 sets forth the regulatory and MPEP guidelines for the abstract of the disclosure.

### Drawings

As noted above, drawings may be provided as part of an application. Section 113 of the Patent Act specifically provides that drawings will be required when necessary to understand the subject matter of the invention; collectively, drawings should illustrate every feature of the invention specified in the claims, containing as many views as necessary. Practically speaking, most utility patent applications will contain at least one drawing, commonly prepared by a professional draftsperson. An examiner will determine the completeness and consistency of any drawings provided. Generally, drawings are numbered as figures (e.g., Fig. 1, Fig. 2, etc.) and are rendered in black ink. Color drawings are permitted only on petition describing the circumstances requiring the submission of color drawings.

Appendix 33 contains the statutory and regulatory guidelines concerning drawings.

### Executed Oath or Declaration

Section 115 of the Patent Act provides that each inventor make an oath or declaration that the inventor is believed to be the original and first inventor of the subject matter of the application. Unlike an oath, a declaration need not be sworn to before a person authorized to administer oaths. Furthermore, the oath or declaration may be filed by way of a form provided by the PTO. The oath or declaration must be signed by the inventor in person, or by the person entitled by law to make application on the inventor's behalf (such as the executor of a deceased inventor's estate). A full first and last name with middle initial or middle name, if any, and the citizenship of each inventor are required. The mailing address of each inventor and foreign priority information (if any) are also required if an application data sheet is not used.

Needless to say, an article may be the product of many inventors. This scenario is addressed in section 116 of the Patent Act, which provides that inventors may apply for a patent jointly even though (1) they did not physically work together or at the same time, (2) each did not make the same type or amount of contribution, or (3) each did not make a contribution to the subject matter of every claim of the patent. However, if in the course of prosecution of an application, one or more claims related to the contribution of an inventor is eliminated and no further grounds exist for the retention of that inventor in the application, then the application must be amended to remove that inventor. Likewise, if the original oath or declaration mistakenly identifies an inventor (without deceptive intent), then the application must be modified and a new oath or declaration must be made by the substituted inventor. In some cases, an additional inventor may be inaccurately listed due to a misconception regarding who is entitled to claim inventor status. For example, if one party has provided all of the ideas of the invention, and the other has only followed instructions in making it or provided the funding for it (such as an employer), then the person who contributed the ideas should be listed as the sole inventor in the patent application. For joint inventorship to arise, therefore, each party must have a share in the ideas forming the invention as defined in the claims, regardless whether the contribution relates only to one claim.

Appendix 34 provides statutory and regulatory references related to inventors and the oath or declaration.

Appendix 35 provides PTO forms for filing a declaration with or without an application data sheet.

### Models or Specimens

Models, specimens, or exhibits are not generally required in a patent application. However, section 114 of the Patent Act provides that, in some instances, the PTO may require an applicant to furnish a model of convenient size to exhibit advantageously several parts of the invention or, in other cases, to submit ingredients to inspect or experiment with a composition of matter. Any such submission should be clearly identified with the filing data of the application to which it relates. Once a submission is no longer needed by the PTO, the applicant must arrange for its return at the applicant's expense.

Appendix 36 contains references from the act and the regulations regarding models, specimens, and exhibits.

### Power of Attorney

As noted previously, a patent applicant may file and prosecute his or her own case or give a power of attorney to one or more patent practitioners. If the power of attorney is not incorporated in the oath or declaration form, then a separate power should be filed. A power previously granted may be revoked by the inventor or an assignee; likewise, a patent practitioner may withdraw from representation upon approval by the PTO.

Appendix 37 sets forth a power of attorney form for filing with the PTO.

### Right of Priority

Applicants are entitled to claim the benefit of an earlier filing date in a previously filed domestic or foreign application under certain conditions. For instance, section 1.78 of the CFR provides that for an applicant in a nonprovisional application to claim the benefit of one or more earlier provisional applications, each earlier provisional application must name as an inventor at least one inventor that appears in the later filed application. The applicant must also disclose the named inventor's invention claimed in at least one claim of the later filed application. Foreign priority may likewise be claimed. Priority is discussed further in Chapter 3 in the section entitled **The Paris Convention for the Protection of Industrial Property**.

Appendix 38 contains statutory and regulatory references to conditions for filing priority claims.

### Receipt for Documents

If a receipt for an application filed with the PTO is desired, then an applicant should include a stamped, self-addressed postcard, detailing each element of the application package and the number of pages, including such elements as the title and number of pages of each PTO form, the number of pages of specification (excluding claims), the number of claims and the number of claim pages, the number of figures of drawings and the number of sheets of drawings, the oath or declaration (if included in the initial filing), and the amount of payment (if included) and the method of payment (i.e., check, credit card, money order, or deposit account). This postcard will be stamped with the date of receipt by the PTO's Mail Room and returned to the applicant, serving as evidence that the reply was received by the Office on that date.

In some cases, a submission may be stamped with the date of deposit of the submission with the United States Postal Service rather than the date of receipt at the PTO. Pursuant to section 21 of the Patent Act and section 1.10 of the CFR, any correspondence received by the PTO (including an application filing) that was delivered by the "Express Mail Post Office to Addressee" service of the United States Postal Service (USPS) will be considered filed in the Office on the date of deposit with the USPS. Before depositing an application with the USPS in accordance with the Express Mail procedure, it is important to place the number of the "Express Mail" mailing label on the application papers. Further, only one application should be mailed in a single "Express Mail" package. This procedure is particularly effective for those applicants needing a specific filing date.

Appendix 39 contains statutory and regulatory provisions concerning the mailing and receipt of documents at the PTO. A list of mailbox designations for PTO applications and other papers is located at http://www.uspto.gov/web/offices/com/sol/og/patboxs.htm.

## ACTIONS DURING PENDENCY OF APPLICATION

### In General

Several activities can occur during the pendency of an application. This chapter will address the following actions: (i) filing such documents as assignments; amendments; publication requests; continuation applications; inventorship changes; correspondence changes; express abandonment; and petitions to revive an abandoned application or to withdraw a holding of abandonment; (ii) responding to office actions; and (iii) interferences.

### Assignments

An issued patent or a patent application may be assigned to a third party—that is, the owner of a right, title, or interest in a patent may convey that entire interest to another party. As indicated in section 261 of the Patent Act, any purported assignment must be in writing and recorded with the PTO to constitute valid notice of the assignment to third parties. Procedurally, the assignment document must be accompanied by a cover sheet and the fee for recording the assignment. The cover sheet includes, among other things, the party giving the assignment (the conveying party) and the party receiving it (the receiving party), the application number(s) or registration number(s) affected by the assignment, and the addressee to whom recordal of the assignment should be sent. Documents sent for recording are examined for compliance with procedural requirements by the PTO's Assignment Division.

Statutory and procedural references related to assignments are set forth in Appendix 40.

### Amendments

Amendments may be made to the specification (e.g., the claims) prior to or as a result of examination of an application. Drawings may be amended upon permission from the PTO.

The manner for making amendments generally is set forth in section 1.121 of the CFR. Amendments received in the Office on or before the mailing date of the first office action are called "preliminary amendments," and their entry is governed by section 1.115 of the CFR. Amendments in reply to a non-final office action are governed by section 1.111 of the CFR. Amendments filed after a final action and after an appeal are governed by sections 1.116 and 41.33, respectively. However, following issuance of the notice of allowance (discussed further below in the section entitled **Issuance of a Patent**), amendments are not available to an applicant as a matter of right. In such an instance, an applicant must specify why a post-allowance amendment is needed.

### Publication

As noted above, many patent applications will be published as a result of being the subject of another application filed abroad unless a certification is made that the application has not and will not be the subject of an application filed in another country or under a multilateral international agreement requiring publication after 18 months. Other instances in which publication will not occur include applications subject to national security requirements, provisional applications, design patents, and patents no longer pending (i.e., abandoned applications). In those cases in which a corresponding international application may not have been contemplated, a decision may thereafter be made to file an international application after the certification referred to above has been tendered. Pursuant to section 122 of the Patent Act, a request not to publish can be rescinded at any time. Moreover, in the event that a subsequent filing is made that would require publication of an earlier application, the PTO must be notified of the filing within 45 days or else the application may be deemed abandoned. Further, applicants may request an accelerated publication date, in which event the PTO will act on the request in due course although no specific date is assured. As a result of the publication requirements, an applicant may assert certain provisional rights such as the opportunity to obtain a reasonable royalty from a third party accused of infringing a published application claim, provided that the third party has received actual notice of the applicant's rights and a patent ultimately issues from the application with a substantially identical claim.

### Continuation Applications

As the name implies, continuations (either continuation applications; continuation-in-part applications; or in some cases, divisional applications) continue, or follow on in some manner, an earlier application (referred to as the "parent" application). For instance, a continuation application is a second application for the same invention claimed in a prior nonprovisional application and filed before the original prior application becomes abandoned or patented. For such a second application to qualify as a continuation, it must have at least one inventor in common with the earlier application and claim the benefit of the filing date (i.e., a right of priority, as discussed above in the section entitled **Right of Priority**) of the earlier application. Continuations are useful to further address claims in situations wherein an examiner may have allowed some but not all claims in a previous application. A continuation-in-part (CIP), on the other hand, relates to an application wherein additional matter not disclosed in the parent application is supplied; it is often used to claim enhancements developed after the parent application was filed and likewise claims the benefit of the filing date of the earlier application. The reader should note that under no circumstances should a nonprovisional application arising from an earlier filed provisional application be referred to as a continuation or CIP application.

Unlike either a continuation or CIP application, a divisional application often results from matter carved out of an original application in cases wherein an earlier application claims more than one distinct invention. In such cases, an examiner will restrict the earlier application to disclosure of a single invention. The divisional application should set forth those portions of the disclosure in the parent application that are relevant to the invention claimed in the divisional application.

### Inventorship Changes

As mentioned earlier, sometimes the wrong inventor may be recited in an application or an inventor may be omitted erroneously, in any case without deceptive intent. In these scenarios, the inventorship stated in the application may be amended by submitting documentation to the PTO observing the following requirements set forth in section 1.48 of the CFR: (i) a request to correct the inventorship that sets forth the desired inventorship change; (ii) a statement from each person being added as an inventor and from each person being omitted as an inventor that the error in inventorship occurred without deceptive intention on his or her part; (iii) an oath or declaration by the actual inventor(s); (iv) payment of the processing fee; and (v) if an assignment has been executed by any of the original named inventors, the written consent of the assignee to the change in inventorship.

### Change of Correspondence Address

The PTO directs all official correspondence related to an application to the individual named as the correspondent in the application. Section 1.33 of the CFR provides the manner in which the correspondence address can be changed. Specifically, if an oath or declaration has not yet been filed by any of the inventors, then the correspondence address may be changed by such parties as the inventor(s), any patent practitioner named in the transmittal papers accompanying the original application, or a party that will be the assignee. If, on the other hand, an oath or declaration has been filed, then the correspondence address may be changed by a patent practitioner of record, an assignee or all of the applicants.

Appendix 41 contains the forms for changing a correspondence address in a pending application and following issuance of the patent.

### Express Abandonment of Application

In some cases, an applicant may intentionally abandon (i.e., withdraw) an application. Such an action may be taken as a result of findings adverse to the continued viability of the claimed invention, or a parent application may be abandoned in favor of a continuation application. An express abandonment may also be filed to avoid publication (if the abandonment can be executed prior to the publication going into effect) or, if eligibility requirements can be met, to claim a refund of search and excess claims fees.

Appendix 42 contains forms to request express abandonment under the conditions discussed above.

### Revival of an Application

The PTO permits the filing of a petition to revive an application as a result of (i) delay that was unavoidable or unintentional; (ii) failure to prosecute an application or make payment of a fee, provided that the appropriate action or reply is taken; (iii) failure to notify the Office of a foreign filing triggering the 18-month publication requirement, provided only that the delay was unintentional; or (iv) failure to meet an Office requirement concerning a provisional application, provided that no such revival will in any event extend the pendency of the application beyond 12 months from its filing date.

A petition to revive an application under the above circumstances should be distinguished from a petition to withdraw a holding of abandonment by the PTO. In the latter case, an applicant contests the finding of an abandonment by the Office by way of a petition filed within two months following the notice of abandonment sent to the applicant. A PTO holding of abandonment may occur as a result of a determination that an office action was ignored or a document was not filed in a timely manner. In such instances, evidence from the applicant showing lack of receipt of the contested communication or a timely filing should result in withdrawal of the abandonment.

### Office Actions

An office action, also referred to as an official action, is a written communication from an examiner at the PTO requesting a response from the applicant concerning a procedural or substantive matter related to the application. For those applicants or their agents eligible to view private PAIR, these communications may be viewed and downloaded by opting in to the PTO's e-Office Action program (http://www.uspto.gov/eoa), thus replacing postal mail notifications of office actions.

An office action may issue under any number of grounds. For instance, an examiner may issue a request for further information, such as information on any competing goods or services embodied in the subject invention or an explanation of technical material in a cited publication. In other cases, the examiner may reject or object to one or more of the aspects of the specification. The distinction between a rejection and an objection is significant. A rejection ensues when the subject matter as claimed is considered unpatentable. In other words, a rejection relates to the merits of a claim, such as its ability to define a useful, novel, nonobvious, and enabled invention. On the other hand, if the form of the claim (as distinguished from its merit, or substance) is at issue, then an objection is made. An example of a matter of form as to which objection is made is the dependency of a claim on a rejected claim, if the dependent claim is otherwise allowable. Procedurally, rejections and objections differ in terms of the venue for an appeal of an adverse decision. A rejection is subject to review by the Board of Patent Appeals and Interferences (mentioned above in the section entitled **A General Overview of the Patent Application Process**); an objection, however, may be reviewed only by way of petition to the Director of the PTO.

Regardless of the nature of the office action, the goal of examination is to clearly articulate any issues with the application early in the prosecution process so that an applicant has the opportunity to provide evidence of patentability and otherwise reply completely at the earliest opportunity. Therefore, if after receiving an office action, an applicant elects to continue prosecution of the application, a timely reply to the action in writing must be submitted. The time for response to an office action is set forth in the office action. Generally, a response to the office action must be made within six months from its mailing date to avoid abandonment of the application. Unless the application is abandoned, the reply should distinctly and specifically point out the supposed errors in the office action and address every objection or rejection in the action, including any amendments desired by the applicant. In some instances, the examiner and the applicant may resolve one or more outstanding issues together in an interview. Interviews are usually only provided when the nature of the case is such that the interview could serve to develop and clarify specific issues and lead to a mutual understanding between the examiner and the applicant, thereby advancing the prosecution of the application.

Upon submission of a reply to an office action, the application will be reconsidered and further examined in view of the applicant's remarks and any amendments included with the reply. The examiner will then either withdraw any refusal and allow the application or, if not persuaded by the remarks and/or amendments submitted, repeat the refusal in a second office action. A second action is generally a final action, and if issues have not been resolved between the examiner and the applicant once an action is made final, the applicant can take an appeal of rejected claims to the Board of Patent Appeals and Interferences (BPAI) or appeal objections to the Director of the PTO.

A notice of appeal filed with the BPAI must be accompanied by an appeal brief within two months following filing of the notice. If a BPAI outcome is unfavorable to the applicant, then the case may be appealed to the United States Court of Appeals for the Federal Circuit (Federal Circuit). The Federal Circuit is one of thirteen circuit appellate courts in the country. In addition to hearing appeals from the BPAI, it hears appeals related to trademarks, international trade, and veterans' benefits, among other things.

Appendix 43 contains a form for filing a notice of appeal.

### Interferences

As noted in Chapter 1, from time to time two or more inventors may lay claim to the same invention in different applications. In such cases (estimated by the PTO to arise in approximately one percent of applications filed), a process known as an interference proceeding (governed by section 135 of the Patent Act) will determine which inventor may claim the invention—that is, which inventor has priority. Interferences may also be initiated between pending applications and issued patents in some circumstances. Generally, an applicant suggests an interference, and the examiner then refers the suggested interference to the BPAI where the interference is officially declared and opened for a hearing and disposition. Each party to such a proceeding must submit evidence of facts proving when the invention was made; absent the required evidence, the filing date of the application will be used as the earliest date. The question of priority with respect to the contested invention is generally determined by examining each party's date of conception of the invention and the date it was reduced to practice. In the case of conception, an inventor's notebook (as discussed above in the section entitled **Documenting an Invention**) could prove especially useful in proving the timing for completion of the means to obtain the patentable matter. The filing of a regular application for patent completely disclosing the invention is treated as equivalent to its reduction to practice. In the simplest of cases, the first party to have conceived the invention and reduced it to practice will be held to be the prior inventor. Like some office actions, an adverse decision may be appealed to the Federal Circuit.

## ISSUANCE OF A PATENT AND POST-ISSUANCE

This section covers the grant, or issuance, of a patent and will also highlight post-issuance matters of maintenance and corrections.

### Issuance of a Patent

If an application is deemed to be in condition for a patent grant, then the examiner will issue a notice of allowance under section 151 of the Patent Act. As the term implies, a notice of allowance is an official communication allowing an application to proceed to the grant of a patent; the notice itself is not a patent grant. Accompanying such a notice is a request for payment of the allowance fee; failure to pay the fee will result in abandonment of the application. The Office of Patent Publication is responsible for the processing of allowed applications. Once the fee and any correspondence and/or drawings are matched with the application and all requirements have been met for issuance of a patent, any required updates will be made to the electronic file and an "Issue Notification" will be mailed approximately three weeks prior to the issue date of the patent. The patent grant, issued in the name of the United States of America under the seal of the PTO, is mailed on the issue date of the patent. The bibliographic data included on the grant certificate include the patent number, the name of the inventor(s), and a brief description of the invention. It is bound in an attractive cover and includes a gold seal and red ribbon. As an original document, the patent grant should be kept in a safe place along with other valuable papers.

### Maintenance

A utility patent grant based on an application filed on or after December 12, 1980, must be maintained to remain in force by the payment of maintenance fees during the life of the patent. Pursuant to section 41(b) of the Patent Act, maintenance payments are due 3 ½ years after the date of issuance, 7 ½ years after the date of issuance, and 11 ½ years after the date of issuance; plant and design patents are exempt from this requirement. Unless payment of the applicable maintenance fee is received at the PTO on or before the date the fee is due or within a grace period of 6 months thereafter (subject to a surcharge), the patent will expire as of the end of the grace period. The practical effect of maintenance payments is to keep only those patents which are still active on the records.

Appendix 44 contains a maintenance fee transmittal form.

### Corrections

An issued patent may generally be corrected or amended in four ways: (i) by means of a certificate of correction that is issued due to an error by the PTO or the applicant; (ii) through a patent reissue; (iii) through a disclaimer; or (iv) by means of reexamination. Section 254 of the Patent Act prescribes the method for correcting an issued patent containing erroneous information due to a mistake by the PTO. Specifically, if the error is one of consequence (i.e., the intended meaning of the grant is not obvious from the context), then the PTO will likely issue a certificate of correction, which is recorded in like manner as the original patent, published in the *Official Gazette,* and made a part of the patent file. The request for such a certificate can be made by the patentee or an assignee and is addressed to the Certificate of Correction Branch at the PTO. In lieu of a certificate of correction, the PTO may in its discretion issue a corrected patent. Alternatively, if the error is deemed minor, the PTO may simply place notice of the error in the file and make no formal corrections. In any event, there is no fee to the patentee or assignee for a correction made as a result of PTO error.

On the other hand, errors made by applicants are subject to fees when corrective action must be taken. Section 255 provides a two-pronged test for correcting patents based on an applicant's error. Under the first prong, the error must be minor, typographical, or clerical in nature. The second prong requires that the correction not materially affect the scope or meaning of the patent. If both requirements are met, then a certificate of correction may issue.

In some cases, the requirements for correction of a patent due to applicant error cannot be met. For instance, a change in the scope of a claim is not ministerial under the provisions of section 255 of the Patent Act. In such an instance, a reissue should be considered as the means by which to correct the patent. Reissues of defective patents, governed by section 251, require an examination in which the proposed changes correcting any defects in the original patent are evaluated. Provided that the claims in a reissue are for the same general invention (and other formalities such as payment of the required fee are met), a reissue patent would be granted to replace the original for the balance of the unexpired term.

Another means of revising a patent is through the use of a disclaimer as provided for in section 253 of the act. A disclaimer is a statement filed by an owner (including an assignee) of a patent (or a patent application) in which certain legal rights to the patent are relinquished. There are two types of disclaimers: a statutory disclaimer and a terminal disclaimer. A statutory disclaimer provides for the surrender of one or more claims in a patent. The disclaimer may arise because of a lawsuit involving one or more of the claims or some holding concerning the validity of a claim. Unlike a statutory disclaimer, a terminal disclaimer disclaims or dedicates to the public the entire term or any portion of the term of a patent or patent to be granted. A terminal disclaimer may be issued in connection with a nonstatutory double patenting rejection, which is a judicially created doctrine intended to prevent prolongation of a patent term by prohibiting claims in a second patent that are not materially distinguishable from claims in a first patent. A nonstatutory double patenting rejection should be distinguished from a statutory double patenting rejection, in which case an application is held to contain more than one invention in violation of section 101 of the Patent Act. In that case, the examiner may require a restriction, resulting in the filing of a divisional application as noted above in the section entitled **Continuation Applications**.

Terminal disclaimers can arise specifically out of reexamination proceedings conducted pursuant to section 302 of the Patent Act and brought in the context of a nonstatutory double patenting rejection. In such a proceeding, any person may file a request for reexamination of a patent, along with the required fee, on the basis of prior art consisting of patents or printed publications that affect one or more of the claims cited in the patent. The PTO will then determine whether any substantial question of patentability has been raised with respect to the patent at issue. At the conclusion of the reexamination proceedings, a certificate setting forth the PTO's findings is issued, which may include canceling any claim of the patent finally determined to be unpatentable, confirming any claim of the patent determined to be patentable, and incorporating in the patent any proposed amended or new claim determined to be patentable.

# CHAPTER 3:
# INTERNATIONAL CONSIDERATIONS

### INTERNATIONAL CONSIDERATIONS GENERALLY

Most countries have laws related to patents, and claimants seeking to protect their inventions outside their home jurisdiction will need to consult the laws of nations of interest to determine the extent of protection accorded to foreign applicants. In other words, there is no single mechanism to protect a patent at once throughout the world; a U.S. patent only covers the United States and its territories. However, various international conventions, or treaties, afford their adherents (i.e., the members, or contracting states) the opportunity to manage intellectual property interests with dozens of countries, thus allowing for patent protection under the terms of that particular treaty. The United States is a signatory to many of the leading treaties affecting patents. This chapter will provide general information on the Paris Convention for the Protection of Industrial Property, the Patent Cooperation Treaty, and TRIPS.

Appendix 45 provides a list of adherents to each of the above-referenced treaties as of this writing.

### THE PARIS CONVENTION FOR THE PROTECTION OF INDUSTRIAL PROPERTY

The Paris Convention for the Protection of Industrial Property (Paris Convention), one of the earliest intellectual property treaties, was signed in Paris, France, on March 20, 1883. It is administered by the World Intellectual Property Organization (WIPO), an agency of the United Nations responsible for the development of laws and regulations that advance the harmonization of intellectual property laws worldwide. The Paris Convention espouses three guiding principles: (i) national treatment; (ii) right of priority, and (iii) common rules.

Simply stated, the principle of national treatment provides that the laws of a contracting state protecting industrial property (e.g., patents and utility models as well as trade names and appellations of origin) are accessible to the nationals of other states adhering to the Paris Convention. Nationals of non-contracting states are also entitled to national treatment under the Paris Convention if they are domiciled or have a real and effective industrial or commercial establishment in a contracting state.

With respect to the second principle, the oft-used expression "right of priority" (as discussed in Chapter 2 in the section entitled **Right of Priority**) means that an applicant from one contracting state can use its first filing date in such a state as the effective filing date in another country, provided that the applicant files another application within 6 months (for design patents) or 12 months (for patents and utility models) from the first filing. These later applications, therefore, have priority over applications for the same invention that may have been filed during the intervening months.

Finally, the Paris Convention provides for common rules that all the contracting parties must follow. One such rule is that the granting of a patent in one contracting state does not oblige the other contracting states to grant a patent. Similarly, a patent cannot be refused, annulled, or terminated in any contracting state on the ground that it has been refused or annulled or has terminated in any other contracting state. An inventor also has the right to be named as such in the patent. Another important precept states that a member nation cannot enact rules providing for compulsory licensing of an inactive invention if the patentee can provide legitimate reasons to justify a failure to work the invention.

### PATENT COOPERATION TREATY

The Patent Cooperation Treaty (PCT), administered by WIPO, is an international agreement negotiated at a diplomatic conference in Washington, D.C., in 1970. The full text of the PCT is provided in Appendix T of the MPEP, and its operative terms are codified beginning at section 351 of the Patent Act. Under the PCT, a U.S. applicant can file one application, known as "an international application," in a standardized format in English at the PTO (the "receiving office") and have that application acknowledged as a regular national or regional filing in as many contracting states to the PCT as the applicant designates. For international applications filed on or after January 1, 2004, the filing of an international application will automatically constitute the designation of all contracting countries to the PCT on that filing date. The PCT likewise enables foreign applicants desiring patent protection in the United States to file a PCT application in their home language and in their home patent office and to have the application acknowledged as a regular U.S. national filing. The PCT simplifies the process of filing patent applications by offering an alternative route to filing patent applications directly in the patent offices of those countries that are members of the treaty. However, the PCT application itself does not mature into a patent; instead, after a period of 30 months (as explained below), the PCT application must be taken into the national stage in those countries where patent protection is being sought. Each of the resulting national applications is then prosecuted before the respective patent offices with a view towards obtaining a foreign issued patent.

Chapter I of the PCT enumerates the filing, search, and publication procedures applicable to PCT applications. Additional procedures for preliminary examination are provided for in Chapter II of the PCT. The timely filing of an international application under Chapter I triggers a prior art search of the invention by an entity designated as the International Searching Authority (ISA). For applications filed with the United States as the receiving office, the applicant may of course choose the PTO to act as the ISA. Other ISAs are the European Patent Office, the Korean Intellectual Property Office, and the Australian Patent Office. Search fees assessed by ISAs vary; therefore, cost is a factor to consider in choosing an ISA. The international search report prepared by the ISA contains a list of documents found to be relevant to patentability of the subject invention and identifies the claims in the application to which they are pertinent. For applications filed on or after January 1, 2004, the ISA will normally issue a written opinion as to whether each claim appears to satisfy the PCT criteria of novelty, inventiveness, and industrial applicability (equivalent to the U.S. patentability standards of novelty, nonobviousness, and usefulness or utility). The written opinion may also comment on the form or clarity of the claims or the drawings. Once the international search report and written opinion are established, the ISA transmits one copy of each to the applicant and WIPO. WIPO acts as the International Bureau (IB), the central coordinating body for all PCT applications.

Publication of the international application generally occurs 18 months from the priority date. In other words, in most instances a national U.S. application is filed first, followed by an international application for the same subject matter within the priority year provided by the Paris Convention, and the priority benefit of the U.S. national application filing date will be claimed. A significant feature of a PCT application is its ability to defer the time for filing national stage applications in foreign jurisdictions because by filing a PCT application, an applicant gains a 30-month period before the payment of national fees and the furnishing of any required translations will be required to subject the application to national procedures for granting of patents in each of the designated countries. This extension of time not only delays the expenses associated with applying for patent protection in foreign countries but also allows the applicant more time to assess the commercial viability of the invention abroad, paying particular attention to any vulnerabilities exposed in the international search report and written opinion.

## TRIPS

Unlike the above treaties, TRIPS (Agreement on Trade-Related Aspects of Intellectual Property Rights) is not administered by WIPO. Instead, the body administering the treaty is the World Trade Organization (WTO), an international organization dealing with the rules of trade between nations. TRIPS is Annex 1C of 18 agreements contained in the Marrakesh Agreement Establishing the World Trade Organization, signed in Marrakesh, Morocco, on April 15, 1994.

TRIPS requires member countries to make patents available for any inventions, whether products or processes, in all fields of technology without discrimination, subject to the tests of novelty, inventiveness, and industrial applicability. The treaty also requires that patents be available and patent rights be enjoyable without discrimination as to the place of invention and regardless whether products are imported or locally produced. Similar to U.S. law, TRIPS also provides exceptions regarding patentable subject matter. For instance, inventions that are dangerous to human, animal or plant life, or health or that seriously impact the environment will be denied patentability. Another exception pertains to the exclusion of diagnostic, therapeutic and surgical methods for the treatment of humans or animals. A third exception involves a country's right to exclude from patentability plants or animals (other than microorganisms) and essentially biological processes for the production of plants or animals (other than microbiological processes). However, any country excluding plant varieties from patent protection must provide another system of protection.

Like U.S. law, the treaty also specifies that contracting nations require an applicant to disclose the invention in a manner sufficiently clear and complete for the invention to be carried out by a person skilled in the art and may require the applicant to indicate the best mode for carrying out the invention known to the inventor at the filing date or, where priority is claimed, at the priority date of the application. In summary, TRIPS complements the rights and obligations afforded applicants under the Paris Convention and the PCT system in the context of promoting international trade.

# CHAPTER 4:
# MONETIZING PATENTS

## A GENERAL OVERVIEW

Like other forms of intellectual property such as trademarks and copyrights, patents are assets capable of producing value for their owners. According to a 2005 study sponsored by USA for Innovation, the value of intellectual property in the United States has increased to over five trillion dollars. The patent monetization industry, in particular, continues to grow and includes activities involving invention promoters, patent aggregators, auctions, and licensing arrangements. This chapter will address basic issues surrounding such methods of extracting value from a patent and will also discuss the effect of joint patent ownership and the need for policing to protect a patent's economic viability.

## INVENTION PROMOTERS

Section 297 of the Patent Act addresses invention promotion. Specifically, an invention promoter is defined as a person or entity engaged in procuring for a patentee or inventor a third party engaged in the development and marketing of products or services that include the invention. The statute also excludes the following operations or scenarios from the general definition of an invention promoter: (i) a governmental department or agency; (ii) a nonprofit, charitable, scientific, or educational organization qualified as such; (iii) any person or entity involved in an evaluation to determine the commercial potential of a utility patent or a previously filed nonprovisional utility patent application (including a sale or license thereof); (iv) any party participating in a transaction involving the sale of the stock or assets of a business; or (v) any party who directly engages in the business of retail sale or distribution of products.

In furtherance of the aim of the American Inventors Protection Act to address improper or deceptive practices of invention promotion companies, the statute also requires invention promoters to make the following disclosures in writing to potential clients: (i) the total number of inventions evaluated by the promoter in the past five years, including the number of positive and negative evaluations; (ii) the number of customers who contracted with the promoter over the last five years; (iii) the total number of customers who received a net financial profit as a direct result of the promoter's services; (iv) the total number of customers who received license agreements for their inventions as a direct result of the promoter's services; and (v) the names and addresses of all previous invention promotion firms with which the invention promoter or its officers have been affiliated for the last 10 years.

The statutory framework addressing invention promotion is not meant to suggest that invention promoters or invention promotion companies are illegitimate. Rather, the law exists to assist potential clients in evaluating offers of invention promotion, particularly considering that many companies may require the expenditure of thousands of dollars for the search, examination, and evaluation of patentable subject matter. Moreover, the PTO provides a public forum for the publication of complaints concerning invention promoters or promotion firms, which are thereafter submitted to the promoter for response. The PTO publishes responses to the complaints as well.

Appendix 46 contains the PTO's sample complaint against an invention promoter or firm.

### SELLING A PATENT

A patent is an article of personal property and as such may be sold to a third party. To sell a patent for the highest possible value, patent owners often use the services of an asset management firm or other entity to undertake a valuation of the patent and to identify potential buyers. Valuation helps patent owners determine their relative position in the marketplace and is used in a variety of contexts besides the outright sale of a patent, such as for licensing, collateralizing a patent for bank financing, or determining damages in an infringement proceeding.

One form of business that buys and sells patents is a patent aggregator. As the term implies, an aggregator buys up patents in bulk from both corporations and individual owners. Some aggregators also buy patents defensively; in other words, they take ownership of patents that may otherwise be targeted by "patent trolls." A patent troll is generally understood as one who buys a patent without a real interest in it to use its subject matter in an infringement proceeding against a company in the relevant industry. Another option for sale of a patent is to engage the services of a broker who will use his or her network to find the best buyer in exchange for a brokerage commission. In addition to the commission (perhaps as much as 25% of the sale price), a broker may charge an upfront fee and require exclusivity. A third option for sale is to submit the patent to public bidding by one of several asset management firms engaged in the business of auctioning patents. Of course, the success of competitive bidding depends on the nature of the patent and the interest generated by the auction. A fourth option is for the seller to list the patent in the *Official Gazette.* In addition to advertising issued patents, the *Gazette* publishes patents for license or sale on the second Tuesday of each month for a current fee of $25 for each published item.

## LICENSING A PATENT

A patent owner's licensing of rights can also reap economic rewards. In many instances, licensing arrangements are entered into voluntarily between or among the parties. However, in some cases, licensing is compulsory. Section 203 of the Patent Act addresses a form of compulsory licensing known as a march-in right. A march-in right applies to government-funded inventions owned by small businesses or nonprofit organizations and grants the government, or its designee, the right to request full access to the patented subject matter. If the request is refused, the funding agency may issue its own license. The statute further sets out limitations for exercise of such a right. Generally, the license may be taken because the inventive entity or its assignee has not taken, or is not expected to take within a reasonable time, effective steps to achieve practical application of the subject invention in the field of use or the license is otherwise in the public interest such as to alleviate health or safety concerns.

In a voluntary licensing arrangement, valuation is one key to effective monetization. In simple terms, if the scope of the claims is broad, then the market value of the patent will be greater if demand is present. Monetization can also be affected by a licensor's lack of oversight concerning licensees. For example, a patent owner should instruct each licensee to mark products covered by the patent with the appropriate notice (as discussed in Chapter 1 in the section entitled **Notice of Patent**). Moreover, a patent owner has a duty to ensure that relevant markings are consistently applied among all licensees. Insufficient marking may preclude the patent owner from collecting pre-filing damages for infringement.

Another issue involving licensing is the potential application of the patent exhaustion doctrine, first applied to patents by the U.S. Supreme Court in 1873. This doctrine is akin to the first sale doctrine in copyright law, which gives the owner of a physical object embodying a copyright the right to dispose of it following the first sale or transfer by the copyright owner. In other words, the owner of a book may sell or otherwise dispose of that article without violating the underlying rights of the copyright owner (i.e., the publisher or the author). Likewise, in patent law, the patent exhaustion doctrine espouses the principle that, once the owner of an invention creates a product from it and sells (or licenses) it, the owner no longer has any rights or claims as to how the product is used or disposed—the owner's patent rights in that regard have been exhausted. The doctrine has been implicated in a wide variety of issues incidental to the licensing of a patent, resulting in rulings by the Federal Circuit that the doctrine is inapplicable in instances wherein the licensor put reasonable restrictions on the scope of the license grant. The inapplicability of the patent exhaustion doctrine in such cases resulted in the structuring of transactions providing for post-sale patent restraints that would apply to end users of the patented product. This erosion of the doctrine was resolved in a 2008 U.S. Supreme Court decision, *Quanta Computer, Inc. v. LG Electronics, Inc.* In that case, LG produced microprocessor technology that it cross licensed to Intel for Intel's manufacture of microprocessors that it subsequently sold to customers like Quanta. LG subsequently sued Quanta for patent infringement on grounds that the Intel-LG license withheld any license to Intel's customers to combine Intel products made under LG's patents with non-Intel products. Quanta combined the microprocessors with semiconductor memory to form a working device that would have infringed the LG patents. The Court decided that LG's rights in its patented technology were exhausted when it entered its transaction with Intel; therefore, an end user like Quanta was free to use the technology for its own purposes. The Supreme Court's reversal of the Federal Circuit's rulings on post-sale patent restraints is likely to affect the structuring of transactions similar to the *Quanta* case.

## EFFECT OF JOINT OWNERSHIP

Joint patent ownership is addressed in section 262 of the Patent Act, which provides that, absent an agreement to the contrary, a joint owner has the right to make, use, sell, offer to sell, or import a patented invention into the United States without the approval of and without accounting to a co-owner for the profits arising from such an activity. The potential effects of a party's right to act in self interest are expansive.

For example, a party may desire to bring an infringement action but be hindered from doing so because a co-owner refuses to join in the litigation as required by a court rule. Alternatively, a co-owner joining in litigation may elect to license an infringer and limit damages in the lawsuit to past infringement.

In other cases, an employee may be established as the inventor and sole (or joint) owner of a patent. Such a circumstance commonly arises due to the absence of a written employee invention agreement. An agreement of this type generally requires an employee to disclose all inventions to the employer, assist in any application for a patent, and assign all rights to any inventions to the employer. Without a written agreement and absent any evidence to prove the employee's hiring or assignment for the purpose of inventing, an employer will likely acquire nothing more than a shop right—that is, a right of the employer, on a nonexclusive basis, to use (but not own) an employee's invention. As a result, costly litigation may arise to resolve ownership issues, the results of which could result in a loss or restriction of a company's patent rights.

## POLICING A PATENT

In addition to addressing potential sources of revenue to enhance the economic vitality of a patent, it is equally important that a patent owner engage resources to monitor the marketplace for instances of infringement or competitive activity that may undermine the value of a patent. Such monitoring is known as a patent watch and is performed by many service companies and patent professionals. A patent watch can encompass a review of newly published patent applications and issued patents in a particular technical area or cover more general activities of competitor companies or inventors. Competitive intelligence is a particularly valuable benefit of a patent watch, allowing a patent owner the opportunity to view trends in a competitor's research and development as well as to uncover any encroachments into a patent owner's own territory. The results of a patent watch can lead to the pursuit of various activities benefiting a patent owner, such as the ability to create collaborative relationships in inventorship or licensing, monitor trends in the owner's field of interest, identify new competitors, and modify any technology under development to avoid infringement of existing patents.

At the corporate level specifically, in addition to properly documenting the obligations of those charged with inventing patentable matter, all employees need to be educated about the economic importance of a company's patents and trade secrets. Indeed, the loss of a competitive advantage arising from an inappropriate disclosure of confidential information can severely undermine a business. Therefore, employees should be educated about the nature of company information, processes, research or development that is considered proprietary. One educational tool is a policy and procedures document outlining the company's privacy guidelines, particularly addressing use of the Internet or social media to disclose company information. Specifically, any company-related posts on blogs or other media should be subject to approval by a certain gatekeeper within the organization. In general, it may be prudent to require employees to sign a confidentiality agreement that addresses such issues as inappropriate disclosure, trade secret theft, and other forms of economic espionage as referred to in Chapter 1 in the section entitled **Patents and Trade Secrets**.

# CHAPTER 5:
# INFRINGEMENT ISSUES

## A GENERAL OVERVIEW

As stated in Chapter 1, the rights accorded a patent owner are derived from federal law; accordingly, a civil claim regarding infringement of a patent is brought in a federal, rather than state, forum. Section 271 of the Patent Act defines infringement as the unauthorized making, using, offering to sell, selling, or importation of any patented invention within the United States during the term of the patent. Proceedings are typically initiated in a federal district court. However, the U.S. International Trade Commission is also empowered to bar the importation of articles that infringe on U.S. patents under section 337 of the Tariff Act of 1930.

Infringement may be direct or indirect; it may also be intentional (willful) or unintentional. Therefore, in some cases a defendant may have been previously unaware of an existing patent that has allegedly been infringed, particularly if the defendant failed to conduct a pre-application search as discussed in Chapter 2. Moreover, there is generally no criminal liability for patent infringement in the United States. Indeed, section 281 of the Patent Act specifically provides that a patentee shall have the right to bring a *civil* action for infringement. However, as noted in Chapter 1 in the section entitled **Patents and Trade Secrets**, proprietary information may be retained as a trade secret and, if misappropriated, may be addressed criminally as trade secret theft under the Economic Espionage Act. Also, under section 497 of title 18 of the United States Code, anyone who alters, forges, or counterfeits a patent may be fined and/or imprisoned for up to 10 years.

The extent of infringement liability is sometimes determined by the nature of the patent. For instance, in the closely watched case, *Cardiac Pacemakers Inc. v. St. Jude Medical Inc.,* the Federal Circuit determined that patents for methods (or processes) are not subject to infringement liability under section 217(f) of the Patent Act if there are no products used in the performance of the methods. Product patents, on the other hand, are not affected by the decision. Section 217(f) provides a cause of action for infringement if the components of a patented invention are supplied for assembly abroad, closing a loophole that allowed infringers to ship unassembled patented components abroad for later assembly. The court decided that, because a step involved in the performance of a method cannot be supplied in the conventional sense of transferring a physical object, no infringement liability existed. In another Federal Circuit case, *Egyptian Goddess, Inc. v. Swisa, Inc.*, the parameters of infringement for design patents were decided. Specifically, the court held that the holder of a design patent need only show that an ordinary observer would find substantial similarity between two designs for infringement liability to attach. Prior to this decision, a more restrictive test required a demonstration that both designs contained the same "points of novelty."

Patent infringement litigation is not an inexpensive process. Accordingly, before commencing any court case, aggrieved patent owners contemplating litigation should assess their position relative to the defending party. This assessment will entail the consideration of several elements including: (i) the competitive position of the defendant; (ii) the likelihood of success of various defenses; (iii) the sufficiency of monetary damages; and (iv) the prospect of obtaining an injunction. This chapter will discuss: (i) direct and equivalents infringement; (ii) indirect infringement; (iii) defenses; (iv) remedies; and (v) insurance.

### Direct Infringement

Direct or literal infringement means that the claim(s) of the defendant's patent match the claim(s) in the plaintiff's patent. Of paramount importance, then, is interpretation of the claim(s) at issue. In a landmark U.S. Supreme Court decision, *Markman v. Westview Instruments, Inc.*, the Court affirmed that claims construction or interpretation is to be determined by a judge and not a jury. As a result, litigants often request a *Markman* hearing—a non-jury hearing for the resolution of claims construction disputes—early in the judicial process.

In addition to literal infringement, a doctrine exists that provides for a cause of action for infringement even when the claims at issue are not identical. Known as the doctrine of equivalents, the principle provides that a defendant's device may still be held infringing despite a lack of identicality in the claims if both devices do the same work in substantially the same way and accomplish essentially the same result.

Thus, a plaintiff applying the doctrine in an action for equivalents infringement seeks to prevent the manufacture of a device that is the essence of the plaintiff's patented product. Not all cases of equivalents infringement are successful, however. For example, if the accused device differs materially from the claims in the plaintiff's patent, the doctrine will not apply. Also, if in the course of prosecution of a patent the plaintiff disclaimed, or surrendered, certain claims of the invention, then the plaintiff would not be able to assert the doctrine of equivalents over the surrendered portions of the claim. This limitation on applicability of the doctrine of equivalents is known alternatively as file wrapper estoppel or prosecution history estoppel.

Over the years, the tension between the doctrines of equivalents and estoppel has been evident. In fact, the Federal Circuit had on many occasions held that the application of estoppel could be overcome on a case-by-case basis. More recently, the circuit court had established a bright-line rule, holding that estoppel was an absolute bar against claiming infringement on the matter amended. This rule was appealed to the U.S. Supreme Court in *Festo Corp. v. Shoketsu Kinzoku Kogyo Kabushiki Co.*

In the *Festo* case, the Court acknowledged that, during the prosecution of an application, the narrowing of certain patent claims may result in the dedication of those claims to the range of equivalents that falls between the original claim and the amended claim. Instead of preventing a patentee from later claiming infringement on this range of equivalents, however, the Court decided that a patentee must be able to demonstrate that at the time of the amendment one skilled in the art could not reasonably be expected to have drafted a claim that would have literally encompassed the alleged equivalents. This important decision created a rebuttable presumption that surrendered claims cannot form the basis of an action for equivalents infringement.

### Indirect Infringement

Indirect infringement includes inducement and contributory infringement. Inducement of infringement is set forth in section 271(b) of the Patent Act, which provides that anyone who actively induces infringement of a patent is liable as an infringer. Although not explicitly stated in the statute, an action for indirect infringement by way of inducement has been held to require some evidence of intent on behalf of the alleged infringer. Contributory infringement is addressed in section 271(c), which provides that anyone who sells or offers to sell or import a material component of a patented invention, knowing the same to be especially made or especially adapted for use in an infringement of such a patent (rather than for a substantial, non-infringing use), is liable as an infringer. In each of the above causes for infringement, it is well settled that underlying proof of direct infringement must be shown.

**Defenses**

Defendants in civil infringement proceedings may avail themselves of any number of defenses to their conduct. For example, a defendant may assert that the case is barred as a result of the six-year statute of limitations set forth in section 286 of the Patent Act or that the patent exhaustion doctrine (discussed in Chapter 4 in the section entitled **Licensing a Patent**) applies. Alternatively, a defendant may rely on section 273(b)(1), which provides a defense to an inventor who actually reduced the subject matter to practice at least one year before the effective filing date of the patent in dispute and commercially used the subject matter before the effective filing date of such patent.

Moreover, section 282 provides for additional defenses such as non-infringement or invalidity. Noninfringement includes assertions of non-equivalence under the doctrine of equivalents, the existence of a disclaimer (as discussed in Chapter 2 in the section entitled **Corrections**), or lack of literal infringement. Invalidity, a popular defense, is a claim rebutting the presumption of validity of a patent. The invalidity defense often involves an assertion of a defect in the patent process (particularly with respect to the specification as discussed in Chapter 2 in the section entitled **Specification**), such as a patentee's failure to disclose the best mode for carrying out the invention or a failure to make an enabling disclosure. Such information is generally known to a defendant as result of conducting a validity study (discussed in Chapter 2 in the section entitled **The Validity Search**). A successful invalidity defense may affect one or more of the patent's claims and potentially mitigates the scope or impact of an infringement claim.

Unlike an invalidity defense, the defense of inequitable conduct will, if successful, disqualify a patent in its entirety because the legitimacy— rather than a flaw—of the invention process is raised. An inequitable conduct defense requires a defendant to prove by clear and convincing evidence that a patentee or other authorized individual failed to disclose material information or submitted false material information regarding the patent with intent to deceive. In other words, the patentee is alleged to have violated the duty of candor and good faith discussed in Chapter 2 in the section entitled **Conducting Patent Searches**. The defense has been used frequently and significantly increases the cost of patent litigation. However, as a result of a recent Federal Circuit case, the defense must now be pleaded with particularity—that is, every instance or circumstance of the alleged misconduct must be described in such detail as to sufficiently establish the facts being alleged or else the claim will fail.

Another defense that can potentially render a patent unenforceable is patent misuse. Patent misuse is a defense alleging that the plaintiff acted outside the scope of the patent (either temporally or in exercising a broader right than allowed under the patent) or engaged in some other form of anticompetitive behavior related to the patent. A scenario that may give rise to anticompetitive behavior is a patentee's requirement that a third party buy staple goods from the patentee as a condition of licensing the patented product, provided that the patentee has market dominance in the field of use of the patented product. If the misuse defense is successful, then the patentee is precluded from claiming infringement for so long as the patent is tainted by its misuse; as a result, the patent may be permanently or temporarily unenforceable. Notwithstanding this and other limitations on a patentee's rights, section 271(d) of the Patent Act makes clear that certain actions will not be susceptible to a claim of misuse. For example, a patentee is not engaged in misuse when seeking to redress contributory infringement or by refusing to grant a license to a third party or by refusing to practice the patented invention.

### Remedies

Sections 283, 284, and 285 of the Patent Act set out various remedies for an aggrieved patent owner, but fundamentally, injunctive relief (provided for in section 283) is a desired outcome for any litigation. Injunctive relief usually includes a request for a temporary restraining order and preliminary injunction during the conduct of the litigation and a permanent injunction following a finding of infringement, thus barring any further infringing use of the patent. Injunctive relief is an equitable remedy exercised by a court, taking into consideration four basic factors: (i) whether irreparable harm will result to the applicant without the issuance of an injunction, (ii) the relative hardship of an injunction on the parties, (iii) the adequacy of money damages; and (iv) the public interest.

Traditionally, in patent cases, injunctive relief was deemed the general rule upon a showing of infringement, together with proof of ownership of the patent and its validity. However, the U.S. Supreme Court rejected the general application of an injunction in its decision in *eBay, Inc. v. MerExchange, LLC.* In that dispute, MerExchange sued eBay for infringement of various patents involved in eBay's online auction process and had subsequently won an award for damages and sought a permanent injunction to prevent any future harm. The district court had denied the injunction, finding that its willingness to license its technology to eBay and its lack of practice of its own invention belied the claim that MerExchange would suffer irreparable harm if an injunction did not issue. This finding was reversed by the Federal Circuit, opting instead for its general rule that an injunction should follow a finding of infringement except in rare instances. The Supreme Court reversed the circuit court's decision, concurring with the district court's traditional analysis of the factors normally considered for the grant of injunctive relief in nonpatent cases as set forth above. Following the *eBay* case, patent owners have found inconsistent results in their quest for an injunction, with many cases turning on whether the parties are direct competitors or whether the patentee is practicing the invention. Interestingly, in some cases courts have encouraged the parties to enter into a licensing arrangement following a denial of an injunction for infringement. Indeed, given the costs of litigation, prospective litigants might be best served by entering into a license (or a cross license in instances where the parties need rights under both patents).

The recovery of monetary damages is another significant remedy sought by plaintiffs. Section 284 of the Patent Act provides that a court shall award damages upon a finding of infringement, in no event less than a reasonable royalty for the use made of the invention by the infringer, together with interest and costs as fixed by the court. Such costs may include the award of attorneys' fees to the prevailing party in exceptional cases as authorized by section 285 of the act. In fact, if willful infringement is found, then enhanced damages of attorneys' fees or treble damages (as provided in section 284) may be awarded. Notably, one key factor used to determine whether a patent owner has proven willful infringement is whether the defendant reasonably relied on a legal opinion of counsel. As noted in Chapter 2 in the section entitled **Professional Services**, prospective patent owners often engage the services of an attorney to express a written opinion regarding such matters as a patent's validity, infringement, or enforceability. In the event that a defendant acts in a manner contrary to that recommended in a legal opinion, then enhanced damages may be indicated in a subsequent litigation. Conversely, a plaintiff may be liable for attorneys' fees if a patent claim is fraudulently asserted.

In lieu of a reasonable royalty, an aggrieved patent owner may claim lost profits. Generally, a plaintiff will choose the option of receiving lost profits if the patentable matter would have been subject to sales in the absence of the infringing activity; lost profits may also be a higher measure of damages than a royalty. Those plaintiffs lacking sales potential for their patents have the statutory option of a reasonable royalty. However, in some instances a patentee with a patent capable of producing sales may not be able to recover lost profits due to the high threshold of proof established by the courts to recover such profits. Specifically, a patentee must prove (i) demand for the patented product and the ability to meet that demand; (ii) the absence of noninfringing substitutes that a purchaser might otherwise have acquired; and (iii) the amount of profit that would have been made. Regardless whether the compensatory method is a measure of lost profits or a reasonable royalty, the goal of the damages statute is not to punish the infringer but rather to put the patent owner in the pecuniary position that would have prevailed in the absence of the infringing activity.

### Insurance

Patent litigation often reaches into the hundreds of thousands (even millions) of dollars. Litigants in the position of defending claims traditionally relied on the "advertising injury" endorsement of their comprehensive general liability (CGL) policy for insurance against claims. However, insurers are increasingly limiting or excluding coverage for infringement under these endorsements. As a result, a specialized policy should be obtained to cover defense and indemnification for damages and legal expenses incurred with respect to alleged infringement.

Likewise, patent owners or inventors should consider obtaining insurance coverage against the often enormous cost of asserting a patent. Known as abatement insurance, policy benefits may include the insurer's provision of notice to an alleged infringer with the goal of early settlement as well as the appointment of an approved attorney to litigate the case if necessary. In some instances, a multi-peril policy may also be available to cover cases where a party may be required to both assert and defend various claims in the same proceeding. Many policies can be crafted to suit the buyer's needs. As a result, insureds now have greater opportunities to find adequate cover against patent-related disputes.

# APPENDIX 1:
# PATENT ACT OF 1790

Patent Act of 1790, Ch. 7, 1 Stat. 109-112 (April 10, 1790) The First United States Patent Statute

CHAP. VII. --An Act to promote the progress of useful Arts.(a )

SEC. 1.

*Be it enacted by the Senate and House of Representatives of the United States of America in Congress assembled,* That upon the petition of any person or persons to the Secretary of State, the Secretary for the department of war, and the Attorney General of the United States, setting forth, that he, she, or they, hath or have invented or discovered any useful art, manufacture, engine, machine, or device, or any improvement therein not before known or used, and praying that a patent may be granted therefor, it shall and may be lawful to and for the Secretary of State, the Secretary for the department of war, and the Attorney General, or any two of them, if they shall deem the invention or discovery sufficiently useful and important, to cause letters patent to be made out in the name of the United States, to bear teste by the President of the United States, reciting the allegations and suggestions of the said petition, and describing the said invention or discovery, clearly, truly and fully, and thereupon granting to such petitioner or petitioners, his, her or their heirs, administrators or assigns for any term not exceeding fourteen years, the sole and exclusive right and liberty of making, constructing, using and vending to others to be used, the said invention or discovery; which letters patent shall be delivered to the Attorney General of the United States to be examined, who shall, within fifteen days next after the delivery to him, if he shall find the same conformable to this act, certify it to be so at the foot thereof, and present the letters patent so certified to the President, who shall cause the seal of the United States to be thereto affixed, and the same shall be good and available to the grantee or grantees by force of this act, to all and every intent and purpose herein contained, and shall be recorded in a book to be kept for that purpose in the office of the Secretary of State, and delivered to the patentee or his agent, and the delivery thereof shall be entered on the record and endorsed on the patent by the said Secretary at the time of granting the same.

SEC 2.

*And be it further enacted,* That the grantee or grantees of each patent shall, at the time of granting the same, deliver to the Secretary of State a specification in writing, containing a description, accompanied with drafts or models, and explanations and models (if the nature of the invention or discovery will admit of a model) of the thing or things, by him or them invented or discovered, and described as aforesaid, in the said patents; which specification shall be so particular, and said models so exact, as not only to distinguish the invention or discovery from other things before known and used, but also to enable a workman or other person skilled in the art or manufacture, whereof it is a branch, or wherewith it may be nearest connected, to make, construct, or use the same, to the end that the public may have the full benefit thereof, after the expiration of the patent term; which specification shall be filed in the office of the said Secretary, and certified copies thereof, shall be competent evidence in all courts and before all jurisdictions, where any matter or thing, touching or concerning such patent, right, or privilege, shall come in question.

SEC. 3.

*And be it further enacted,* That upon the application of any person to the Secretary of State, for a copy of any such specification, and for permission to have similar model or models made, it shall be the duty of the Secretary to give such copy, and to permit the person so applying for a similar model or models, to take, or make, or cause the same to be taken or made, at the expense of such applicant.

SEC. 4.

*And be it further enacted,* That if any person or persons shall devise, make, construct, use, employ, or vend within these United States, any art, manufacture, engine, machine or device, or any invention or improvement upon, or in any art, manufacture, engine, machine or device, the sole and exclusive right of which shall be so as aforesaid granted by patent to any person or persons, by virtue and in pursuance of this act, without the consent of the patentee or patentees, their executors, administrators or assigns, first had and obtained in writing, every person so offending, shall forfeit and pay to the said patentee or patentees, his, her or their executors, administrators or assigns such damages as shall be as - sessed by a jury, and moreover shall forfeit to the person aggrieved, the thing or things so devised, made, constructed, used, employed or vended, contrary to the true intent of this act, which may be recovered in an action on the case founded on this act.

SEC. 5.

And be it further enacted, That upon oath or affirmation made before the judge of the district court, where the defendant resides, that any patent which shall be issued in pursuance of this act, was obtained surreptitiously by, or upon false suggestion, and motion made to the said court, within one year after issuing the said patent, but not afterwards, it shall and may be lawful to and for the judge of the said district court, if the matter alleged shall appear to him to be sufficient, to grant a rule that the patentee or patentees, his, her, or their executors, administrators or assigns, show cause why process should not issue against him, her, or them, to repeal such patents; and if sufficient cause shall not be shown to the contrary, the rule shall be made absolute, and thereupon the said judge shall order process to be issued as aforesaid, against such patentee or patentees, his, her, or their executors, administrators, or assigns. And in case no sufficient cause shall be shown to the contrary, or if it shall appear that the patentee was not the first and true inventor or discoverer, judgment shall be rendered by such court for the repeal of such patent or patents; and if the party at whose complaint the process issued, shall have judgment given against him, he shall pay all such costs as the defendant shall be put to in defending the suit, to be taxed by the court, and recovered in such manner as costs expended by defendants, shall be recovered in due course of law.

SEC. 6.

*And be it further enacted,* That in all actions to be brought by such patentee or patentees, his, her, or their executors, administrators or assigns, for any penalty incurred by virtue of this act, the said patents or specifications shall be *prima facie* evidence, that the said patentee or patentees was or were the first and true inventor or inventors, discoverer or discoverers of the thing so specified, and that the same is truly specified; but that nevertheless the defendant or defendants may plead the general issue, and give this act, and any special matter whereof notice in writing shall have been given to the plaintiff, or his attorney, thirty days before the trial, in evidence, tending to prove that the specification filed by the plaintiff does not contain the whole of the truth concerning his invention or discovery; or that it contains more than is necessary to produce the effect described; and if the concealment of part, or the addition of more than is necessary, shall appear to have been intended to mislead, or shall actually mislead the public, so as the effect described cannot be produced by the means specified, then, and in such cases, the verdict and judgment shall be for the defendant.

SEC. 7.

*And be it further enacted,* That such patentee as aforesaid, shall, before he receives his patent, pay the following fees to the several officers employed in making out and perfecting the same, to wit: For receiving and filing the petition, fifty cents; for filing specifications, per copy-sheet containing one hundred words, ten cents; for making out patent, two dollars; for affixing great seal, one dollar; for indorsing the day of delivering the same to the patentee, including all intermediate services, twenty cents.

**Legislative History**

APPROVED, April 10, 1790.

Understanding Patent Law: A Beginner's Guide

# APPENDIX 2:
# AMERICAN INVENTORS PROTECTION ACT OF 1999

*Excerpts from the American Inventors Protection Act of 1999,*
*Nov. 29, 1999, Public Law 106–113*

**TITLE IV—INVENTOR PROTECTION**

**SEC. 4001. SHORT TITLE**

This title may be cited as the "American Inventors Protection Act of 1999."

Subtitle A—Inventors' Rights

**SEC. 4101. SHORT TITLE**

This subtitle may be cited as the "Inventors' Rights Act of 1999."

**SEC. 4102. INTEGRITY IN INVENTION PROMOTION SERVICES**

(a) In General.—Chapter 29 of title 35, United States Code, is amended by adding at the end the following new section:

"Sec. 297. Improper and deceptive invention promotion

"(a) In General.—An invention promoter shall have a duty to disclose the following information to a customer in writing, prior to entering into a contract for invention promotion services—

"(1) the total number of inventions evaluated by the invention promoter for commercial potential in the past 5 years, as well as the number of those inventions that received positive evaluations, and the number of those inventions that received negative evaluations;

"(2) the total number of customers who have contracted with the invention promoter in the past 5 years, not including customers who have purchased trade show services, research, advertising, or other nonmarketing services from the invention promoter, or who have defaulted in their payment to the invention promoter;

"(3) the total number of customers known by the invention promoter to have received a net financial profit as a direct result of the invention promotion services provided by such invention promoter;

"(4) the total number of customers known by the invention promoter to have received license agreements for their inventions as a direct result of the invention promotion services provided by such invention promoter; and

"(5) the names and addresses of all previous invention promotion companies with which the invention promoter or its officers have collectively or individually been affiliated in the previous 10 years.

"(b) Civil Action.—(1) Any customer who enters into a contract with an invention promoter and who is found by a court to have been injured by any material false or fraudulent statement or representation, or any omission of material fact, by that invention promoter (or any agent, employee, director, officer, partner, or independent contractor of such invention promoter), or by the failure of that invention promoter to disclose such information as required under subsection (a), may recover in a civil action against the invention promoter (or the officers, directors, or partners of such invention promoter), in addition to reasonable costs and attorneys' fees—

"(A) the amount of actual damages incurred by the customer; or

"(B) at the election of the customer at any time before final judgment is rendered, statutory damages in a sum of not more than $5,000, as the court considers just.

"(2) Notwithstanding paragraph (1), in a case where the customer sustains the burden of proof, and the court finds, that the invention promoter intentionally misrepresented or omitted a material fact to such customer, or willfully failed to disclose such information as required under subsection (a), with the purpose of deceiving that customer, the court may increase damages to not more than three times the amount awarded, taking into account past complaints made against the invention promoter that resulted in regulatory sanctions or other corrective actions based on those records compiled by the Commissioner of Patents under subsection (d).

"(c) Definitions.—For purposes of this section—

"(1) a 'contract for invention promotion services' means a contract by which an invention promoter undertakes invention promotion services for a customer;

"(2) a 'customer' is any individual who enters into a contract with an invention promoter for invention promotion services;

"(3) the term 'invention promoter' means any person, firm, partnership, corporation, or other entity who offers to perform or performs invention promotion services for, or on behalf of, a customer, and who holds itself out through advertising in any mass media as providing such services, but does not include—

"(A) any department or agency of the Federal Government or of a State or local government;

"(B) any nonprofit, charitable, scientific, or educational organization, qualified under applicable State law or described under section 170(b)(1)(A) of the Internal Revenue Code of 1986;

"(C) any person or entity involved in the evaluation to determine commercial potential of, or offering to license or sell, a utility patent or a previously filed nonprovisional utility patent application;

"(D) any party participating in a transaction involving the sale of the stock or assets of a business; or

"(E) any party who directly engages in the business of retail sales of products or the distribution of products; and

"(4) the term 'invention promotion services' means the procurement or attempted procurement for a customer of a firm, corporation, or other entity to develop and market products or services that include the invention of the customer.

"(d) Records of Complaints.—

"(1) Release of complaints.—The Commissioner of Patents shall make all complaints received by the Patent and Trademark Office involving invention promoters publicly available, together with any response of the invention promoters. The Commissioner of Patents shall notify the invention promoter of a complaint and provide a reasonable opportunity to reply prior to making such complaint publicly available.

"(2) Request for complaints.—The Commissioner of Patents may request complaints relating to invention promotion services from any Federal or State agency and include such complaints in the records maintained under paragraph (1), together with any response of the invention promoters."

Subtitle E—Domestic Publication of Patent Applications Published Abroad

### SEC. 4501. SHORT TITLE

This subtitle may be cited as the "Domestic Publication of Foreign Filed Patent Applications Act of 1999."

### SEC. 4502. PUBLICATION

(a) Publication.—Section 122 of title 35, United States Code, is amended to read as follows:

"Sec. 122. Confidential status of applications; publication of patent applications

"(a) Confidentiality.—Except as provided in subsection (b), applications for patents shall be kept in confidence by the Patent and Trademark Office and no information concerning the same given without authority of the applicant or owner unless necessary to carry out the provisions of an Act of Congress or in such special circumstances as may be determined by the Director.

"(b) Publication.—

"(1) In general.—(A) Subject to paragraph (2), each application for a patent shall be published, in accordance with procedures determined by the Director, promptly after the expiration of a period of 18 months from the earliest filing date for which a benefit is sought under this title. At the request of the applicant, an application may be published earlier than the end of such 18-month period.

"(B) No information concerning published patent applications shall be made available to the public except as the Director determines.

"(C) Notwithstanding any other provision of law, a determination by the Director to release or not to release information concerning a published patent application shall be final and nonreviewable.

"(2) Exceptions.—(A) An application shall not be published if that application is—

"(i) no longer pending;

"(ii) subject to a secrecy order under section 181 of this title;

"(iii) a provisional application filed under section 111(b) of this title; or

"(iv) an application for a design patent filed under chapter 16 of this title.

"(B)(i) If an applicant makes a request upon filing, certifying that the invention disclosed in the application has not and will not be the subject of an application filed in another country, or under a multilateral international agreement, that requires publication of applications 18 months after filing, the application shall not be published as provided in paragraph (1).

"(ii) An applicant may rescind a request made under clause (i) at any time.

"(iii) An applicant who has made a request under clause (i) but who subsequently files, in a foreign country or under a multilateral international agreement specified in clause (i), an application directed to the invention disclosed in the application filed in the Patent and Trademark Office, shall notify the Director of such filing not later than 45 days after the date of the filing of such foreign or international application. A failure of the applicant to provide such notice within the prescribed period shall result in the application being regarded as abandoned, unless it is shown to the satisfaction of the Director that the delay in submitting the notice was unintentional.

"(iv) If an applicant rescinds a request made under clause (i) or notifies the Director that an application was filed in a foreign country or under a multilateral international agreement specified in clause (i), the application shall be published in accordance with the provisions of paragraph (1) on or as soon as is practical after the date that is specified in clause (i).

"(v) If an applicant has filed applications in one or more foreign countries, directly or through a multilateral international agreement, and such foreign filed applications corresponding to an application filed in the Patent and Trademark Office or the description of the invention in such foreign filed applications is less extensive than the application or description of the invention in the application filed in the Patent and Trademark Office, the applicant may submit a redacted copy of the application filed in the Patent and Trademark Office eliminating any part or description of the invention in such application that is not also contained in any of the corresponding applications filed in a foreign country. The Director may only publish the redacted copy of the application unless the redacted copy of the application is not received within 16 months after the earliest effective filing date for which a benefit is sought under this title. The provisions of section 154(d) shall not apply to a claim if the description of the invention published in the redacted application filed under this clause with respect to the claim does not enable a person skilled in the art to make and use the subject matter of the claim.

"(c) Protest and Pre-Issuance Opposition.—The Director shall establish appropriate procedures to ensure that no protest or other form of pre-issuance opposition to the grant of a patent on an application may be initiated after publication of the application without the express written consent of the applicant.

"(d) National Security.—No application for patent shall be published under subsection (b)(1) if the publication or disclosure of such invention would be detrimental to the national security. The Director shall establish appropriate procedures to ensure that such applications are promptly identified and the secrecy of such inventions is maintained in accordance with chapter 17 of this title."

# APPENDIX 3:
# DEFINITIONS AND CONDITIONS
# FOR PATENTABILITY

## DEFINITIONS

### Section 100 of the Patent Act:

When used in this title unless the context otherwise indicates—

(a) The term "invention" means invention or discovery.

(b) The term "process" means process, art, or method, and includes a new use of a known process, machine, manufacture, composition of matter, or material.

(c) The terms "United States" and "this country" mean the United States of America, its territories and possessions.

(d) The word "patentee" includes not only the patentee to whom the patent was issued but also the successors in title to the patentee.

(e) The term "third-party requester" means a person requesting ex parte reexamination under section 302 or inter partes reexamination under section 311 who is not the patent owner.

## CONDITIONS FOR PATENTABILITY

### Section 101 of the Patent Act:

Whoever invents or discovers any new and useful process, machine, manufacture, or composition of matter, or any new and useful improvement thereof, may obtain a patent therefor, subject to the conditions and requirements of this title.

**Section 102 of the Patent Act:**

A person shall be entitled to a patent unless—

(a) the invention was known or used by others in this country, or patented or described in a printed publication in this or a foreign country, before the invention thereof by the applicant for patent, or

(b) the invention was patented or described in a printed publication in this or a foreign country or in public use or on sale in this country, more than one year prior to the date of the application for patent in the United States, or

(c) he has abandoned the invention, or

(d) the invention was first patented or caused to be patented, or was the subject of an inventor's certificate, by the applicant or his legal representatives or assigns in a foreign country prior to the date of the application for patent in this country on an application for patent or inventor's certificate filed more than twelve months before the filing of the application in the United States, or

(e) the invention was described in—

(1) an application for patent, published under section 122(b), by another filed in the United States before the invention by the applicant for patent or (2) a patent granted on an application for patent by another filed in the United States before the invention by the applicant for patent, except that an international application filed under the treaty defined in section 351(a) shall have the effects for the purposes of this subsection of an application filed in the United States only if the international application designated the United States and was published under Article 21(2) of such treaty in the English language; or

(f) he did not himself invent the subject matter sought to be patented, or

(g)(1) during the course of an interference conducted under section 135 or section 291, another inventor involved therein establishes, to the extent permitted in section 104, that before such person's invention thereof the invention was made by such other inventor and not abandoned, suppressed, or concealed, or (2) before such person's invention thereof, the invention was made in this country by another inventor who had not abandoned, suppressed, or concealed it. In determining priority of invention under this subsection, there shall be considered not only the respective dates of conception and reduction to practice of the invention, but also the reasonable diligence of one who was first to conceive and last to reduce to practice, from a time prior to conception by the other.

### Section 103 of the Patent Act:

(a) A patent may not be obtained though the invention is not identically disclosed or described as set forth in section 102 of this title, if the differences between the subject matter sought to be patented and the prior art are such that the subject matter as a whole would have been obvious at the time the invention was made to a person having ordinary skill in the art to which said subject matter pertains. Patentability shall not be negatived by the manner in which the invention was made.

(b)(1) Notwithstanding subsection (a), and upon timely election by the applicant for patent to proceed under this subsection, a biotechnological process using or resulting in a composition of matter that is novel under section 102 and nonobvious under subsection (a) of this section shall be considered nonobvious if—

(A) claims to the process and the composition of matter are contained in either the same application for patent or in separate applications having the same effective filing date; and

(B) the composition of matter, and the process at the time it was invented, were owned by the same person or subject to an obligation of assignment to the same person.

(2) A patent issued on a process under paragraph (1)—

(A) shall also contain the claims to the composition of matter used in or made by that process, or

(B) shall, if such composition of matter is claimed in another patent, be set to expire on the same date as such other patent, notwithstanding section 154.

(3) For purposes of paragraph (1), the term "biotechnological process" means—

(A) a process of genetically altering or otherwise inducing a single- or multi-celled organism to—

(i) express an exogenous nucleotide sequence,

(ii) inhibit, eliminate, augment, or alter expression of an endogenous nucleotide sequence, or

(iii) express a specific physiological characteristic not naturally associated with said organism;

(B) cell fusion procedures yielding a cell line that expresses a specific protein, such as a monoclonal antibody; and

(C) a method of using a product produced by a process defined by subparagraph (A) or (B), or a combination of subparagraphs (A) and (B).

# APPENDIX 4:
# PATENT MARKING PROVISIONS

**Excerpt from Section 287 of the Patent Act:**

(a) Patentees, and persons making, offering for sale, or selling within the United States any patented article for or under them, or importing any patented article into the United States, may give notice to the public that the same is patented, either by fixing thereon the word "patent" or the abbreviation "pat.," together with the number of the patent, or when, from the character of the article, this cannot be done, by fixing to it, or to the package wherein one or more of them is contained, a label containing a like notice. In the event of failure so to mark, no damages shall be recovered by the patentee in any action for infringement, except on proof that the infringer was notified of the infringement and continued to infringe thereafter, in which event damages may be recovered only for infringement occurring after such notice. Filing of an action for infringement shall constitute such notice.

**Section 292 of the Patent Act:**

(a) Whoever, without the consent of the patentee, marks upon, or affixes to, or uses in advertising in connection with anything made, used, offered for sale, or sold by such person within the United States, or imported by the person into the United States, the name or any imitation of the name of the patentee, the patent number, or the words "patent," "patentee," or the like, with the intent of counterfeiting or imitating the mark of the patentee, or of deceiving the public and inducing them to believe that the thing was made, offered for sale, sold, or imported into the United States by or with the consent of the patentee; or

Whoever marks upon, or affixes to, or uses in advertising in connection with any unpatented article the word "patent" or any word or number importing the same is patented, for the purpose of deceiving the public; or

Whoever marks upon, or affixes to, or uses in advertising in connection with any article the words "patent applied for," "patent pending," or any word importing that an application for patent has been made, when no application for patent has been made, or if made, is not pending, for the purpose of deceiving the public—

Shall be fined not more than $500 for every such offense.

(b) Any person may sue for the penalty, in which event one-half shall go to the person suing and the other to the use of the United States.

# APPENDIX 5:
# PATENT DURATION AND ADJUSTMENT

**Excerpt from Section 154 of the Patent Act:**

(2) TERM—Subject to the payment of fees under this title, such grant shall be for a term beginning on the date on which the patent issues and ending 20 years from the date on which the application for the patent was filed in the United States or, if the application contains a specific reference to an earlier filed application or applications under section 120, 121, or 365(c) of this title, from the date on which the earliest such application was filed.

. . .

(b) ADJUSTMENT OF PATENT TERM—

(1) PATENT TERM GUARANTEES—

(A) GUARANTEE OF PROMPT PATENT AND TRADEMARK OFFICE RESPONSES—Subject to the limitations under paragraph (2), if the issue of an original patent is delayed due to the failure of the Patent and Trademark Office to—

(i) provide at least one of the notifications under section 132 of this title or a notice of allowance under section 151 of this title not later than 14 months after—

(I) the date on which an application was filed under section 111(a) of this title; or

(II) the date on which an international application fulfilled the requirements of section 371 of this title;

(ii) respond to a reply under section 132, or to an appeal taken under section 134, within 4 months after the date on which the reply was filed or the appeal was taken;

(iii) act on an application within 4 months after the date of a decision by the Board of Patent Appeals and Interferences under section 134 or 135 or a decision by a Federal court under section 141, 145, or 146 in a case in which allowable claims remain in the application; or

(iv) issue a patent within 4 months after the date on which the issue fee was paid under section 151 and all outstanding requirements were satisfied, the term of the patent shall be extended 1 day for each day after the end of the period specified in clause (i), (ii), (iii), or (iv), as the case may be, until the action described in such clause is taken.

(B) GUARANTEE OF NO MORE THAN 3-YEAR APPLICATION PENDENCY—Subject to the limitations under paragraph (2), if the issue of an original patent is delayed due to the failure of the United States Patent and Trademark Office to issue a patent within 3 years after the actual filing date of the application in the United States, not including—

(i) any time consumed by continued examination of the application requested by the applicant under section 132(b);

(ii) any time consumed by a proceeding under section 135(a), any time consumed by the imposition of an order under section 181, or any time consumed by appellate review by the Board of Patent Appeals and Interferences or by a Federal court; or

(iii) any delay in the processing of the application by the United States Patent and Trademark Office requested by the applicant except as permitted by paragraph (3)(C), the term of the patent shall be extended 1 day for each day after the end of that 3-year period until the patent is issued.

(C) GUARANTEE OR ADJUSTMENTS FOR DELAYS DUE TO INTERFERENCES, SECRECY ORDERS, AND APPEALS—Subject to the limitations under paragraph (2), if the issue of an original patent is delayed due to—

(i) a proceeding under section 135(a);

(ii) the imposition of an order under section 181; or

(iii) appellate review by the Board of Patent Appeals and Interferences or by a Federal court in a case in which the patent was issued under a decision in the review reversing an adverse determination of patentability, the term of the patent shall be extended 1 day for each day of the pendency of the proceeding, order, or review, as the case may be.

(2) LIMITATIONS—

(A) IN GENERAL—To the extent that periods of delay attributable to grounds specified in paragraph (1) overlap, the period of any adjustment granted under this subsection shall not exceed the actual number of days the issuance of the patent was delayed.

(B) DISCLAIMED TERM—No patent of the term of which has been disclaimed beyond a specified date may be adjusted under this section beyond the expiration date specified in the disclaimer.

(C) REDUCTION OF PERIOD OF ADJUSTMENT—

(i) The period of adjustment of the term of a patent under paragraph (1) shall be reduced by a period equal to the period of time during which the applicant failed to engage in reasonable efforts to conclude prosecution of the application.

## Section 155 of the Patent Act:

Notwithstanding the provisions of section 154, the term of a patent which encompasses within its scope a composition of matter or a process for using such composition shall be extended if such composition or process has been subjected to a regulatory review by the Federal Food and Drug Administration pursuant to the Federal Food, Drug, and Cosmetic Act leading to the publication of regulation permitting the interstate distribution and sale of such composition or process and for which there has thereafter been a stay of regulation of approval imposed pursuant to section 409 of the Federal Food, Drug, and Cosmetic Act, which stay was in effect on January 1, 1981, by a length of time to be measured from the date such stay of regulation of approval was imposed until such proceedings are finally resolved and commercial marketing permitted. The patentee, his heirs, successors, or assigns shall notify the Director within 90 days of the date of enactment of this section or the date the stay of regulation of approval has been removed, whichever is later, of the number of the patent to be extended and the date the stay was imposed and the date commercial marketing was permitted. On receipt of such notice, the Director shall promptly issue to the owner of record of the patent a certificate of extension, under seal, stating the fact and length of the extension and identifying the composition of matter or process for using such composition to which such extension is applicable. Such certificate shall be recorded in the official file of each patent extended and such certificate shall be considered as part of the original patent, and an appropriate notice shall be published in the Official Gazette of the Patent and Trademark Office.

**SECTIONS 1.701–1.705 OF TITLE 37 OF THE CFR**

**Section 1.701:**

(a) A patent, other than for designs, issued on an application filed on or after June 8, 1995, is entitled to extension of the patent term if the issuance of the patent was delayed due to:

(1) Interference proceedings under 35 U.S.C.135(a); and/or

(2) The application being placed under a secrecy order under 35 U.S.C. 181; and/or

(3) Appellate review by the Board of Patent Appeals and Interferences or by a Federal court under 35 U.S.C. 141 or 145, if the patent was issued pursuant to a decision in the review reversing an adverse determination of patentability and if the patent is not subject to a terminal disclaimer due to the issuance of another patent claiming subject matter that is not patentably distinct from that under appellate review. If an application is remanded by a panel of the Board of Patent Appeals and Interferences, and the remand is the last action by a panel of the Board of Patent Appeals and Interferences prior to the mailing of a notice of allowance under 35 U.S.C. 151 in the application, the remand shall be considered a decision in the review reversing an adverse determination of patentability as that phrase is used in 35 U.S.C. 154(b)(2) as amended by section 532(a) of the Uruguay Round Agreements Act, Public Law 103–465, 108 Stat. 4809, 4983–85 (1994), and a final decision in favor of the applicant under paragraph (c)(3) of this section. A remand by a panel of the Board of Patent Appeals and Interferences shall not be considered a decision in the review reversing an adverse determination of patentability as provided in this paragraph if there is filed a request for continued examination under 35 U.S.C. 132(b) that was not first preceded by the mailing, after such remand, of at least one of an action under 35 U.S.C. 132 or a notice of allowance under 35 U.S.C. 151.

(b) The term of a patent entitled to extension under paragraph (a) of this section shall be extended for the sum of the periods of delay calculated under paragraphs (c)(1), (c)(2), (c)(3), and (d) of this section, to the extent that these periods are not overlapping, up to a maximum of five years. The extension will run from the expiration date of the patent. (c)(1) The period of delay under paragraph (a)(1) of this section for an application is the sum of the following periods, to the extent that the periods are not overlapping:

(i) With respect to each interference in which the application was involved, the number of days, if any, in the period beginning on the date the interference was declared or redeclared to involve the application in the interference and ending on the date that the interference was terminated with respect to the application; and

(ii) The number of days, if any, in the period beginning on the date that prosecution in the application was suspended by the Patent and Trademark Office due to interference proceedings under 35 U.S.C. 135(a) not involving the application and ending on the date of the termination of the suspension.

(2) The period of delay under paragraph (a)(2) of this section for an application is the sum of the following periods, to the extent that the periods are not overlapping:

(i) The number of days, if any, the application was maintained in a sealed condition under 35 U.S.C. 181;

(ii) The number of days, if any, in the period beginning on the date of mailing of an examiner's answer under § 41.39 of this title in the application under secrecy order and ending on the date the secrecy order and any renewal thereof was removed;

(iii) The number of days, if any, in the period beginning on the date applicant was notified that an interference would be declared but for the secrecy order and ending on the date the secrecy order and any renewal thereof was removed; and

(iv) The number of days, if any, in the period beginning on the date of notification under § 5.3(c) and ending on the date of mailing of the notice of allowance under § 1.311.

(3) The period of delay under paragraph (a)(3) of this section is the sum of the number of days, if any, in the period beginning on the date on which an appeal to the Board of Patent Appeals and Interferences was filed under 35 U.S.C. 134 and ending on the date of a final decision in favor of the applicant by the Board of Patent Appeals and Interferences or by a Federal court in an appeal under 35 U.S.C. 141 or a civil action under 35 U.S.C. 145.

(d) The period of delay set forth in paragraph (c)(3) shall be reduced by:

(1) Any time during the period of appellate review that occurred before 3 years from the filing of the first national application for patent presented for examination; and

(2) Any time during the period of appellate review, as determined by the Director, during which the applicant for patent did not act with due diligence. In determining the due diligence of an applicant, the Director may examine the facts and circumstances of the applicant's actions during the period of appellate review to determine whether the applicant exhibited that degree of timeliness as may reasonably be expected from, and which is ordinarily exercised by, a person during a period of appellate review.

(e) The provisions of this section apply only to original patents, except for design patents, issued on applications filed on or after June 8, 1995, and before May 29, 2000.

## Section 1.702:

(a) *Failure to take certain actions within specified time frames.* Subject to the provisions of 35 U.S.C. 154(b) and this subpart, the term of an original patent shall be adjusted if the issuance of the patent was delayed due to the failure of the Office to:

(1) Mail at least one of a notification under 35 U.S.C. 132 or a notice of allowance under 35 U.S.C. 151 not later than 14 months after the date on which the application was filed under 35 U.S.C. 111(a) or fulfilled the requirements of 35 U.S.C. 371 in an international application;

(2) Respond to a reply under 35 U.S.C. 132 or to an appeal taken under 35 U.S.C. 134 not later than 4 months after the date on which the reply was filed or the appeal was taken;

(3) Act on an application not later than four months after the date of a decision by the Board of Patent Appeals and Interferences under 35 U.S.C. 134 or 135 or a decision by a Federal court under 35 U.S.C. 141, 145, or 146 where at least one allowable claim remains in the application; or

(4) Issue a patent not later than four months after the date on which the issue fee was paid under 35 U.S.C. 151 and all outstanding requirements were satisfied.

(b) *Failure to issue a patent within three years of the actual filing date of the application.* Subject to the provisions of 35 U.S.C. 154(b) and this subpart, the term of an original patent shall be adjusted if the issuance of the patent was delayed due to the failure of the Office to issue a patent within three years after the date on which the application was filed under 35 U.S.C. 111(a) or the national stage commenced under 35 U.S.C. 371(b) or (f) in an international application, but not including:

(1) Any time consumed by continued examination of the application under 35 U.S.C. 132(b);

(2) Any time consumed by an interference proceeding under 35 U.S.C. 135(a);

(3) Any time consumed by the imposition of a secrecy order under 35 U.S.C. 181;

(4) Any time consumed by review by the Board of Patent Appeals and Interferences or a Federal court; or

(5) Any delay in the processing of the application by the Office that was requested by the applicant.

(c) *Delays caused by interference proceedings.* Subject to the provisions of 35 U.S.C. 154(b) and this subpart, the term of an original patent shall be adjusted if the issuance of the patent was delayed due to interference proceedings under 35 U.S.C. 135(a).

(d) *Delays caused by secrecy order.* Subject to the provisions of 35 U.S.C. 154(b) and this subpart, the term of an original patent shall be adjusted if the issuance of the patent was delayed due to the application being placed under a secrecy order under 35 U.S.C. 181.

(e) *Delays caused by successful appellate review.* Subject to the provisions of 35 U.S.C. 154(b) and this subpart, the term of an original patent shall be adjusted if the issuance of the patent was delayed due to review by the Board of Patent Appeals and Interferences under 35 U.S.C. 134 or by a Federal court under 35 U.S.C. 141 or 145, if the patent was issued under a decision in the review reversing an adverse determination of patentability. If an application is remanded by a panel of the Board of Patent Appeals and Interferences, and the remand is the last action by a panel of the Board of Patent Appeals and Interferences prior to the mailing of a notice of allowance under 35 U.S.C. 151 in the application, the remand shall be considered a decision by the Board of Patent Appeals and Interferences as that phrase is used in 35 U.S.C. 154(b)(1)(A)(iii), a decision in the review reversing an adverse determination of patentability as that phrase is used in 35 U.S.C. 154(b)(1)(C)(iii), and a final decision in favor of the applicant under §1.703(e). A remand by a panel of the Board of Patent Appeals and Interferences shall not be considered a decision in the review reversing an adverse determination of patentability as provided in this paragraph if there is filed a request for continued examination under 35 U.S.C. 132(b) that was not first preceded by the mailing, after such remand, of at least one of an action under 35 U.S.C. 132 or a notice of allowance under 35 U.S.C. 151.

(f) The provisions of this section and §§1.703 through 1.705 apply only to original applications, except applications for a design patent, filed on or after May 29, 2000, and patents issued on such applications.

## Section 1.703

(a) The period of adjustment under § 1.702(a) is the sum of the following periods:

(1) The number of days, if any, in the period beginning on the day after the date that is fourteen months after the date on which the application was filed under 35 U.S.C. 111(a) or fulfilled the requirements of 35 U.S.C. 371 and ending on the date of mailing of either an action under 35 U.S.C. 132, or a notice of allowance under 35 U.S.C. 151, whichever occurs first;

(2) The number of days, if any, in the period beginning on the day after the date that is four months after the date a reply under § 1.111 was filed and ending on the date of mailing of either an action under 35 U.S.C. 132, or a notice of allowance under 35 U.S.C. 151, whichever occurs first;

(3) The number of days, if any, in the period beginning on the day after the date that is four months after the date a reply in compliance with § 1.113(c) was filed and ending on the date of mailing of either an action under 35 U.S.C. 132, or a notice of allowance under 35 U.S.C. 151, whichever occurs first;

(4) The number of days, if any, in the period beginning on the day after the date that is four months after the date an appeal brief in compliance with §41.37 of this title was filed and ending on the date of mailing of any of an examiner's answer under § 41.39 of this title, an action under 35 U.S.C. 132, or a notice of allowance under 35 U.S.C. 151, whichever occurs first;

(5) The number of days, if any, in the period beginning on the day after the date that is four months after the date of a final decision by the Board of Patent Appeals and Interferences or by a Federal court in an appeal under 35 U.S.C. 141 or a civil action

under 35 U.S.C. 145 or 146 where at least one allowable claim remains in the application and ending on the date of mailing of either an action under 35 U.S.C. 132 or a notice of allowance under 35 U.S.C. 151, whichever occurs first; and

(6) The number of days, if any, in the period beginning on the day after the date that is four months after the date the issue fee was paid, and all outstanding requirements were satisfied and ending on the date a patent was issued.

(b) The period of adjustment under § 1.702(b) is the number of days, if any, in the period beginning on the day after the date that is three years after the date on which the application was filed under 35 U.S.C. 111(a) or the national stage commenced under 35 U.S.C. 371(b) or (f) in an international application and ending on the date a patent was issued, but not including the sum of the following periods:

(1) The number of days, if any, in the period beginning on the date on which a request for continued examination of the application under 35 U.S.C. 132(b) was filed and ending on the date the patent was issued;

(2)(i) The number of days, if any, in the period beginning on the date that an interference was declared or redeclared to involve the application in the interference and ending on the date that the interference was terminated with respect to the application; and

(ii) The number of days, if any, in the period beginning on the date prosecution in the application was suspended by the Office due to interference proceedings under 35 U.S.C. 135(a) not involving the application and ending on the date of the termination of the suspension;

(3)(i) The number of days, if any, the application was maintained in a sealed condition under 35 U.S.C. 181;

(ii) The number of days, if any, in the period beginning on the date of mailing of an examiner's answer under § 41.39 of this title in the application under secrecy order and ending on the date the secrecy order was removed;

(iii) The number of days, if any, in the period beginning on the date applicant was notified that an interference would be declared but for the secrecy order and ending on the date the secrecy order was removed; and

(iv) The number of days, if any, in the period beginning on the date of notification under § 5.3(c) of this chapter and ending on the date of mailing of the notice of allowance under 35 U.S.C. 151; and,

(4) The number of days, if any, in the period beginning on the date on which a notice of appeal to the Board of Patent Appeals and Interferences was filed under 35 U.S.C. 134 and § 41.31 of this title and ending on the date of the last decision by the Board of Patent Appeals and Interferences or by a Federal court in an appeal under 35 U.S.C. 141 or a civil action under 35 U.S.C. 145, or on the date of mailing of either an action under 35 U.S.C. 132, or a notice of allowance under 35 U.S.C. 151, whichever occurs first, if the appeal did not result in a decision by the Board of Patent Appeals and Interferences.

(c) The period of adjustment under § 1.702(c) is the sum of the following periods, to the extent that the periods are not overlapping:

(1) The number of days, if any, in the period beginning on the date an interference was declared or redeclared to involve the application in the interference and ending on the date that the interference was terminated with respect to the application; and

(2) The number of days, if any, in the period beginning on the date prosecution in the application was suspended by the Office due to interference proceedings under 35 U.S.C. 135(a) not involving the application and ending on the date of the termination of the suspension.

(d) The period of adjustment under § 1.702(d) is the sum of the following periods, to the extent that the periods are not overlapping:

(1) The number of days, if any, the application was maintained in a sealed condition under 35 U.S.C. 181;

(2) The number of days, if any, in the period beginning on the date of mailing of an examiner's answer under § 41.39 of this title in the application under secrecy order and ending on the date the secrecy order was removed;

(3) The number of days, if any, in the period beginning on the date applicant was notified that an interference would be declared but for the secrecy order and ending on the date the secrecy order was removed; and

(4) The number of days, if any, in the period beginning on the date of notification under § 5.3(c) of this chapter and ending

on the date of mailing of the notice of allowance under 35 U.S.C. 151.

(e) The period of adjustment under § 1.702(e) is the sum of the number of days, if any, in the period beginning on the date on which a notice of appeal to the Board of Patent Appeals and Interferences was filed under 35 U.S.C. 134 and § 41.31 of this title and ending on the date of a final decision in favor of the applicant by the Board of Patent Appeals and Interferences or by a Federal court in an appeal under 35 U.S.C. 141 or a civil action under 35 U.S.C. 145.

(f) The adjustment will run from the expiration date of the patent as set forth in 35 U.S.C. 154(a)(2). To the extent that periods of delay attributable to the grounds specified in §1.702 overlap, the period of adjustment granted under this section shall not exceed the actual number of days the issuance of the patent was delayed. The term of a patent entitled to adjustment under § 1.702 and this section shall be adjusted for the sum of the periods calculated under paragraphs (a) through (e) of this section, to the extent that such periods are not overlapping, less the sum of the periods calculated under § 1.704. The date indicated on any certificate of mailing or transmission under § 1.8 shall not be taken into account in this calculation.

(g) No patent, the term of which has been disclaimed beyond a specified date, shall be adjusted under § 1.702 and this section beyond the expiration date specified in the disclaimer.

### Section 1.704:

(a) The period of adjustment of the term of a patent under § 1.703(a) through (e) shall be reduced by a period equal to the period of time during which the applicant failed to engage in reasonable efforts to conclude prosecution (processing or examination) of the application.

(b) With respect to the grounds for adjustment set forth in §§ 1.702(a) through (e), and in particular the ground of adjustment set forth in § 1.702(b), an applicant shall be deemed to have failed to engage in reasonable efforts to conclude processing or examination of an application for the cumulative total of any periods of time in excess of three months that are taken to reply to any notice or action by the Office making any rejection, objection, argument, or other request, measuring such three-month period from the date the notice or action was mailed or given to the applicant, in which case the period of adjustment set forth in § 1.703 shall be reduced by the number of days, if any, beginning on the day after the date that is three months after the date of mailing or transmission of the Office communication notifying the applicant of the rejection, objection, argument, or other request and ending on the date the reply was filed. The period, or shortened statutory period, for reply that is set in the Office action or notice has no effect on the three-month period set forth in this paragraph.

(c) Circumstances that constitute a failure of the applicant to engage in reasonable efforts to conclude processing or examination of an application also include the following circumstances, which will result in the following reduction of the period of adjustment set forth in § 1.703 to the extent that the periods are not overlapping:

(1) Suspension of action under § 1.103 at the applicant's request, in which case the period of adjustment set forth in § 1.703 shall be reduced by the number of days, if any, beginning on the date a request for suspension of action under § 1.103 was filed and ending on the date of the termination of the suspension;

(2) Deferral of issuance of a patent under § 1.314, in which case the period of adjustment set forth in § 1.703 shall be reduced by the number of days, if any, beginning on the date a request for deferral of issuance of a patent under § 1.314 was filed and ending on the date the patent was issued;

(3) Abandonment of the application or late payment of the issue fee, in which case the period of adjustment set forth in §1.703 shall be reduced by the number of days, if any, beginning on the date of abandonment or the date after the date the issue fee was due and ending on the earlier of:

(i) The date of mailing of the decision reviving the application or accepting late payment of the issue fee; or

(ii) The date that is four months after the date the grantable petition to revive the application or accept late payment of the issue fee was filed;

(4) Failure to file a petition to withdraw the holding of abandonment or to revive an application within two months from the mailing date of a notice of abandonment, in which case the period of adjustment set forth in § 1.703 shall be reduced by the number of days, if any, beginning on the day after the date two months from the mailing date of a notice of abandonment and ending on the date a petition to withdraw the holding of abandonment or to revive the application was filed;

(5) Conversion of a provisional application under 35 U.S.C. 111(b) to a nonprovisional application under 35 U.S.C. 111(a) pursuant to 35 U.S.C.111(b)(5), in which case the period of adjustment set forth in § 1.703 shall be reduced by the number of days, if any, beginning on the date the application was filed under 35 U.S.C. 111(b) and ending on the date a request in compliance with §1.53(c)(3) to convert the provisional application into a nonprovisional application was filed;

(6) Submission of a preliminary amendment or other preliminary paper less than one month before the mailing of an Office action under 35 U.S.C. 132 or notice of allowance under 35 U.S.C. 151 that requires the mailing of a supplemental Office action or notice of allowance, in which case the period of adjustment set forth in § 1.703 shall be reduced by the lesser of:

(i) The number of days, if any, beginning on the day after the mailing date of the original Office action or notice of allowance and ending on the date of mailing of the supplemental Office action or notice of allowance; or

(ii) Four months;

(7) Submission of a reply having an omission (§1.135(c)), in which case the period of adjustment set forth in § 1.703 shall be reduced by the number of days, if any, beginning on the day after the date the reply having an omission was filed and ending on the date that the reply or other paper correcting the omission was filed;

(8) Submission of a supplemental reply or other paper, other than a supplemental reply or other paper expressly requested by the examiner, after a reply has been filed, in which case the period of adjustment set forth in § 1.703 shall be reduced by the number of days, if any, beginning on the day after the date the initial reply was filed and ending on the date that the supplemental reply or other such paper was filed;

(9) Submission of an amendment or other paper after a decision by the Board of Patent Appeals and Interferences, other than a decision designated as containing a new ground of rejection under § 41.50 (b) of this title or statement under § 41.50(c) of this title, or a decision by a Federal court, less than one month before the mailing of an Office action under 35 U.S.C. 132 or notice of allowance under 35 U.S.C.151 that requires the mailing of a

supplemental Office action or supplemental notice of allowance, in which case the period of adjustment set forth in § 1.703 shall be reduced by the lesser of:

(i) The number of days, if any, beginning on the day after the mailing date of the original Office action or notice of allowance and ending on the mailing date of the supplemental Office action or notice of allowance; or

(ii) Four months;

(10) Submission of an amendment under § 1.312 or other paper after a notice of allowance has been given or mailed, in which case the period of adjustment set forth in § 1.703 shall be reduced by the lesser of:

(i) The number of days, if any, beginning on the date the amendment under § 1.312 or other paper was filed and ending on the mailing date of the Office action or notice in response to the amendment under § 1.312 or such other paper; or

(ii) Four months; and

(11) Further prosecution via a continuing application, in which case the period of adjustment set forth in § 1.703 shall not include any period that is prior to the actual filing date of the application that resulted in the patent.

(d) A paper containing only an information disclosure statement in compliance with §§ 1.97 and 1.98 will not be considered a failure to engage in reasonable efforts to conclude prosecution (processing or examination) of the application under paragraphs (c)(6), (c)(8), (c)(9), or (c)(10) of this section if it is accompanied by a statement that each item of information contained in the information disclosure statement was first cited in any communication from a foreign patent office in a counterpart application and that this communication was not received by any individual designated in § 1.56(c) more than thirty days prior to the filing of the information disclosure statement. This thirty-day period is not extendable.

(e) Submission of an application for patent term adjustment under § 1.705(b) (with or without request under § 1.705(c) for reinstatement of reduced patent term adjustment) will not be considered a failure to engage in reasonable efforts to conclude prosecution (processing or examination) of the application under paragraph (c)(10) of this section.

## § 1.705 Patent term adjustment determination.

(a) The notice of allowance will include notification of any patent term adjustment under 35 U.S.C. 154(b).

(b) Any request for reconsideration of the patent term adjustment indicated in the notice of allowance, except as provided in paragraph (d) of this section, and any request for reinstatement of all or part of the term reduced pursuant to § 1.704(b) must be by way of an application for patent term adjustment. An application for patent term adjustment under this section must be filed no later than the payment of the issue fee but may not be filed earlier than the date of mailing of the notice of allowance. An application for patent term adjustment under this section must be accompanied by:

(1) The fee set forth in § 1.18(e); and

(2) A statement of the facts involved, specifying:

(i) The correct patent term adjustment and the basis or bases under § 1.702 for the adjustment;

(ii) The relevant dates as specified in §§1.703(a) through (e) for which an adjustment is sought and the adjustment as specified in § 1.703(f) to which the patent is entitled;

(iii) Whether the patent is subject to a terminal disclaimer and any expiration date specified in the terminal disclaimer; and

(iv)(A) Any circumstances during the prosecution of the application resulting in the patent that constitute a failure to engage in reasonable efforts to conclude processing or examination of such application as set forth in § 1.704; or

(B) That there were no circumstances constituting a failure to engage in reasonable efforts to conclude processing or examination of such application as set forth in § 1.704.

(c) Any application for patent term adjustment under this section that requests reinstatement of all or part of the period of adjustment reduced pursuant to §1.704(b) for failing to reply to a rejection, objection, argument, or other request within three months of the date of mailing of the Office communication notifying the applicant of the rejection, objection, argument, or other request must also be accompanied by:

(1) The fee set forth in § 1.18(f); and

(2) A showing to the satisfaction of the Director that, in spite of all due care, the applicant was unable to reply to the rejection,

objection, argument, or other request within three months of the date of mailing of the Office communication notifying the applicant of the rejection, objection, argument, or other request. The Office shall not grant any request for reinstatement for more than three additional months for each reply beyond three months from the date of mailing of the Office communication notifying the applicant of the rejection, objection, argument, or other request.

(d) If there is a revision to the patent term adjustment indicated in the notice of allowance, the patent will indicate the revised patent term adjustment. If the patent indicates or should have indicated a revised patent term adjustment, any request for reconsideration of the patent term adjustment indicated in the patent must be filed within two months of the date the patent issued and must comply with the requirements of paragraphs (b)(1) and (b)(2) of this section. Any request for reconsideration under this section that raises issues that were raised, or could have been raised, in an application for patent term adjustment under paragraph (b) of this section shall be dismissed as untimely as to those issues.

(e) The periods set forth in this section are not extendable.

(f) No submission or petition on behalf of a third party concerning patent term adjustment under 35 U.S.C. 154(b) will be considered by the Office. Any such submission or petition will be returned to the third party, or otherwise disposed of, at the convenience of the Office.

# APPENDIX 6:
# UNIFORM TRADE SECRETS ACT

**1985 AMENDMENTS**

**SECTION 1. DEFINITIONS**

As used in this [Act], unless the context requires otherwise:

(1) "Improper means" includes theft, bribery, misrepresentation, breach or inducement of a breach of a duty to maintain secrecy, or espionage through electronic or other means;

(2) "Misappropriation" means:

(i) acquisition of a trade secret of another by a person who knows or has reason to know that the trade secret was acquired by improper means; or

(ii) disclosure or use of a trade secret of another without express or implied consent by a person who

(A) used improper means to acquire knowledge of the trade secret; or

(B) at the time of disclosure or use, knew or had reason to know that his knowledge of the trade secret was

(I) derived from or through a person who had utilized improper means to acquire it;

(II) acquired under circumstances giving rise to a duty to maintain its secrecy or limit its use; or

(III) derived from or through a person who owed a duty to the person seeking relief to maintain its secrecy or limit its use; or

(C) before a material change of his [or her] position, knew or had reason to know that it was a trade secret and that knowledge of it had been acquired by accident or mistake.

(3) "Person" means a natural person, corporation, business trust, estate, trust, partnership, association, joint venture, government, governmental subdivision or agency, or any other legal or commercial entity.

(4) "Trade secret" means information, including a formula, pattern, compilation, program, device, method, technique, or process, that:

(i) derives independent economic value, actual or potential, from not being generally known to, and not being readily ascertainable by proper means by, other persons who can obtain economic value from its disclosure or use, and

(ii) is the subject of efforts that are reasonable under the circumstances to maintain its secrecy.

## Comment

One of the broadly stated policies behind trade secret law is "the maintenance of standards of commercial ethics." *Kewanee Oil Co. v. Bicron Corp.,* 416 U.S. 470 (1974). The Restatement of Torts, Section 757, Comment (f), notes: "A complete catalogue of improper means is not possible," but Section 1(1) includes a partial listing.

Proper means include:

1. Discovery by independent invention;

2. Discovery by "reverse engineering," that is, by starting with the known product and working backward to find the method by which it was developed. The acquisition of the known product must, of course, also be by a fair and honest means, such as purchase of the item on the open market for reverse engineering to be lawful;

3. Discovery under a license from the owner of the trade secret;

4. Observation of the item in public use or on public display;

5. Obtaining the trade secret from published literature.

Improper means could include otherwise lawful conduct which is improper under the circumstances; e.g., an airplane overflight used as aerial reconnaissance to determine the competitor's plant layout during construction of the plant. *E. I. du Pont de Nemours & Co., Inc. v. Christopher,* 431 F.2d 1012 (CA5, 1970), cert. den., 400 U.S. 1024 (1970). Because the trade secret can be destroyed through public knowledge, the unauthorized disclosure of a trade secret is also a misappropriation.

The type of accident or mistake that can result in a misappropriation under Section 1(2)(ii)(C) involves conduct by a person seeking relief that does not constitute a failure of efforts that are reasonable under the circumstances to maintain its secrecy under Section 1(4)(ii).

The definition of "trade secret" contains a reasonable departure from the Restatement of Torts (First) definition which required that a trade secret be "continuously used in one's business." The broader definition in the proposed Act extends protection to a plaintiff who has not yet had an opportunity or acquired the means to put a trade secret to use. The definition includes information that has commercial value from a negative viewpoint, for example, the results of lengthy and expensive research which proves that a certain process will not work could be of great value to a competitor.

*Cf. Telex Corp. v. IBM Corp.*, 510 F.2d 894 (CA10, 1975) per curiam, cert. dismissed, 423 U.S. 802 (1975) (liability imposed for developmental cost savings with respect to product not marketed). Because a trade secret need not be exclusive to confer a competitive advantage, different independent developers can acquire rights in the same trade secret.

The words "method, technique" are intended to include the concept of "know-how."

The language "not being generally known to and not being readily ascertainable by proper means by other persons" does not require that information be generally known to the public for trade secret rights to be lost. If the principal ~~person~~ *persons* who can obtain economic benefit from information ~~is~~ *are* aware of it, there is no trade secret. A method of casting metal, for example, may be unknown to the general public but readily known within the foundry industry.

Information is readily ascertainable if it is available in trade journals, reference books, or published materials. Often, the nature of a product lends itself to being readily copied as soon as it is available on the market. On the other hand, if reverse engineering is lengthy and expensive, a person who discovers the trade secret through reverse engineering can have a trade secret in the information obtained from reverse engineering.

Finally, reasonable efforts to maintain secrecy have been held to include advising employees of the existence of a trade secret, limiting access to a trade secret on "need to know basis," and controlling plant access. On the other hand, public disclosure of information through display, trade journal publications, advertising, or other carelessness can preclude protection.

The efforts required to maintain secrecy are those "reasonable under the circumstances." The courts do not require that extreme and unduly expensive procedures be taken to protect trade secrets against flagrant industrial espionage. See *E. I. du Pont de Nemours & Co., Inc. v. Christopher,* supra. It follows that reasonable use of a trade secret, including controlled disclosure to employees and licensees, is consistent with the requirement of relative secrecy.

## SECTION 2. INJUNCTIVE RELIEF

(a) Actual or threatened misappropriation may be enjoined. Upon application to the court, an injunction shall be terminated when the trade secret has ceased to exist, but the injunction may be continued for an additional reasonable period of time in order to eliminate commercial advantage that otherwise would be derived from the misappropriation.

(b) ~~If the court determines that it would be unreasonable to prohibit future use~~ *In exceptional circumstances,* an injunction may condition future use upon payment of a reasonable royalty for no longer than the period of time ~~the~~ *for which* use could have been prohibited. *Exceptional circumstances include, but are not limited to, a material and prejudicial change of position prior to acquiring knowledge or reason to know of misappropriation that renders a prohibitive injunction inequitable.*

(c) In appropriate circumstances, affirmative acts to protect a trade secret may be compelled by court order.

## Comment

Injunctions restraining future use and disclosure of misappropriated trade secrets frequently are sought. Although punitive perpetual injunctions have been granted, e.g., *Elcor Chemical Corp. v. Agri-Sul, Inc.,* 494 S.W.2d 204 (Tex. Civ. App. 1973), Section 2(a) of this Act adopts the position of the trend of authority limiting the duration of injunctive relief to the extent of the temporal advantage over good faith competitors gained by a misappropriator. See, e.g., *K-2 Ski Co. v. Head Ski Co., Inc.,* 506 F.2d 471 (CA9, 1974) (maximum appropriate duration of both temporary and permanent injunctive relief is the period of time it would have taken defendant to discover trade secrets lawfully through either independent development or reverse engineering of plaintiff's products).

The general principle of Section 2(a) and (b) is that an injunction should last for as long as is necessary, but no longer than is necessary, to eliminate the commercial advantage or "lead time" with respect to good faith competitors that a person has obtained through misappropriation. Subject to any additional period of restraint necessary to negate lead time, an injunction accordingly should terminate when a former trade secret becomes either generally known to good faith competitors or generally knowable to them because of the lawful availability of products that can be reverse engineered to reveal a trade secret.

For example, assume that A has a valuable trade secret of which B and C, the other industry members, are originally unaware. If B subsequently misappropriates the trade secret and is enjoined from use, but C later lawfully reverse engineers the trade secret, the injunction restraining B is subject to termination as soon as B's lead time has been dissipated. All of the persons who could derive economic value from use of the information are now aware of it, and there is no longer a trade secret under Section 1(4). It would be anticompetitive to continue to restrain B after any lead time that B had derived from misappropriation had been removed.

If a misappropriator either has not taken advantage of lead time or good faith competitors already have caught up with a misappropriator at the time that a case is decided, future disclosure and use of a former trade secret by a misappropriator will not damage a trade secret owner and no injunctive restraint of future disclosure and use is appropriate. See, e.g., *Northern Petrochemical Co. v. Tomlinson,* 484 F.2d 1057 (CA7, 1973) (affirming trial court's denial of preliminary injunction in part because an explosion at its plant prevented an alleged misappropriator from taking advantage of lead time); *Kubik, Inc. v. Hull,* 185 USPQ 391 (Mich.App.1974) (discoverability of trade secret by lawful reverse engineering made by injunctive relief punitive rather than compensatory).

Section 2(b) deals with a distinguishable *the special* situation in which future use by a misappropriator will damage a trade secret owner but an injunction against future use nevertheless is unreasonable under the particular *inappropriate due to exceptional* circumstances of a case. Situations in which this unreasonableness can exist *Exceptional circumstances* include the existence of an overriding public interest which requires the denial of a prohibitory injunction against future damaging use and a person's reasonable reliance upon acquisition of a misappropriated trade secret in good faith and without reason to know of its prior misappropriation that would be prejudiced by a prohibitory injunction against future damaging use. *Republic Aviation Corp. v. Schenk,* 152 USPQ 830 (N.Y. Sup. Ct. 1967) illustrates the public interest justification for withholding prohibitory injunctive relief. The court considered that enjoining a misappropriator from supplying the United States with an aircraft weapons control system would have endangered military personnel in Vietnam. The prejudice to a good faith third-party justification for withholding prohibitory injunctive relief can arise upon a trade secret owner's notification to a good faith third party that the third party has knowledge of a trade secret as a result of misappropriation by another. This notice suffices to make the third party a misappropriator thereafter under Section 1(2)(ii)(B)(I). In weighing an aggrieved person's interests and the interests of a third party who has relied in good faith upon his or her ability to utilize information, a court may conclude that restraining future use of the information by the third party is unwarranted. With respect to innocent acquirers of misappropriated trade secrets, Section 2(b) is consistent with the principle of 4 Restatement Torts (First) § 758(b) (1939), but rejects the Restatement's literal conferral of absolute immunity upon all third parties who have paid value in good faith for a trade secret misappropriated by another. The position taken by the Uniform Act is supported by *Forest Laboratories, Inc. v. Pillsbury Co.*, 452 F.2d 621 (CA7, 1971) in which a defendant's purchase of assets of a corporation to which a trade secret had been disclosed in confidence was not considered to confer immunity upon the defendant.

When Section 2(b) applies, a court is given *has* discretion to substitute an injunction conditioning future use upon payment of a reasonable royalty for an injunction prohibiting future use. Like all injunctive relief for misappropriation, a royalty order injunction is appropriate only if a misappropriator has obtained a competitive advantage through misappropriation and only for the duration of that competitive advantage. In some situations, typically those involving good faith acquirers of trade secrets misappropriated by others, a court may conclude that the same considerations that render a prohibitory injunction against future use inappropriate also render a royalty order injunction inappropriate. See, generally, *Prince Manufacturing, Inc. v. Automatic Partner, Inc.*, 198 USPQ 618 (N.J. Super. Ct. 1976) (purchaser of misappropriator's assets from receiver after trade secret disclosed to public through sale of product not subject to liability for misappropriation).

*A royalty order injunction under Section 2(b) should be distinguished from a reasonable royalty alternative measure of damages under Section 3(a). See the Comment to Section 3 for discussion of the differences in the remedies.*

Section 2(c) authorizes mandatory injunctions requiring that a misappropriator return the fruits of misappropriation to an aggrieved person, e.g., the return of stolen blueprints or the surrender of surreptitious photographs or recordings.

Where more than one person is entitled to trade secret protection with respect to the same information, only that one from whom misappropriation occurred is entitled to a remedy.

## SECTION 3. DAMAGES

(a) ~~In addition to or in lieu of injunctive relief~~ *Except to the extent that a material and prejudicial change of position prior to acquiring knowledge or reason to know of misappropriation renders a monetary recovery inequitable,* a complainant ~~may~~ *is entitled to* recover damages for ~~the actual loss caused by~~ misappropriation. ~~A complainant also may recover for~~ *Damages can include both the actual loss caused by misappropriation and* the unjust enrichment caused by misappropriation that is not taken into account in computing ~~damages for~~ actual loss. *In lieu of damages measured by any other methods, the damages caused by misappropriation may be measured by imposition of liability for a reasonable royalty for a misappropriator's unauthorized disclosure or use of a trade secret.*

(b) If willful and malicious misappropriation exists, the court may award exemplary damages in an amount not exceeding twice any award made under subsection (a).

## Comment

Like injunctive relief, a monetary recovery for trade secret misappropriation is appropriate only for the period in which information is entitled to protection as a trade secret, plus the additional period, if any, in which a misappropriator retains an advantage over good faith competitors because of misappropriation. Actual damage to a complainant and unjust benefit to a misappropriator are caused by misappropriation during this time alone. See *Conmar Products Corp. v. Universal Slide Fastener Co.,* 172 F.2d 150 (CA2, 1949) (no remedy for period subsequent to disclosure of trade secret by issued patent); *Carboline Co. v. Jarboe,* 454 S.W.2d 540 (MO., 1970) (recoverable monetary relief limited to period that it would have taken misappropriator to discover trade secret without misappropriation). A claim for actual damages and net profits can be combined with a claim for injunctive relief, but, if both claims are granted, the injunctive relief ordinarily will preclude a monetary award for a period in which the injunction is effective.

As long as there is no double counting, Section 3(a) adopts the principle of the recent cases allowing recovery of both a complainant's actual losses and a misappropriator's unjust benefit that are caused by misappropriation. E.g., *Tri-Tron International v. Velto,* 525 F.2d 432 (CA9, 1975) (complainant's loss and misappropriator's benefit can be combined).

Because certain cases may have sanctioned double counting in a combined award of losses and unjust benefit, e.g., *Telex Corp. v. IBM Corp.,* 510 F.2d 894 (CA10, 1975) (per curiam), cert. dismissed, 423 U.S. 802 (1975) (IBM recovered rentals lost due to displacement by misappropriator's products without deduction for expenses saved by displacement; as a result of rough approximations adopted by the trial judge, IBM also may have recovered developmental costs saved by misappropriator through misappropriation with respect to the same customers), the Act adopts an express prohibition upon the counting of the same item as both a loss to a complainant and an unjust benefit to a misappropriator.

*As an alternative to all other methods of measuring damages caused by a misappropriator's past conduct, a complainant can request that damages be based upon a demonstrably reasonable royalty for a misappropriator's unauthorized disclosure or use of a trade secret. In order to justify this alternative measure of damages, there must be competent evidence of the amount of a reasonable royalty.*

*The reasonable royalty alternative measure of damages for a misappropriator's past conduct under Section 3(a) is readily distinguishable from a Section 2(b) royalty order injunction, which conditions a misappropriator's future ability to use a trade secret upon payment of a reasonable royalty. A Section 2(b) royalty order injunction is appropriate only in exceptional circumstances; whereas a reasonable royalty measure of damages is a general option. Because Section 3(a) damages are awarded for a misappropriator's past conduct and a Section 2(b) royalty order injunction regulates a misappropriator's future conduct, both remedies cannot be awarded for the same conduct. If a royalty order injunction is appropriate because of a person's material and prejudicial change of position prior to having reason to know that a trade secret has been acquired from a misappropriator, damages, moreover, should not be awarded for past conduct that occurred prior to notice that a misappropriated trade secret has been acquired.*

Monetary relief can be appropriate whether or not injunctive relief is granted under Section 2. If a person charged with misappropriation has ~~acquired~~ *materially and prejudicially changed position in reliance upon* knowledge of a trade secret *acquired* in good faith *and* without reason to know of its misappropriation by another, however, the same considerations that can justify denial of all injunctive relief also can justify denial of all monetary relief. See *Conmar Products Corp. v. Universal Slide Fastener Co.,* 172 F.2d 1950 (CA2, 1949) (no relief against new employer of employee subject to contractual obligation not to disclose former employer's trade secrets where new employer innocently had committed $40,000 to develop the trade secrets prior to notice of misappropriation).

If willful and malicious misappropriation is found to exist, Section 3(b) authorizes the court to award a complainant exemplary damages in addition to the actual recovery under Section 3(a) an amount not exceeding twice that recovery. This provision follows federal patent law in leaving discretionary trebling to the judge even though there may be a jury, compare 35 U.S.C. Section 284 (1976).

Whenever more than one person is entitled to trade secret protection with respect to the same information, only that one from whom misappropriation occurred is entitled to a remedy.

## SECTION 4. ATTORNEYS' FEES

If (i) a claim of misappropriation is made in bad faith, (ii) a motion to terminate an injunction is made or resisted in bad faith, or (iii) willful and malicious misappropriation exists, the court may award reasonable attorneys' fees to the prevailing party.

### Comment

Section 4 allows a court to award reasonable attorneys' fees to a prevailing party in specified circumstances as a deterrent to specious claims of misappropriation, to specious efforts by a misappropriator to terminate injunctive relief, and to willful and malicious misappropriation. In the latter situation, the court should take into consideration the extent to which a complainant will recover exemplary damages in determining whether additional attorneys' fees should be awarded. Again, patent law is followed in allowing the judge to determine whether attorneys' fees should be awarded even if there is a jury, compare 35 U.S.C. Section 285 (1976).

## SECTION 5. PRESERVATION OF SECRECY

In an action under this [Act], a court shall preserve the secrecy of an alleged trade secret by reasonable means, which may include granting protective orders in connection with discovery proceedings, holding in-camera hearings, sealing the records of the action, and ordering any person involved in the litigation not to disclose an alleged trade secret without prior court approval.

### Comment

If reasonable assurances of maintenance of secrecy could not be given, meritorious trade secret litigation would be chilled. In fashioning safeguards of confidentiality, a court must ensure that a respondent is provided sufficient information to present a defense and a trier of fact sufficient information to resolve the merits. In addition to the illustrative techniques specified in the statute, courts have protected secrecy in these cases by restricting disclosures to a party's counsel and his or her assistants and by appointing a disinterested expert as a special master to hear secret information and report conclusions to the court.

## SECTION 6. STATUTE OF LIMITATIONS

An action for misappropriation must be brought within 3 years after the misappropriation is discovered or by the exercise of reasonable diligence should have been discovered. For the purposes of this section, a continuing misappropriation constitutes a single claim.

### Comment

There presently is a conflict of authority as to whether trade secret misappropriation is a continuing wrong. Compare *Monolith Portland Midwest Co. v. Kaiser Aluminum & Chemical Corp.*, 407 F.2d 288 (CA9, 1969) (no *not a* continuing wrong under California law—limitation period upon all recovery begins upon initial misappropriation) with *Underwater Storage, Inc. v. U.S. Rubber Co.*, 371 F.2d 950 (CADC, 1966), cert. den., 386 U.S. 911 (1967) (continuing wrong under general principles—limitation period with respect to a specific act of misappropriation begins at the time that the act of misappropriation occurs).

This Act rejects a continuing wrong approach to the statute of limitations but delays the commencement of the limitation period until an aggrieved person discovers or reasonably should have discovered the existence of misappropriation. If objectively reasonable notice of misappropriation exists, three years is sufficient time to vindicate one's legal rights.

## SECTION 7. EFFECT ON OTHER LAW

(a) This *Except as provided in subsection (b), this* [Act] displaces conflicting tort, restitutionary, and other law of this State pertaining to *providing* civil liability *remedies* for misappropriation of a trade secret.

(b) This [Act] does not affect:

(1) contractual or other civil liability or relief that is *remedies, whether or* not based upon misappropriation of a trade secret; or

(2) criminal liability for *other civil remedies that are not based upon* misappropriation of a trade secret.; *or*

(3) *criminal remedies, whether or not based upon misappropriation of a trade secret.*

## Comment

This Act ~~is not a comprehensive remedy~~ *does not deal with criminal remedies for trade secret misappropriation and is not a comprehensive statement of civil remedies.* It applies to ~~duties imposed by law in order~~ *a duty* to protect competitively significant secret information *that is imposed by law.* It does not apply to ~~duties~~ *a duty* voluntarily assumed through an express or an implied-in-fact contract. The enforceability of covenants not to disclose trade secrets and covenants not to compete that are intended to protect trade secrets, for example, ~~are~~ *is* governed by other law. The Act also does not apply to ~~duties~~ *a duty* imposed by law that ~~are~~ *is* not dependent upon the existence of competitively significant secret information, like an agent's duty of loyalty to his or her principal.

## SECTION 8. UNIFORMITY OF APPLICATION AND CONSTRUCTION

This [Act] shall be applied and construed to effectuate its general purpose to make uniform the law with respect to the subject of this [Act] among states enacting it.

## SECTION 9. SHORT TITLE

This [Act] may be cited as the Uniform Trade Secrets Act.

## SECTION 10. SEVERABILITY

If any provision of this [Act] or its application to any person or circumstances is held invalid, the invalidity does not affect other provisions or applications of the [Act] which can be given effect without the invalid provision or application, and to this end the provisions of this [Act] are severable.

## SECTION 11. TIME OF TAKING EFFECT

This [Act] takes effect on _____, and does not apply to misappropriation occurring prior to the effective date. *With respect to a continuing misappropriation that began prior to the effective date, the [Act] also does not apply to the continuing misappropriation that occurs after the effective date.*

## Comment

*The Act applies exclusively to misappropriation that begins after its effective date. Neither misappropriation that began and ended before the effective date nor misappropriation that began before the effective date and continued thereafter is subject to the Act.*

## SECTION 12. REPEAL

The following Acts and parts of Acts are repealed:

(1)

(2)

(3)

### STATE ADOPTIONS OF 1979 UTSA:

Arkansas
California
Connecticut
Indiana
Louisiana
Rhode Island
Washington

### ADOPTIONS WITH 1985 AMENDMENTS:

| | | |
|---|---|---|
| Alabama | Kentucky | Ohio |
| Alaska | Maine | Oklahoma |
| Arizona | Maryland | Oregon |
| Colorado | Michigan | Pennsylvania |
| Delaware | Minnesota | South Carolina |
| District of Columbia | Mississippi | South Dakota |
| Florida | Missouri | Tennessee |
| Georgia | Montana | U.S. Virgin Islands |
| Hawaii | Nebraska | Utah |
| Idaho | Nevada | Vermont |
| Illinois | New Hampshire | Virginia |
| Iowa | New Mexico | West Virginia |
| Kansas | North Dakota | Wisconsin |
| | | Wyoming |

### 2009 INTRODUCTIONS:

Massachusetts
New York

Source: http://www.nccusl.org

# APPENDIX 7:
# ECONOMIC ESPIONAGE ACT

## SECTION 1. SHORT TITLE

This Act may be cited as the "Economic Espionage Act of 1996."

**TITLE I—PROTECTION OF TRADE SECRETS**

**SEC. 101. PROTECTION OF TRADE SECRETS**

(a) IN GENERAL— Title 18, United States Code, is amended by inserting after chapter 89 the following:

CHAPTER 90—PROTECTION OF TRADE SECRETS

"Sec.

"1831. Economic espionage.

"1832. Theft of trade secrets.

"1833. Exceptions to prohibitions.

"1834. Criminal forfeiture.

"1835. Orders to preserve confidentiality.

"1836. Civil proceedings to enjoin violations.

"1837. Conduct outside the United States.

"1838. Construction with other laws.

"1839. Definitions.

"Sec. 1831. Economic espionage

"(a) IN GENERAL— Whoever, intending or knowing that the offense will benefit any foreign government, foreign instrumentality, or foreign agent, knowingly—

"(1) steals, or without authorization appropriates, takes, carries away, or conceals, or by fraud, artifice, or deception obtains a trade secret;

"(2) without authorization copies, duplicates, sketches, draws, photographs, downloads, uploads, alters, destroys, photocopies, replicates, transmits, delivers, sends, mails, communicates, or conveys a trade secret;

"(3) receives, buys, or possesses a trade secret, knowing the same to have been stolen or appropriated, obtained, or converted without authorization;

"(4) attempts to commit any offense described in any of paragraphs (1) through (3); or

"(5) conspires with one or more other persons to commit any offense described in any of paragraphs (1) through (3), and one or more of such persons do any act to effect the object of the conspiracy, shall, except as provided in subsection (b), be fined not more than $500,000 or imprisoned not more than 15 years, or both.

"(b) ORGANIZATIONS— Any organization that commits any offense described in subsection (a) shall be fined not more than $10,000,000.

"Sec. 1832. Theft of trade secrets

"(a) Whoever, with intent to convert a trade secret, that is related to or included in a product that is produced for or placed in interstate or foreign commerce, to the economic benefit of anyone other than the owner thereof, and intending or knowing that the offense will, injure any owner of that trade secret, knowingly—

"(1) steals, or without authorization appropriates, takes, carries away, or conceals, or by fraud, artifice, or deception obtains such information;

"(2) without authorization copies, duplicates, sketches, draws, photographs, downloads, uploads, alters, destroys, photocopies, replicates, transmits, delivers, sends, mails, communicates, or conveys such information;

"(3) receives, buys, or possesses such information, knowing the same to have been stolen or appropriated, obtained, or converted without authorization;

"(4) attempts to commit any offense described in paragraphs (1) through (3); or

"(5) conspires with one or more other persons to commit any offense described in paragraphs (1) through (3), and one or more of such persons do any act to effect the object of the conspiracy, shall, except as provided in subsection (b), be fined under this title or imprisoned not more than 10 years, or both.

"(b) Any organization that commits any offense described in subsection (a) shall be fined not more than $5,000,000.

"Sec. 1833. Exceptions to prohibitions

"This chapter does not prohibit—

"(1) any otherwise lawful activity conducted by a governmental entity of the United States, a State, or a political subdivision of a State; or

"(2) the reporting of a suspected violation of law to any governmental entity of the United States, a State, or a political subdivision of a State, if such entity has lawful authority with respect to that violation.

"Sec. 1834. Criminal forfeiture

"(a) The court, in imposing sentence on a person for a violation of this chapter, shall order, in addition to any other sentence imposed, that the person forfeit to the United States—

"(1) any property constituting, or derived from, any proceeds the person obtained, directly or indirectly, as the result of such violation; and

"(2) any of the person's property used, or intended to be used, in any manner or part, to commit or facilitate the commission of such violation, if the court in its discretion so determines, taking into consideration the nature, scope, and proportionality of the use of the property in the offense.

"(b) Property subject to forfeiture under this section, any seizure and disposition thereof, and any administrative or judicial proceeding in relation thereto, shall be governed by section 413 of the Comprehensive Drug Abuse Prevention and Control Act of 1970 (21 U.S.C. 853), except for subsections (d) and (j) of such section, which shall not apply to forfeitures under this section.

"Sec. 1835. Orders to preserve confidentiality

"In any prosecution or other proceeding under this chapter, the court shall enter such orders and take such other action as may be necessary and appropriate to preserve the confidentiality of trade secrets, consistent with the requirements of the Federal Rules of Criminal and Civil Procedure, the Federal Rules of Evidence, and all other applicable laws. An interlocutory appeal by the United States shall lie from a decision or order of a district court authorizing or directing the disclosure of any trade secret.

"Sec. 1836. Civil proceedings to enjoin violations

"(a) The Attorney General may, in a civil action, obtain appropriate injunctive relief against any violation of this section.

"(b) The district courts of the United States shall have exclusive original jurisdiction of civil actions under this subsection.

"Sec. 1837. Applicability to conduct outside the United States

This chapter also applies to conduct occurring outside the United States if—

"(1) the offender is a natural person who is a citizen or permanent resident alien of the United States, or an organization organized under the laws of the United States or a State or political subdivision thereof; or

"(2) an act in furtherance of the offense was committed in the United States.

"Sec. 1838. Construction with other laws

"This chapter shall not be construed to preempt or displace any other remedies, whether civil or criminal, provided by United States Federal, State, commonwealth, possession, or territory law for the misappropriation of a trade secret, or to affect the otherwise lawful disclosure of information by any Government employee under section 552 of title 5 (commonly known as the Freedom of Information Act).

"Sec. 1839. Definitions

"As used in this chapter—

"(1) the term 'foreign instrumentality' means any agency, bureau, ministry, component, institution, association, or any legal, commercial, or business organization, corporation, firm, or entity that is substantially owned, controlled, sponsored, commanded, managed, or dominated by a foreign government;

"(2) the term 'foreign agent' means any officer, employee, proxy, servant, delegate, or representative of a foreign government;

"(3) the term 'trade secret' means all forms and types of financial, business, scientific, technical, economic, or engineering information, including patterns, plans, compilations, program devices, formulas, designs, prototypes, methods, techniques, processes, procedures, programs, or codes, whether tangible or intangible, and whether or how stored, compiled, or memorialized physically, electronically, graphically, photographically, or in writing if—

"(A) the owner thereof has taken reasonable measures to keep such information secret; and

"(B) the information derives independent economic value, actual or potential, from not being generally known to, and not being readily ascertainable through proper means by, the public; and

"(4) the term 'owner,' with respect to a trade secret, means the person or entity in whom or in which rightful legal or equitable title to, or license in, the trade secret is reposed."

# APPENDIX 8:
# PLANT AND DESIGN PATENTS

**PLANT PATENTS: SECTIONS 161, 162, AND 163 OF THE PATENT ACT**

## Section 161:

Whoever invents or discovers and asexually reproduces any distinct and new variety of plant, including cultivated sports, mutants, hybrids, and newly found seedlings, other than a tuber propagated plant or a plant found in an uncultivated state, may obtain a patent therefor, subject to the conditions and requirements of this title.

The provisions of this title relating to patents for inventions shall apply to patents for plants, except as otherwise provided.

## Section 162:

No plant patent shall be declared invalid for noncompliance with section 112 of this title if the description is as complete as is reasonably possible.

## Section 163:

In the case of a plant patent, the grant shall include the right to exclude others from asexually reproducing the plant, and from using, offering for sale, or selling the plant so reproduced, or any of its parts, throughout the United States, or from importing the plant so reproduced, or any parts thereof, into the United States.

**DESIGN PATENTS**

## Section 171:

Whoever invents any new, original, and ornamental design for an article of manufacture may obtain a patent therefor, subject to the conditions and requirements of this title.

The provisions of this title relating to patents for inventions shall apply to patents for designs, except as otherwise provided.

# APPENDIX 9:
# NONPROVISIONAL PLANT PATENT
# APPLICATION TRANSMITTAL

PTO/SB/19 (08-08)
Approved for use through 06/30/2010. OMB 0651-0032
U.S. Patent and Trademark Office; U.S. DEPARTMENT OF COMMERCE
Under the Paperwork Reduction Act of 1995, no persons are required to respond to a collection of information unless it displays a valid OMB control number.

| **PLANT** | Attorney Docket No. | |
|---|---|---|
| **PATENT APPLICATION** | First Named Inventor | |
| **TRANSMITTAL** | Title | |
| *(Only for new nonprovisional applications filed under 37 CFR 1.53(b))* | Express Mail Label No. | |

**Commissioner for Patents**
**ADDRESS TO:**    **P.O. Box 1450**
**Alexandria, VA 22313-1450**

| APPLICATION ELEMENTS | ACCOMPANYING APPLICATION PARTS |
|---|---|
| *See MPEP chapters 600 & 1600 concerning plant patent application contents.* | **ACCOMPANYING APPLICATION PARTS** |

**APPLICATION ELEMENTS**
*See MPEP chapters 600 & 1600 concerning plant patent application contents.*

1. ☐ Fee Transmittal Form *(e.g., PTO/SB/17)*

2. ☐ Applicant claims small entity status. See 37 CFR 1.27.

3. ☐ Specification                      [Total Pages _____]
   *(preferred arrangement set forth below)*
   - Descriptive title of the invention
   - Cross References to Related Applications
   - Statement Regarding Fed sponsored R & D
   - Latin name of genus and species
   - Variety denomination
   - Background of the Invention
   - Brief Description of the Drawings
   - Detailed Botanical Description
   - A single claim
   - Abstract of the Disclosure

4. ☐ Color drawing(s)          [Total Sheets _____]
   (2 copies required – 37 CFR 1.165(b))

5. ☐ Oath or Declaration          [Total Pages _____]
   a. ☐ Newly executed (original or copy)
   b. ☐ A copy from a prior application (37 CFR 1.63(d))
      *(for continuation/divisional with Box 16 completed)*
      i ☐ DELETION OF INVENTOR(S)
         Signed statement attached deleting
         inventor(s) named in the prior application,
         see 37 CFR 1.63(d)(2) and 1.33(b).

6. ☐ Application Data Sheet. See 37 CFR 1.76.

**ACCOMPANYING APPLICATION PARTS**

7. ☐ Assignment Papers *(cover sheet & document(s))*

8. ☐ 37 CFR 3.73(b) Statement   ☐ Power of
   *(when there is an assignee)*          Attorney

9. ☐ English Translation Document *(if applicable)*

10. ☐ Information Disclosure Statement (IDS)
    PTO/SB/08 or PTO-1449
    ☐ Copies of foreign patent documents, NPL &
       Pending U.S. patent applications

11. ☐ Preliminary Amendment

12. ☐ Return Receipt Postcard (MPEP 503)
    *(Should be specifically itemized)*

13. ☐ Certified Copy of Priority Document(s)
    *(if foreign priority is claimed)*

14. ☐ Request Nonpublication under 35 U.S.C. 122(b)(2)(B)(i)
    Applicant must attach form PTO/SB/35 or equivalent.

15. ☐ Other:

Note: Please state the Latin name and variety denomination of the plant
claimed in a separate section of the specification.

16. *If a CONTINUING APPLICATION*, check appropriate box, and supply the requisite information below and in the first sentence of the specification following the title, or in an Application Data Sheet under 37 CFR 1.76.

☐ Continuation   ☐ Divisional   ☐ Continuation-in-part (CIP) of prior application No.: _____

*Prior application information:* Examiner _____ Art Unit: _____

## 17. CORRESPONDENCE ADDRESS

☐ The address associated with Customer Number: [ _____ ]   OR   ☐ Correspondence address below

| Name | |
|---|---|
| Address | |

| City | | State | | Zip Code | |
|---|---|---|---|---|---|
| Country | | Telephone | | Email | |

| Signature | | Date | |
|---|---|---|---|
| Name (Print/Typed) | | Registration No. | |

This collection of information is required by 37 CFR 1.53(b). The information is required to obtain or retain a benefit by the public which is to file (and by the USPTO to process) an application. Confidentiality is governed by 35 U.S.C. 122 and 37 CFR 1.11 and 1.14. This collection is estimated to take 12 minutes to complete, including gathering, preparing, and submitting the completed application form to the USPTO. Time will vary depending upon the individual case. Any comments on the amount of time you require to complete this form and/or suggestions for reducing this burden, should be sent to the Chief Information Officer, U.S. Patent and Trademark Office, U.S. Department of Commerce, P.O. Box 1450, Alexandria, VA 22313-1450. DO NOT SEND FEES OR COMPLETED FORMS TO THIS ADDRESS. **SEND TO: Commissioner for Patents, P.O. Box 1450, Alexandria, VA 22313-1450.**

*If you need assistance in completing the form, call 1-800-PTO-9199 and select option 2.*

## Privacy Act Statement

The **Privacy Act of 1974 (P.L. 93-579)** requires that you be given certain information in connection with your submission of the attached form related to a patent application or patent. Accordingly, pursuant to the requirements of the Act, please be advised that: (1) the general authority for the collection of this information is 35 U.S.C. 2(b)(2); (2) furnishing of the information solicited is voluntary; and (3) the principal purpose for which the information is used by the U.S. Patent and Trademark Office is to process and/or examine your submission related to a patent application or patent. If you do not furnish the requested information, the U.S. Patent and Trademark Office may not be able to process and/or examine your submission, which may result in termination of proceedings or abandonment of the application or expiration of the patent.

The information provided by you in this form will be subject to the following routine uses:

1. The information on this form will be treated confidentially to the extent allowed under the Freedom of Information Act (5 U.S.C. 552) and the Privacy Act (5 U.S.C 552a). Records from this system of records may be disclosed to the Department of Justice to determine whether disclosure of these records is required by the Freedom of Information Act.
2. A record from this system of records may be disclosed, as a routine use, in the course of presenting evidence to a court, magistrate, or administrative tribunal, including disclosures to opposing counsel in the course of settlement negotiations.
3. A record in this system of records may be disclosed, as a routine use, to a Member of Congress submitting a request involving an individual, to whom the record pertains, when the individual has requested assistance from the Member with respect to the subject matter of the record.
4. A record in this system of records may be disclosed, as a routine use, to a contractor of the Agency having need for the information in order to perform a contract. Recipients of information shall be required to comply with the requirements of the Privacy Act of 1974, as amended, pursuant to 5 U.S.C. 552a(m).
5. A record related to an International Application filed under the Patent Cooperation Treaty in this system of records may be disclosed, as a routine use, to the International Bureau of the World Intellectual Property Organization, pursuant to the Patent Cooperation Treaty.
6. A record in this system of records may be disclosed, as a routine use, to another federal agency for purposes of National Security review (35 U.S.C. 181) and for review pursuant to the Atomic Energy Act (42 U.S.C. 218(c)).
7. A record from this system of records may be disclosed, as a routine use, to the Administrator, General Services, or his/her designee, during an inspection of records conducted by GSA as part of that agency's responsibility to recommend improvements in records management practices and programs, under authority of 44 U.S.C. 2904 and 2906. Such disclosure shall be made in accordance with the GSA regulations governing inspection of records for this purpose, and any other relevant (*i.e.*, GSA or Commerce) directive. Such disclosure shall not be used to make determinations about individuals.
8. A record from this system of records may be disclosed, as a routine use, to the public after either publication of the application pursuant to 35 U.S.C. 122(b) or issuance of a patent pursuant to 35 U.S.C. 151. Further, a record may be disclosed, subject to the limitations of 37 CFR 1.14, as a routine use, to the public if the record was filed in an application which became abandoned or in which the proceedings were terminated and which application is referenced by either a published application, an application open to public inspection or an issued patent.
9. A record from this system of records may be disclosed, as a routine use, to a Federal, State, or local law enforcement agency, if the USPTO becomes aware of a violation or potential violation of law or regulation.

# APPENDIX 10:
# DESIGN PATENT APPLICATION
# TRANSMITTAL

PTO/SB/18 (08-08)
Approved for use through 06/30/2010. OMB 0651-0032
U.S. Patent and Trademark Office; U.S. DEPARTMENT OF COMMERCE
Under the Paperwork Reduction Act of 1995, no persons are required to respond to a collection of information unless it displays a valid OMB control number.

**DESIGN PATENT APPLICATION TRANSMITTAL**

*(Only for new nonprovisional applications under 37 CFR 1.53(b))*

| | |
|---|---|
| Attorney Docket No. | |
| First Named Inventor | |
| Title | |
| Express Mail Label No. | |

ADDRESS TO:
**Commissioner for Patents**
P.O. Box 1450
Alexandria, VA 22313-1450

*DESIGN V. UTILITY: A "design patent" protects an article's ornamental appearance (e.g., the way an article looks) (35 U.S.C. 171), while a "utility patent" protects the way an article is used and works (35 U.S.C. 101). The ornamental appearance of an article includes its shape/configuration or surface ornamentation upon the article, or both. Both a design and a utility patent may be obtained on an article if invention resides both in its ornamental appearance and its utility. For more information, see MPEP 1502.01.*

## APPLICATION ELEMENTS
*See MPEP 1500 concerning design patent application contents.*

1. ☐ Fee Transmittal Form *(e.g., PTO/SB/17)*

2. ☐ Applicant claims small entity status. See 37 CFR 1.27.

3. ☐ Specification [Total Pages _____]
   *(preferred arrangement set forth below, MPEP 1503.01)*
   - Preamble
   - Cross References to Related Applications
   - Statement Regarding Fed sponsored R & D
   - Description of the figure(s) of the drawings
   - Feature description
   - Claim (only one (1) claim permitted, MPEP 1503.03)

4. ☐ Drawing(s) (37 CFR 1.152) [Total Sheets _____]

5. Oath or Declaration [Total Pages _____]
   a. ☐ Newly executed (original or copy)
   b. ☐ A copy from a prior application (37 CFR 1.63(d))
      *(for continuation/divisional with Box 16 completed)*
      *DELETION OF INVENTOR(S)*
      i. ☐ Signed statement attached deleting inventor(s) named in the prior application, see 37 CFR 1.63(d)(2) and 1.33(b)

6. ☐ Application Data Sheet. See 37 CFR 1.76

## ACCOMPANYING APPLICATION PARTS

7. ☐ Assignment Papers (cover sheet & document(s))

8. ☐ 37 CFR 3.73(b) Statement ☐ Power of Attorney *(when there is an assignee)*

9. ☐ English Translation Document *(if applicable)*

10. ☐ Information Disclosure Statement (IDS) PTO/SB/08 or PTO-1449
    ☐ Copies of foreign patent documents, publications, & other information

11. ☐ Preliminary Amendment

12. ☐ Return Receipt Postcard (MPEP 503) *(Should be specifically itemized)*

13. ☐ Certified Copy of Priority Document(s) (if foreign priority is claimed)

14. ☐ Request for Expedited Examination of a Design Application (37 CFR 1.155) (NOTE: Use "Mail Stop Expedited Design")

15. ☐ Other:

**16.** If a CONTINUING APPLICATION, check appropriate box, and supply the requisite information below and in the first sentence of the specification following the title, or in an Application Data Sheet under 37 CFR 1.76:

☐ Continuation   ☐ Divisional   ☐ Continuation-in-part (CIP) of prior application No.: _____

Prior application information: Examiner _____ Art Unit: _____

## 17. CORRESPONDENCE ADDRESS

☐ The address associated with Customer Number: _____   **OR**   ☐ Correspondence address below

| Name | |
|---|---|
| Address | |
| City | State | Zip Code |
| Country | Telephone | Email |
| Signature | Date |
| Name (Print/Type) | Registration No. (Attorney/Agent) |

This collection of information is required by 37 CFR 1.53(b). The information is required to obtain or retain a benefit by the public which is to file (and by the USPTO to process) an application. Confidentiality is governed by 35 U.S.C. 122 and 37 CFR 1.11 and 1.14. This collection is estimated to take 12 minutes to complete, including gathering, preparing, and submitting the completed application form to the USPTO. Time will vary depending upon the individual case. Any comments on the amount of time you require to complete this form and/or suggestions for reducing this burden, should be sent to the Chief Information Officer, U.S. Patent and Trademark Office, U.S. Department of Commerce, P.O. Box 1450, Alexandria, VA 22313-1450. DO NOT SEND FEES OR COMPLETED FORMS TO THIS ADDRESS. **SEND TO: Commissioner for Patents, P.O. Box 1450, Alexandria, VA 22313-1450.**
*If you need assistance in completing the form, call 1-800-PTO-9199 and select option 2.*

## Privacy Act Statement

The **Privacy Act of 1974 (P.L. 93-579)** requires that you be given certain information in connection with your submission of the attached form related to a patent application or patent. Accordingly, pursuant to the requirements of the Act, please be advised that: (1) the general authority for the collection of this information is 35 U.S.C. 2(b)(2); (2) furnishing of the information solicited is voluntary; and (3) the principal purpose for which the information is used by the U.S. Patent and Trademark Office is to process and/or examine your submission related to a patent application or patent. If you do not furnish the requested information, the U.S. Patent and Trademark Office may not be able to process and/or examine your submission, which may result in termination of proceedings or abandonment of the application or expiration of the patent.

The information provided by you in this form will be subject to the following routine uses:

1. The information on this form will be treated confidentially to the extent allowed under the Freedom of Information Act (5 U.S.C. 552) and the Privacy Act (5 U.S.C 552a). Records from this system of records may be disclosed to the Department of Justice to determine whether disclosure of these records is required by the Freedom of Information Act.
2. A record from this system of records may be disclosed, as a routine use, in the course of presenting evidence to a court, magistrate, or administrative tribunal, including disclosures to opposing counsel in the course of settlement negotiations.
3. A record in this system of records may be disclosed, as a routine use, to a Member of Congress submitting a request involving an individual, to whom the record pertains, when the individual has requested assistance from the Member with respect to the subject matter of the record.
4. A record in this system of records may be disclosed, as a routine use, to a contractor of the Agency having need for the information in order to perform a contract. Recipients of information shall be required to comply with the requirements of the Privacy Act of 1974, as amended, pursuant to 5 U.S.C. 552a(m).
5. A record related to an International Application filed under the Patent Cooperation Treaty in this system of records may be disclosed, as a routine use, to the International Bureau of the World Intellectual Property Organization, pursuant to the Patent Cooperation Treaty.
6. A record in this system of records may be disclosed, as a routine use, to another federal agency for purposes of National Security review (35 U.S.C. 181) and for review pursuant to the Atomic Energy Act (42 U.S.C. 218(c)).
7. A record from this system of records may be disclosed, as a routine use, to the Administrator, General Services, or his/her designee, during an inspection of records conducted by GSA as part of that agency's responsibility to recommend improvements in records management practices and programs, under authority of 44 U.S.C. 2904 and 2906. Such disclosure shall be made in accordance with the GSA regulations governing inspection of records for this purpose, and any other relevant (*i.e.*, GSA or Commerce) directive. Such disclosure shall not be used to make determinations about individuals.
8. A record from this system of records may be disclosed, as a routine use, to the public after either publication of the application pursuant to 35 U.S.C. 122(b) or issuance of a patent pursuant to 35 U.S.C. 151. Further, a record may be disclosed, subject to the limitations of 37 CFR 1.14, as a routine use, to the public if the record was filed in an application which became abandoned or in which the proceedings were terminated and which application is referenced by either a published application, an application open to public inspection or an issued patent.
9. A record from this system of records may be disclosed, as a routine use, to a Federal, State, or local law enforcement agency, if the USPTO becomes aware of a violation or potential violation of law or regulation.

# APPENDIX 11:
# PROVISIONAL PATENT APPLICATION PROCESS

**Excerpt from Section 111 of the Patent Act:**

(b) PROVISIONAL APPLICATION—

(1) AUTHORIZATION—A provisional application for patent shall be made or authorized to be made by the inventor, except as otherwise provided in this title, in writing to the Director. Such application shall include—

(A) a specification as prescribed by the first paragraph of section 112 of this title; and

(B) a drawing as prescribed by section 113 of this title.

(2) CLAIM—A claim, as required by the second through fifth paragraphs of section 112, shall not be required in a provisional application.

(3) FEE—

(A) The application must be accompanied by the fee required by law.

(B) The fee may be submitted after the specification and any required drawing are submitted, within such period and under such conditions, including the payment of a surcharge, as may be prescribed by the Director.

(C) Upon failure to submit the fee within such prescribed period, the application shall be regarded as abandoned, unless it is shown to the satisfaction of the Director that the delay in submitting the fee was unavoidable or unintentional.

(4) FILING DATE—The filing date of a provisional application shall be the date on which the specification and any required drawing are received in the Patent and Trademark Office.

(5) ABANDONMENT—Notwithstanding the absence of a claim, upon timely request and as prescribed by the Director, a provisional application may be treated as an application filed under subsection (a). Subject to section 119(e)(3) of this title, if no such request is made, the provisional application shall be regarded as abandoned 12 months after the filing date of such application and shall not be subject to revival after such 12-month period.

(6) OTHER BASIS FOR PROVISIONAL APPLICATION—Subject to all the conditions in this subsection and section 119(e) of this title, and as prescribed by the Director, an application for patent filed under subsection (a) may be treated as a provisional application for patent.

(7) NO RIGHT OF PRIORITY OR BENEFIT OF EARLIEST FILING DATE—A provisional application shall not be entitled to the right of priority of any other application under section 119 or 365(a) of this title or to the benefit of an earlier filing date in the United States under section 120, 121, or 365(c) of this title.

(8) APPLICABLE PROVISIONS—The provisions of this title relating to applications for patent shall apply to provisional applications for patent, except as otherwise provided, and except that provisional applications for patent shall not be subject to sections 115, 131, 135, and 157 of this title.

## Excerpt from Section 119 of the Patent Act:

(e)(1) An application for patent filed under section 111(a) or section 363 of this title for an invention disclosed in the manner provided by the first paragraph of section 112 of this title in a provisional application filed under section 111(b) of this title, by an inventor or inventors named in the provisional application, shall have the same effect, as to such invention, as though filed on the date of the provisional application filed under section 111(b) of this title, if the application for patent filed under section 111(a) or section 363 of this title is filed not later than 12 months after the date on which the provisional application was filed and if it contains or is amended to contain a specific reference to the provisional application. No application shall be entitled to the benefit of an earlier filed provisional application under this subsection unless an amendment containing the specific reference to the earlier filed provisional application is submitted at such time during the pendency of the application as required by the Director. The Director may consider the failure to submit such an amendment within that time period as a waiver of any benefit under this subsection. The Director may establish procedures, including the payment of a surcharge, to accept an unintentionally delayed submission of an amendment under this subsection during the pendency of the application.

(2) A provisional application filed under section 111(b) of this title may not be relied upon in any proceeding in the Patent and Trademark Office unless the fee set forth in subparagraph (A) or (C) of section 41(a)(1) of this title has been paid.

(3) If the day that is 12 months after the filing date of a provisional application falls on a Saturday, Sunday, or Federal holiday within the District of Columbia, the period of pendency of the provisional application shall be extended to the next succeeding secular or business day.

## Section 1.51(c) of Title 37 of the CFR:

(c) A complete provisional application filed under § 1.53(c) comprises:

(1) A cover sheet identifying:

(i) The application as a provisional application,

(ii) The name or names of the inventor or inventors, (see § 1.41(a)(2)),

(iii) The residence of each named inventor,

(iv) The title of the invention,

(v) The name and registration number of the attorney or agent (if applicable),

(vi) The docket number used by the person filing the application to identify the application (if applicable),

(vii) The correspondence address, and

(viii) The name of the U.S. Government agency and Government contract number (if the invention was made by an agency of the U.S. Government or under a contract with an agency of the U.S. Government);

(2) A specification as prescribed by the first paragraph of 35 U.S.C. 112, see § 1.71;

(3) Drawings, when necessary, see §§ 1.81 to 1.85; and

(4) The prescribed filing fee and application size fee, see § 1.16.

# APPENDIX 12:
# PROVISIONAL UTILITY APPLICATION
# COVER SHEET

PTO/SB/16 (12-08)
Approved for use through 06/30/2010. OMB 0651-0032
U.S. Patent and Trademark Office; U.S. DEPARTMENT OF COMMERCE
Under the Paperwork Reduction Act of 1995, no persons are required to respond to a collection of information unless it displays a valid OMB control number.

**PROVISIONAL APPLICATION FOR PATENT COVER SHEET – Page 1 of 2**
This is a request for filing a PROVISIONAL APPLICATION FOR PATENT under 37 CFR 1.53(c).

Express Mail Label No. _____

| INVENTOR(S) | | |
|---|---|---|
| Given Name (first and middle [if any]) | Family Name or Surname | Residence (City and either State or Foreign Country) |
| | | |
| | | |
| | | |
| | | |
| | | |

Additional inventors are being named on the _____ separately numbered sheets attached hereto.

**TITLE OF THE INVENTION (500 characters max):**



*Direct all correspondence to:* **CORRESPONDENCE ADDRESS**

☐ The address corresponding to Customer Number: [_____]

**OR**

☐ Firm or Individual Name

Address

| City | State | Zip |
|---|---|---|
| Country | Telephone | Email |

**ENCLOSED APPLICATION PARTS (check all that apply)**

☐ Application Data Sheet. See 37 CFR 1.76  ☐ CD(s), Number of CDs _____

☐ Drawing(s)  *Number of Sheets* _____  ☐ Other (specify) _____

☐ Specification (e.g. description of the invention) *Number of Pages* _____

Fees Due: Filing Fee of $220 ($110 for small entity). If the specification and drawings exceed 100 sheets of paper, an application size fee is also due, which is $270 ($135 for small entity) for each additional 50 sheets or fraction thereof. See 35 U.S.C. 41(a)(1)(G) and 37 CFR 1.16(s).

**METHOD OF PAYMENT OF THE FILING FEE AND APPLICATION SIZE FEE FOR THIS PROVISIONAL APPLICATION FOR PATENT**

☐ Applicant claims small entity status. See 37 CFR 1.27.

☐ A check or money order made payable to the *Director of the United States Patent and Trademark Office* is enclosed to cover the filing fee and application size fee (if applicable).

☐ Payment by credit card. Form PTO-2038 is attached.

☐ The Director is hereby authorized to charge the filing fee and application size fee (if applicable) or credit any overpayment to Deposit Account Number: _____ .

[_____]

**TOTAL FEE AMOUNT ($)**

*USE ONLY FOR FILING A PROVISIONAL APPLICATION FOR PATENT*
This collection of information is required by 37 CFR 1.51. The information is required to obtain or retain a benefit by the public which is to file (and by the USPTO to process) an application. Confidentiality is governed by 35 U.S.C. 122 and 37 CFR 1.11 and 1.14. This collection is estimated to take 8 hours to complete, including gathering, preparing, and submitting the completed application form to the USPTO. Time will vary depending upon the individual case. Any comments on the amount of time you require to complete this form and/or suggestions for reducing this burden, should be sent to the Chief Information Officer, U.S. Patent and Trademark Office, U.S. Department of Commerce, P.O. Box 1450, Alexandria, VA 22313-1450. DO NOT SEND FEES OR COMPLETED FORMS TO THIS ADDRESS. **SEND TO: Commissioner for Patents, P.O. Box 1450, Alexandria, VA 22313-1450.**
*If you need assistance in completing the form, call 1-800-PTO-9199 and select option 2.*

PROVISIONAL APPLICATION COVER SHEET
Page 2 of 2

PTO/SB/16 (12-08)
Approved for use through 06/30/2010. OMB 0651-0032
U.S. Patent and Trademark Office; U.S. DEPARTMENT OF COMMERCE
Under the Paperwork Reduction Act of 1995, no persons are required to respond to a collection of information unless it displays a valid OMB control number.

The invention was made by an agency of the United States Government or under a contract with an agency of the United States Government.

☐ No.

☐ Yes, the name of the U.S. Government agency and the Government contract number are: _____
_____

## WARNING:

Petitioner/applicant is cautioned to avoid submitting personal information in documents filed in a patent application that may contribute to identity theft. Personal information such as social security numbers, bank account numbers, or credit card numbers (other than a check or credit card authorization form PTO-2038 submitted for payment purposes) is never required by the USPTO to support a petition or an application. If this type of personal information is included in documents submitted to the USPTO, petitioners/applicants should consider redacting such personal information from the documents before submitting them to the USPTO. Petitioner/applicant is advised that the record of a patent application is available to the public after publication of the application (unless a non-publication request in compliance with 37 CFR 1.213(a) is made in the application) or issuance of a patent. Furthermore, the record from an abandoned application may also be available to the public if the application is referenced in a published application or an issued patent (see 37 CFR 1.14). Checks and credit card authorization forms PTO-2038 submitted for payment purposes are not retained in the application file and therefore are not publicly available.

SIGNATURE _____ Date _____

TYPED or PRINTED NAME _____ REGISTRATION NO. _____
(if appropriate)

TELEPHONE _____ Docket Number: _____

## Privacy Act Statement

The **Privacy Act of 1974 (P.L. 93-579)** requires that you be given certain information in connection with your submission of the attached form related to a patent application or patent. Accordingly, pursuant to the requirements of the Act, please be advised that: (1) the general authority for the collection of this information is 35 U.S.C. 2(b)(2); (2) furnishing of the information solicited is voluntary; and (3) the principal purpose for which the information is used by the U.S. Patent and Trademark Office is to process and/or examine your submission related to a patent application or patent. If you do not furnish the requested information, the U.S. Patent and Trademark Office may not be able to process and/or examine your submission, which may result in termination of proceedings or abandonment of the application or expiration of the patent.

The information provided by you in this form will be subject to the following routine uses:

1. The information on this form will be treated confidentially to the extent allowed under the Freedom of Information Act (5 U.S.C. 552) and the Privacy Act (5 U.S.C 552a). Records from this system of records may be disclosed to the Department of Justice to determine whether disclosure of these records is required by the Freedom of Information Act.
2. A record from this system of records may be disclosed, as a routine use, in the course of presenting evidence to a court, magistrate, or administrative tribunal, including disclosures to opposing counsel in the course of settlement negotiations.
3. A record in this system of records may be disclosed, as a routine use, to a Member of Congress submitting a request involving an individual, to whom the record pertains, when the individual has requested assistance from the Member with respect to the subject matter of the record.
4. A record in this system of records may be disclosed, as a routine use, to a contractor of the Agency having need for the information in order to perform a contract. Recipients of information shall be required to comply with the requirements of the Privacy Act of 1974, as amended, pursuant to 5 U.S.C. 552a(m).
5. A record related to an International Application filed under the Patent Cooperation Treaty in this system of records may be disclosed, as a routine use, to the International Bureau of the World Intellectual Property Organization, pursuant to the Patent Cooperation Treaty.
6. A record in this system of records may be disclosed, as a routine use, to another federal agency for purposes of National Security review (35 U.S.C. 181) and for review pursuant to the Atomic Energy Act (42 U.S.C. 218(c)).
7. A record from this system of records may be disclosed, as a routine use, to the Administrator, General Services, or his/her designee, during an inspection of records conducted by GSA as part of that agency's responsibility to recommend improvements in records management practices and programs, under authority of 44 U.S.C. 2904 and 2906. Such disclosure shall be made in accordance with the GSA regulations governing inspection of records for this purpose, and any other relevant (*i.e.*, GSA or Commerce) directive. Such disclosure shall not be used to make determinations about individuals.
8. A record from this system of records may be disclosed, as a routine use, to the public after either publication of the application pursuant to 35 U.S.C. 122(b) or issuance of a patent pursuant to 35 U.S.C. 151. Further, a record may be disclosed, subject to the limitations of 37 CFR 1.14, as a routine use, to the public if the record was filed in an application which became abandoned or in which the proceedings were terminated and which application is referenced by either a published application, an application open to public inspection or an issued patent.
9. A record from this system of records may be disclosed, as a routine use, to a Federal, State, or local law enforcement agency, if the USPTO becomes aware of a violation or potential violation of law or regulation.

# APPENDIX 13:
# PETITION TO ACCELERATE
# EXAMINATION (AGE)

Doc code : PET.OP.AGE
Description : Petition to make special based on Age/Health

PTO/SB/130 (07-09)
Approved for use through 07/31/2012. OMB 0651- 0031
U.S. Patent and Trademark Office, U.S. DEPARTMENT OF COMMERCE
Under the Paperwork Reduction Act of 1995, no persons are required to respond to a collection of information unless it contains a valid OMB control number

**PETITION TO MAKE SPECIAL BASED ON AGE FOR ADVANCEMENT OF EXAMINATION
UNDER 37 CFR 1.102(c)(1)**

**Application Information**

| Application Number | | Confirmation Number | | Filing Date | |
|---|---|---|---|---|---|
| Attorney Docket Number (optional) | | Art Unit | | Examiner | |
| First Named Inventor | | | | | |
| Title of Invention | | | | | |

**Attention: Office of Petitions**
An application may be made special for advancement of examination upon filing of a petition showing that the applicant is 65 years of age, or more. No fee is required with such a petition. See 37 CFR 1.102(c)(1) and MPEP 708.02 (IV).

APPLICANT HEREBY PETITIONS TO MAKE SPECIAL FOR ADVANCEMENT OF EXAMINATION IN THIS APPLICATION UNDER 37 CFR 1.102(c)(1) and MPEP 708.02 (IV) ON THE BASIS OF THE APPLICANT'S AGE.

A grantable petition requires one of the following items:
(1) Statement by one named inventor in the application that he/she is 65 years of age, or more; or

**Name of Inventor who is 65 years of age, or older**

A signature of the applicant or representative is required in accordance with 37 CFR 1.33 and 10.18.
Please see 37 CFR 1.4(d) for the format of the signature.

Select (1) or (2) :

- 

| Signature | |
|---|---|

EFSWeb 1.0.18

Doc code : PET.OP.AGE
Description : Petition to make special based on Age/Health

PTO/SB/130 (07-09)
Approved for use through 07/31/2012. OMB 0651- 0031
U.S. Patent and Trademark Office; U.S. DEPARTMENT OF COMMERCE
Under the Paperwork Reduction Act of 1995, no persons are required to respond to a collection of information unless it contains a valid OMB control number

# Privacy Act Statement

The Privacy Act of 1974 (P.L. 93-579) requires that you be given certain information in connection with your submission of the attached form related to a patent application or patent. Accordingly, pursuant to the requirements of the Act, please be advised that: (1) the general authority for the collection of this information is 35 U.S.C. 2(b)(2); (2) furnishing of the information solicited is voluntary; and (3) the principal purpose for which the information is used by the U.S. Patent and Trademark Office is to process and/or examine your submission related to a patent application or patent. If you do not furnish the requested information, the U.S. Patent and Trademark Office may not be able to process and/or examine your submission, which may result in termination of proceedings or abandonment of the application or expiration of the patent.

The information provided by you in this form will be subject to the following routine uses:

1. The information on this form will be treated confidentially to the extent allowed under the Freedom of Information Act (5 U.S.C. 552) and the Privacy Act (5 U.S.C. 552a). Records from this system of records may be disclosed to the Department of Justice to determine whether the Freedom of Information Act requires disclosure of these records.

2. A record from this system of records may be disclosed, as a routine use, in the course of presenting evidence to a court, magistrate, or administrative tribunal, including disclosures to opposing counsel in the course of settlement negotiations.

3. A record in this system of records may be disclosed, as a routine use, to a Member of Congress submitting a request involving an individual, to whom the record pertains, when the individual has requested assistance from the Member with respect to the subject matter of the record.

4. A record in this system of records may be disclosed, as a routine use, to a contractor of the Agency having need for the information in order to perform a contract. Recipients of information shall be required to comply with the requirements of the Privacy Act of 1974, as amended, pursuant to 5 U.S.C. 552a(m).

5. A record related to an International Application filed under the Patent Cooperation Treaty in this system of records may be disclosed, as a routine use, to the International Bureau of the World Intellectual Property Organization, pursuant to the Patent Cooperation Treaty.

6. A record in this system of records may be disclosed, as a routine use, to another federal agency for purposes of National Security review (35 U.S.C. 181) and for review pursuant to the Atomic Energy Act (42 U.S.C. 218(c)).

7. A record from this system of records may be disclosed, as a routine use, to the Administrator, General Services, or his/her designee, during an inspection of records conducted by GSA as part of that agency's responsibility to recommend improvements in records management practices and programs, under authority of 44 U.S.C. 2904 and 2906. Such disclosure shall be made in accordance with the GSA regulations governing inspection of records for this purpose, and any other relevant (i.e., GSA or Commerce) directive. Such disclosure shall not be used to make determinations about indivi duals.

8. A record from this system of records may be disclosed, as a routine use, to the public after either publication of the application pursuant to 35 U.S.C. 122(b) or issuance of a patent pursuant to 35 U.S.C. 151. Further, a record may be disclosed, subject to the limitations of 37 CFR 1.14, as a routine use, to the public if the record was filed in an

EFSWeb 1.0.18

# APPENDIX 14:
# PETITION TO PROCEED UNDER ACCELERATED EXAM PROGRAM

Doc Code: PET.SPRE.ACX
Doc Description: Petition for 12-month Accelerated Exam

PTO/SB/28 (07-09)
Approved for use through 07/31/2012. OMB 0651-0031
U.S. Patent and Trademark Office; U. S. DEPARTMENT OF COMMERCE
Under the Paperwork Reduction Act of 1995, no persons are required to respond to a collection of information unless it displays a valid OMB control number.

## PETITION TO MAKE SPECIAL UNDER ACCELERATED EXAMINATION PROGRAM

| Attorney Docket Number | | First Named Inventor | |
|---|---|---|---|
| Application Number (if Known) | | | |
| Title of Invention | | | |

**APPLICANT HEREBY PETITIONS TO MAKE THE ABOVE-IDENTIFIED APPLICATION SPECIAL UNDER THE REVISED ACCELERATED EXAMINATION PROGRAM. See Instruction sheet on page 3.**

1. **Claims of the application:**
   a. The application must contain three (3) or fewer independent claims and twenty (20) or fewer total claims. The application may not contain any multiple dependent claims.

   b. **Applicant hereby agrees not to separately argue the patentability of any dependent claim during any appeal in the application.** Specifically, the applicant agrees that the dependent claims will be grouped together with and not argued separately from the independent claim from which they depend in any appeal brief filed in the application (37 CFR 41.37(c)(1)(vii)).

   c. The claims must be directed to **a single invention.**

2. **Interviews:**
   Applicant hereby agrees to have (if requested by examiner):
   a. An interview (including an interview before a first Office action) to discuss the prior art and any potential rejections or objections with the intention of clarifying and possibly resolving all issues with respect to patentability at that time, and

   b. A telephonic interview to make an election without traverse if the Office determines that the claims are not obviously directed to a single invention.

3. **Preexamination Search Statement and Accelerated Examination Support Document:**
   With this petition, applicant is providing: a **preexamination search statement**, in compliance with the requirements set forth in item 8 of the instruction sheet, and an **"accelerated examination support document"** that includes:
   a. An **information disclosure statement** in compliance with 37 CFR 1.98 citing each reference deemed most closely related to the subject matter of each of the claims;

   b. For each reference cited, **an identification of all the limitations of the claims** that are disclosed by the reference specifying where the limitation is disclosed in the cited reference;

   c. A **detailed explanation of how each of the claims are patentable** over the references cited with the particularity required by 37 CFR 1.111(b) and (c);

   d. A concise **statement of the utility** of the invention as defined in each of the independent claims (unless the application is a design application);

   e. An identification of any cited references that may be disqualified as prior art under 35 U.S.C. 103(c) as amended by the CREATE act; and

   f. **A showing of where each limitation of the claims finds support under the first paragraph of 35 U.S.C. 112** in the written description of the specification. If applicable, the showing must also identify: (1) each means- (or step-) plus-function claim element that invokes consideration under 35 U.S.C. 112, ¶6; and (2) the structure, material, or acts that correspond to any means- (or step-) plus-function claim element that invokes consideration under 35 U.S.C. 112, ¶6. If the application claims the benefit of one or more applications under title 35, United States Code, the showing must also include where each limitation of the claims finds support under the first paragraph of 35 U.S.C. 112 in each such application in which such support exists.

The information is required to obtain or retain a benefit by the public which is to file (and by the USPTO to process) an application. Confidentiality is governed by 35 U.S.C. 122 and 37 CFR 1.11 and 1.14. This form is estimated to take 12 hours to complete, including gathering, preparing, and submitting the completed application form to the USPTO. Time will vary depending upon the individual case. Any comments on the amount of time you require to complete this form and/or suggestions for reducing this burden, should be sent to the Chief Information Officer, U.S. Patent and Trademark Office, U.S. Department of Commerce, P.O. Box 1450, Alexandria, VA 22313-1450. DO NOT SEND FEES OR COMPLETED FORMS TO THIS ADDRESS. *If you need assistance in completing the form, call 1-800-PTO-9199 and select option 2.*
EFS Web 2.2.20

Doc Code: PET.SPRE.ACX
Doc Description: Petition for 12-month Accelerated Exam

PTO/SB/28 (07-09)
Approved for use through 07/31/2012. OMB 0651-0031
U.S. Patent and Trademark Office; U. S. DEPARTMENT OF COMMERCE
Under the Paperwork Reduction Act of 1995, no persons are required to respond to a collection of information unless it displays a valid OMB control number.

## PETITION TO MAKE SPECIAL UNDER ACCELERATED EXAMINATION PROGRAM
## (Continued)

| Attorney Docket Number | | First Named Inventor | |
|---|---|---|---|

**Attachments:**

| a. | | Accelerated Examination Support Document (see item 3 above). |
|---|---|---|
| b. | | A statement, in compliance with the requirements set forth in item 8 of the instruction sheet, detailing the preexamination search which was conducted. |
| c. | | Information Disclosure Statement. |
| d. | ☐ | Other (e.g., a statement that the claimed subject matter is directed to environmental quality, energy, or countering terrorism (37 CFR 1.102(c)(2)). |

**Fees: The following fees must be filed electronically via EFS or EFS-Web:**

| a. | The basic filing fee, search fee, examination fee, and application size fee (if required) under 37 CFR 1.16. |
|---|---|
| b. | Petition fee under 37 CFR 1.17(h) - unless the petition is filed with a showing under 37 CFR 1.102(c)(2). |

**Signature:**

| Click Remove if you wish to remove this signatory | | | Remove |
|---|---|---|---|
| Signature | | Date | |
| Name (Print/Typed) | | Registration Number | |
| Click Add if you wish to add additional signatory | | | Add |

**Note:** Signatures of all the inventors or assignees of record of the entire interest or their representative(s) are required in accordance with 37 CFR 1.33 and 10.18. Please see 37 CFR 1.4(d) for the form of the signature.

Doc Code: PET.SPRE.ACX
Doc Description: Petition for 12-month Accelerated Exam

PTO/SB/28 (07-09)
Approved for use through 07/31/2012. OMB 0651-0031
U.S. Patent and Trademark Office; U. S. DEPARTMENT OF COMMERCE
Under the Paperwork Reduction Act of 1995, no persons are required to respond to a collection of information unless it displays a valid OMB control number.

## Instruction Sheet Petition to Make Special Under the Accelerated Examination

*A grantable petition must meet the following conditions:*

1. The petition to make special under the accelerated examination program must be filed with the application and accompanied by the fee set forth in 37 CFR 1.17(h) or a statement that the claimed subject matter is directed to environmental quality, energy, or countering terrorism.

2. The application must be a non-reissue utility or design application filed under 35 U.S.C. 111(a).

3. The application must be **filed electronically** using the Office electronic filing system (EFS) or EFS-Web.

4. The application must be complete under 37 CFR 1.51 and in condition for examination on filing. For example, the application must be filed together with the basic filing fee, search fee, examination fee, and application size fee (if applicable), and an oath or declaration under 37 CFR 1.63.

5. The application must contain three (3) or fewer independent claims and twenty (20) or fewer total claims. The application may not contain any multiple dependent claims. The petition must include a statement that **applicant will agree not to separately argue the patentability of any dependent claim during any appeal** in the application. Specifically, the applicant is agreeing that the dependent claims will be grouped together with and not argued separately from the independent claim from which they depend in any appeal brief filed in the application (37 CFR 41.37(c)(1)(vii)).

6. The claims must be directed to a **single invention**. The petition must include a statement that applicant will agree to have a telephonic interview to make an election without traverse in a telephonic interview if the Office determines that all the claims are not directed to a single invention.

7. The petition must include a statement that **applicant will agree** to have an interview (including an interview before a first Office action) to discuss the prior art and any potential rejections or objections with the intention of clarifying and possibly resolving all issues with respect to patentability at that time.

8. At the time of filing, applicant must provide a statement that a **preexamination search was conducted**, including an identification of the field of search by United States class and subclass and the date of the search, where applicable, and, for database searches, the search logic or chemical structure or sequence used as a query, the name of the file or files searched and the database service, and the date of the search.
   a. This preexamination search must involve U.S. patents and patent application publications, foreign patent documents, and nonpatent literature, unless the applicant can justify with reasonable certainty that no references more pertinent than those already identified are likely to be found in the eliminated source and includes such a justification with this statement.
   b. This preexamination search must be directed to the claimed invention and encompass all of the features of the independent claims, giving the claims the broadest reasonable interpretation.
   c. The preexamination search must also encompass the disclosed features that may be claimed, in that an amendment to the claims (including any new claim) that is not encompassed by the preexamination search will be treated as non-responsive and will not be entered.
   d. A search report from a foreign patent office will not be accepted unless the search report satisfies the requirements set forth above.
   e. Any statement in support of a petition to make special must be based on a good faith belief that the preexamination search was conducted in compliance with these requirement. See 37 CFR 1.56 and 10.18.

9. At the time of filing, applicant must provide in support of the petition an **accelerated examination support document** that includes:
   a. An **information disclosure statement** in compliance with 37 CFR 1.98 citing each reference deemed most closely related to the subject matter of each of the claims;
   b. For each reference cited, **an identification of all the limitations of the claims** that are disclosed by the reference specifying where the limitation is disclosed in the cited reference;
   c. A **detailed explanation of how each of the claims are patentable** over the references cited with the particularity required by 37 CFR 1.111(b) and (c);
   d. A concise **statement of the utility** of the invention as defined in each of the independent claims (unless the application is a design application);
   e. An identification of any cited references that may be disqualified as prior art under 35 U.S.C. 103(c) as am ende d by the CREATE act; and
   f. A **showing of where each limitation of the claims finds support under the first paragraph of 35 U.S.C. 112** in the written description of the specification. If applicable, the showing must also identify: (1) each means- (or step-) plus-function claim element that invokes consideration under 35 U.S.C. 112, ¶6; and (2) the structure, material, or acts that correspond to any means- (or step-) plus-function claim element that invokes consideration under 35 U.S.C. 112, ¶6. If the application claims the benefit of one or more applications under title 35, United States Code, the showing must also include where each limitation of the claims finds support under the first paragraph of 35 U.S.C. 112 in each such application in which such support exists.
   *For more information, see notice "Changes to Practice for Petitions in Patent Applications to Make Special and for Accelerated Examination" available on the USPTO web site at http://www.uspto.gov/web/office s/pac/dapp/ogsheet.html*

EFS Web 2.2.20

## Privacy Act Statement

The Privacy Act of 1974 (P.L. 93-579) requires that you be given certain information in connection with your submission of the attached form related to a patent application or patent. Accordingly, pursuant to the requirements of the Act, please be advised that: (1) the general authority for the collection of this information is 35 U.S.C. 2(b)(2); (2) furnishing of the information solicited is voluntary; and (3) the principal purpose for which the information is used by the U.S. Patent and Trademark Office is to process and/or examine your submission related to a patent application or patent. If you do not furnish the requested information, the U.S. Patent and Trademark Office may not be able to process and/or examine your submission, which may result in termination of proceedings or abandonment of the application or expiration of the patent.

The information provided by you in this form will be subject to the following routine uses:

1.  The information on this form will be treated confidentially to the extent allowed under the Freedom of Information Act (5 U.S.C. 552) and the Privacy Act (5 U.S.C. 552a). Records from this system of records may be disclosed to the Department of Justice to determine whether the Freedom of Information Act requires disclosure of these records.

2.  A record from this system of records may be disclosed, as a routine use, in the course of presenting evidence to a court, magistrate, or administrative tribunal, including disclosures to opposing counsel in the course of settlement negotiations.

3.  A record in this system of records may be disclosed, as a routine use, to a Member of Congress submitting a request involving an individual, to whom the record pertains, when the individual has requested assistance from the Member with respect to the subject matter of the record.

4.  A record in this system of records may be disclosed, as a routine use, to a contractor of the Agency having need for the information in order to perform a contract. Recipients of information shall be required to comply with the requirements of the Privacy Act of 1974, as amended, pursuant to 5 U.S.C. 552a(m).

5.  A record related to an International Application filed under the Patent Cooperation Treaty in this system of records may be disclosed, as a routine use, to the International Bureau of the World Intellectual Property Organization, pursuant to the Patent Cooperation Treaty.

6.  A record in this system of records may be disclosed, as a routine use, to another federal agency for purposes of National Security review (35 U.S.C. 181) and for review pursuant to the Atomic Energy Act (42 U.S.C. 218(c)).

7.  A record from this system of records may be disclosed, as a routine use, to the Administrator, General Services, or his/her designee, during an inspection of records conducted by GSA as part of that agency's responsibility to recommend improvements in records management practices and programs, under authority of 44 U.S.C. 2904 and 2906. Such disclosure shall be made in accordance with the GSA regulations governing inspection of records for this purpose, and any other relevant (i.e., GSA or Commerce) directive. Such disclosure shall not be used to make determinations about individuals.

8.  A record from this system of records may be disclosed, as a routine use, to the public after either publication of the application pursuant to 35 U.S.C. 122(b) or issuance of a patent pursuant to 35 U.S.C. 151. Further, a record may be disclosed, subject to the limitations of 37 CFR 1.14, as a routine use, to the public if the record was filed in an application which became abandoned or in which the proceedings were terminated and which application is referenced by either a published application, an application open to public inspections or an issued patent.

9.  A record from this system of records may be disclosed, as a routine use, to a Federal, State, or local law enforcement agency, if the USPTO becomes aware of a violation or potential violation of law or regulation.

# APPENDIX 15:
# CONTENT AND ORDER OF
# AN APPLICATION

**Excerpt from Section 111 of the Patent Act:**

(a) IN GENERAL—

(1) WRITTEN APPLICATION—An application for patent shall be made, or authorized to be made, by the inventor, except as otherwise provided in this title, in writing to the Director.

(2) CONTENTS—Such application shall include—

(A) a specification as prescribed by section 112 of this title;

(B) a drawing as prescribed by section 113 of this title; and

(C) an oath by the applicant as prescribed by section 115 of this title.

(3) FEE AND OATH—The application must be accompanied by the fee required by law. The fee and oath may be submitted after the specification and any required drawing are submitted, within such period and under such conditions, including the payment of a surcharge, as may be prescribed by the Director.

(4) FAILURE TO SUBMIT—Upon failure to submit the fee and oath within such prescribed period, the application shall be regarded as abandoned, unless it is shown to the satisfaction of the Director that the delay in submitting the fee and oath was unavoidable or unintentional. The filing date of an application shall be the date on which the specification and any required drawing are received in the Patent and Trademark Office.

**Excerpt from Section 1.51 of Title 37 of the CFR:**

(a) Applications for patents must be made to the Director of the United States Patent and Trademark Office.

(b) A complete application filed under § 1.53(b) or § 1.53(d) comprises:

(1) A specification as prescribed by 35 U.S.C. 112, including a claim or claims, see §§ 1.71 to 1.77;

(2) An oath or declaration, see §§ 1.63 and 1.68;

(3) Drawings, when necessary, see §§ 1.81 to 1.85; and

(4) The prescribed filing fee, search fee, examination fee, and application size fee, see § 1.16.

. . .

(d) Applicants are encouraged to file an information disclosure statement in nonprovisional applications. See § 1.97 and § 1.98. No information disclosure statement may be filed in a provisional application.

**Excerpt from Section 1.52 of Title 37 of the CFR:**

(a) *Papers that are to become a part of the permanent United States Patent and Trademark Office records in the file of a patent application or a reexamination proceeding.*

(1) All papers, other than drawings, that are submitted on paper or by facsimile transmission, and are to become a part of the permanent United States Patent and Trademark Office records in the file of a patent application or reexamination proceeding, must be on sheets of paper that are the same size, not permanently bound together, and:

(i) Flexible, strong, smooth, non-shiny, durable, and white;

(ii) Either 21.0 cm by 29.7 cm (DIN size A4) or 21.6 cm by 27.9 cm (8 1/2 by 11 inches), with each sheet including a top margin of at least 2.0 cm (3/4 inch), a left side margin of at least 2.5 cm (1 inch), a right side margin of at least 2.0 cm (3/4 inch), and a bottom margin of at least 2.0 cm (3/4 inch);

(iii) Written on only one side in portrait orientation;

(iv) Plainly and legibly written either by a typewriter or machine printer in permanent dark ink or its equivalent; and

(v) Presented in a form having sufficient clarity and contrast between the paper and the writing thereon to permit the direct reproduction of readily legible copies in any number by use of photographic, electrostatic, photo-offset, and microfilming processes and electronic capture by use of digital imaging and optical character recognition.

(2) All papers that are submitted on paper or by facsimile transmission and are to become a part of the permanent records of the United States Patent and Trademark Office should have no holes in the sheets as submitted.

(3) The provisions of this paragraph and paragraph (b) of this section do not apply to the preprinted information on paper forms provided by the Office, or to the copy of the patent submitted on paper in double column format as the specification in a reissue application or request for reexamination.

(4) See § 1.58 for chemical and mathematical formulae and tables, and § 1.84 for drawings.

(5) Papers that are submitted electronically to the Office must be formatted and transmitted in compliance with the Office's electronic filing system requirements.

(b) *The application (specification, including the claims, drawings, and oath or declaration) or reexamination proceeding and any amendments or corrections to the application or reexamination proceeding.*

(1) The application or proceeding and any amendments or corrections to the application (including any translation submitted pursuant to paragraph (d) of this section) or proceeding, except as provided for in § 1.69 and paragraph (d) of this section, must:

(i) Comply with the requirements of paragraph (a) of this section; and

(ii) Be in the English language or be accompanied by a translation of the application and a translation of any corrections or amendments into the English language together with a statement that the translation is accurate.

(2) The specification (including the abstract and claims) for other than reissue applications and reexamination proceedings, and any amendments for applications (including reissue applications) and reexamination proceedings to the specification, except as provided for in §§ 1.821 through 1.825, must have:

(i) Lines that are 1 1/2 or double spaced;

(ii) Text written in a nonscript type font (e.g., Arial, Times Roman, or Courier, preferably a font size of 12) lettering style having capital letters which should be at least 0.3175 cm. (0.125 inch) high, but may be no smaller than 0.21 cm. (0.08 inch) high (e.g., a font size of 6); and

(iii) Only a single column of text.

(3) The claim or claims must commence on a separate physical sheet or electronic page (§ 1.75(h)).

(4) The abstract must commence on a separate physical sheet or electronic page or be submitted as the first page of the patent in a reissue application or reexamination proceeding (§ 1.72(b)).

(5) Other than in a reissue application or reexamination proceeding, the pages of the specification including claims and abstract must be numbered consecutively, starting with 1, the numbers being centrally located above or preferably below, the text.

(6) Other than in a reissue application or reexamination proceeding, the paragraphs of the specification, other than in the claims or abstract, may be numbered at the time the application is filed, and should be individually and consecutively numbered using Arabic numerals, so as to unambiguously identify each paragraph. The number should consist of at least four numerals enclosed in square brackets, including leading zeros (e.g., [0001]). The numbers and enclosing brackets should appear to the right of the left margin as the first item in each paragraph, before the first word of the paragraph, and should be highlighted in bold. A gap, equivalent to approximately four spaces, should follow the number. Nontext elements (e.g., tables, mathematical or chemical formulae, chemical structures, and sequence data) are considered part of the numbered paragraph around or above the elements, and should not be independently numbered. If a nontext element extends to the left margin, it should not be numbered as a separate and independent paragraph. A list is also treated as part of the paragraph around or above the list and should not be independently numbered. Paragraph or section headers (titles), whether abutting the left margin or centered on the page, are not considered paragraphs and should not be numbered.

(c)(1) Any interlineation, erasure, cancellation, or other alteration of the application papers filed must be made before the signing of any accompanying oath or declaration pursuant to § 1.63 referring to those application papers and should be dated and initialed or signed by the applicant on the same sheet of paper. Application papers containing alterations made after the signing of an oath or declaration referring to those application papers must be supported by a supplemental oath or declaration under § 1.67. In either situation, a substitute specification (§ 1.125) is required if the application papers do not comply with paragraphs (a) and (b) of this section.

(2) After the signing of the oath or declaration referring to the application papers, amendments may only be made in the manner provided by § 1.121.

(3) Notwithstanding the provisions of this paragraph, if an oath or declaration is a copy of the oath or declaration from a prior application, the application for which such copy is submitted may contain alterations that do not introduce matter that would have been new matter in the prior application.

(d) A nonprovisional or provisional application may be in a language other than English.

(1) *Nonprovisional application.* If a nonprovisional application is filed in a language other than English, an English language translation of the non- English language application, a statement that the translation is accurate, and the processing fee set forth in § 1.17(i) are required. If these items are not filed with the application, applicant will be notified and given a period of time within which they must be filed in order to avoid abandonment.

(2) *Provisional application.* If a provisional application is filed in a language other than English, an English language translation of the non-English language provisional application will not be required in the provisional application. See § 1.78(a) for the requirements for claiming the benefit of such provisional application in a nonprovisional application.

### Excerpt from Section 1.53 of Title 37 of the CFR:

(b) *Application filing requirements—Nonprovisional application.* The filing date of an application for patent filed under this section, except for a provisional application under paragraph (c) of this section or a continued prosecution application under paragraph (d) of this section, is the date on which a specification as prescribed by 35 U.S.C. 112 containing a description pursuant to § 1.71 and at least one claim pursuant to § 1.75, and any drawing required by § 1.81(a) are filed in the Patent and Trademark Office. No new matter may be introduced into an application after its filing date. A continuing application, which may be a continuation, divisional, or continuation-in-part application, may be filed under the conditions specified in 35 U.S.C. 120, 121 or 365(c) and § 1.78(a).

**Excerpt from Section 1.77 of Title 37 of the CFR:**

(a) The elements of the application, if applicable, should appear in the following order:

(1) Utility application transmittal form.

(2) Fee transmittal form.

(3) Application data sheet (see § 1.76).

(4) Specification.

(5) Drawings.

(6) Executed oath or declaration.

# APPENDIX 16:
# NONPROVISIONAL UTILITY PATENT
# APPLICATION TRANSMITTAL

| UTILITY PATENT APPLICATION TRANSMITTAL | Attorney Docket No. | |
| --- | --- | --- |
| | First Inventor | |
| | Title | |
| *(Only for new nonprovisional applications under 37 CFR 1.53(b))* | Express Mail Label No. | |

| **APPLICATION ELEMENTS** | ADDRESS TO: | **Commissioner for Patents** |
| --- | --- | --- |
| *See MPEP chapter 600 concerning utility patent application contents.* | | P.O. Box 1450 Alexandria VA 22313-1450 |

**APPLICATION ELEMENTS**

1. ☐ **Fee Transmittal Form** (e.g., PTO/SB/17)

2. ☐ **Applicant claims small entity status.** See 37 CFR 1.27.

3. ☐ **Specification** [Total Pages_____]
   Both the claims and abstract must start on a new page
   *(For information on the preferred arrangement, see MPEP 608.01(a))*

4. ☐ **Drawing(s)** (35 U.S.C. 113) [Total Sheets_____]

5. **Oath or Declaration** [Total Sheets_____]
   a. ☐ Newly executed (original or copy)
   b. ☐ A copy from a prior application (37 CFR 1.63(d))
      *(for continuation/divisional with Box 18 completed)*
      i. ☐ DELETION OF INVENTOR(S)
         Signed statement attached deleting inventor(s)
         name in the prior application, see 37 CFR
         1.63(d)(2) and 1.33(b).

6. ☐ **Application Data Sheet.** See 37 CFR 1.76

7. ☐ **CD-ROM or CD-R** in duplicate, large table or
      Computer Program *(Appendix)*
      ☐ Landscape Table on CD

8. **Nucleotide and/or Amino Acid Sequence Submission**
   *(if applicable, items a. – c. are required)*
   a. ☐ Computer Readable Form (CRF)
   b. ☐ Specification Sequence Listing on:
      i. ☐ CD-ROM or CD-R (2 copies); or
      ii. ☐ Paper
   c. ☐ Statements verifying identity of above copies

**ACCOMPANYING APPLICATION PARTS**

9. ☐ **Assignment Papers** (cover sheet & document(s))
   Name of Assignee_____

10. ☐ **37 CFR 3.73(b) Statement** (when there is an assignee)    ☐ **Power of Attorney**

11. ☐ **English Translation Document** *(if applicable)*

12. ☐ **Information Disclosure Statement** (PTO/SB/08 or PTO-1449)
    ☐ Copies of citations attached

13. ☐ **Preliminary Amendment**

14. ☐ **Return Receipt Postcard** (MPEP 503)
    *(Should be specifically itemized)*

15. ☐ **Certified Copy of Priority Document(s)**
    *(if foreign priority is claimed)*

16. ☐ **Nonpublication Request** under 35 U.S.C. 122(b)(2)(B)(i).
    Applicant must attach form PTO/SB/35 or equivalent.

17. ☐ **Other:**_____

18. If a CONTINUING APPLICATION, check appropriate box, and supply the requisite information below and in the first sentence of the specification following the title, or in an Application Data Sheet under 37 CFR 1.76:

☐ Continuation    ☐ Divisional    ☐ Continuation-in-part (CIP)    of prior application No.: ...............................

Prior application information:    Examiner _____    Art Unit: _____

**19. CORRESPONDENCE ADDRESS**

☐ The address associated with Customer Number: _____    OR ☐ Correspondence address below

| Name | | | |
| --- | --- | --- | --- |
| Address | | | |
| City | State | Zip Code | |
| Country | Telephone | Email | |
| Signature | | Date | |
| Name (Print/Type) | | Registration No. (Attorney/Agent) | |

## Privacy Act Statement

The **Privacy Act of 1974 (P.L. 93-579)** requires that you be given certain information in connection with your submission of the attached form related to a patent application or patent. Accordingly, pursuant to the requirements of the Act, please be advised that: (1) the general authority for the collection of this information is 35 U.S.C. 2(b)(2); (2) furnishing of the information solicited is voluntary; and (3) the principal purpose for which the information is used by the U.S. Patent and Trademark Office is to process and/or examine your submission related to a patent application or patent. If you do not furnish the requested information, the U.S. Patent and Trademark Office may not be able to process and/or examine your submission, which may result in termination of proceedings or abandonment of the application or expiration of the patent.

The information provided by you in this form will be subject to the following routine uses:

1. The information on this form will be treated confidentially to the extent allowed under the Freedom of Information Act (5 U.S.C. 552) and the Privacy Act (5 U.S.C 552a). Records from this system of records may be disclosed to the Department of Justice to determine whether disclosure of these records is required by the Freedom of Information Act.
2. A record from this system of records may be disclosed, as a routine use, in the course of presenting evidence to a court, magistrate, or administrative tribunal, including disclosures to opposing counsel in the course of settlement negotiations.
3. A record in this system of records may be disclosed, as a routine use, to a Member of Congress submitting a request involving an individual, to whom the record pertains, when the individual has requested assistance from the Member with respect to the subject matter of the record.
4. A record in this system of records may be disclosed, as a routine use, to a contractor of the Agency having need for the information in order to perform a contract. Recipients of information shall be required to comply with the requirements of the Privacy Act of 1974, as amended, pursuant to 5 U.S.C. 552a(m).
5. A record related to an International Application filed under the Patent Cooperation Treaty in this system of records may be disclosed, as a routine use, to the International Bureau of the World Intellectual Property Organization, pursuant to the Patent Cooperation Treaty.
6. A record in this system of records may be disclosed, as a routine use, to another federal agency for purposes of National Security review (35 U.S.C. 181) and for review pursuant to the Atomic Energy Act (42 U.S.C. 218(c)).
7. A record from this system of records may be disclosed, as a routine use, to the Administrator, General Services, or his/her designee, during an inspection of records conducted by GSA as part of that agency's responsibility to recommend improvements in records management practices and programs, under authority of 44 U.S.C. 2904 and 2906. Such disclosure shall be made in accordance with the GSA regulations governing inspection of records for this purpose, and any other relevant (*i.e.*, GSA or Commerce) directive. Such disclosure shall not be used to make determinations about individuals.
8. A record from this system of records may be disclosed, as a routine use, to the public after either publication of the application pursuant to 35 U.S.C. 122(b) or issuance of a patent pursuant to 35 U.S.C. 151. Further, a record may be disclosed, subject to the limitations of 37 CFR 1.14, as a routine use, to the public if the record was filed in an application which became abandoned or in which the proceedings were terminated and which application is referenced by either a published application, an application open to public inspection or an issued patent.
9. A record from this system of records may be disclosed, as a routine use, to a Federal, State, or local law enforcement agency, if the USPTO becomes aware of a violation or potential violation of law or regulation.

# APPENDIX 17:
# ONGOING SUBMISSIONS
# TRANSMITTAL FORM

Doc Code: TRAN.LET
Document Description: Transmittal Letter

PTO/SB/21 (07-09)
Approved for use through 07/31/2012. OMB 0651-0031
U.S. Patent and Trademark Office; U.S. DEPARTMENT OF COMMERCE
Under the Paperwork Reduction Act of 1995, no persons are required to respond to a collection of information unless it displays a valid OMB control number.

| | |
|---|---|
| **TRANSMITTAL FORM** | Application Number |
| | Filing Date |
| | First Named Inventor |
| | Art Unit |
| (to be used for all correspondence after initial filing) | Examiner Name |
| Total Number of Pages in This Submission | Attorney Docket Number |

## ENCLOSURES    (Check all that apply)

- Fee Transmittal Form
  - Fee Attached
- Amendment/Reply
  - After Final
  - Affidavits/declaration(s)
- Extension of Time Request
- Express Abandonment Request
- Information Disclosure Statement
- Certified Copy of Priority Document(s)
- Reply to Missing Parts/ Incomplete Application
  - Reply to Missing Parts under 37 CFR 1.52 or 1.53

- Drawing(s)
- Licensing-related Papers
- Petition
- Petition to Convert to a Provisional Application
- Power of Attorney, Revocation Change of Correspondence Address
- Terminal Disclaimer
- Request for Refund
- CD, Number of CD(s) _____
  - Landscape Table on CD

Remarks

- After Allowance Communication to TC
- Appeal Communication to Board of Appeals and Interferences
- Appeal Communication to TC (Appeal Notice, Brief, Reply Brief)
- Proprietary Information
- Status Letter
- Other Enclosure(s) (please identify below):

## SIGNATURE OF APPLICANT, ATTORNEY, OR AGENT

| | |
|---|---|
| Firm Name | |
| Signature | |
| Printed name | |
| Date | Reg. No. |

## CERTIFICATE OF TRANSMISSION/MAILING

I hereby certify that this correspondence is being facsimile transmitted to the USPTO or deposited with the United States Postal Service with sufficient postage as first class mail in an envelope addressed to: Commissioner for Patents, P.O. Box 1450, Alexandria, VA 22313-1450 on the date shown below:

| | |
|---|---|
| Signature | |
| Typed or printed name | Date |

This collection of information is required by 37 CFR 1.5. The information is required to obtain or retain a benefit by the public which is to file (and by the USPTO to process) an application. Confidentiality is governed by 35 U.S.C. 122 and 37 CFR 1.11 and 1.14. This collection is estimated to 2 hours to complete, including gathering, preparing, and submitting the completed application form to the USPTO. Time will vary depending upon the individual case. Any comments on the amount of time you require to complete this form and/or suggestions for reducing this burden, should be sent to the Chief Information Officer, U.S. Patent and Trademark Office, U.S. Department of Commerce, P.O. Box 1450, Alexandria, VA 22313-1450. DO NOT SEND FEES OR COMPLETED FORMS TO THIS ADDRESS. **SEND TO: Commissioner for Patents, P.O. Box 1450, Alexandria, VA 22313-1450.**

*If you need assistance in completing the form, call 1-800-PTO-9199 and select option 2.*

## Privacy Act Statement

The **Privacy Act of 1974 (P.L. 93-579)** requires that you be given certain information in connection with your submission of the attached form related to a patent application or patent. Accordingly, pursuant to the requirements of the Act, please be advised that: (1) the general authority for the collection of this information is 35 U.S.C. 2(b)(2); (2) furnishing of the information solicited is voluntary; and (3) the principal purpose for which the information is used by the U.S. Patent and Trademark Office is to process and/or examine your submission related to a patent application or patent. If you do not furnish the requested information, the U.S. Patent and Trademark Office may not be able to process and/or examine your submission, which may result in termination of proceedings or abandonment of the application or expiration of the patent.

The information provided by you in this form will be subject to the following routine uses:

1. The information on this form will be treated confidentially to the extent allowed under the Freedom of Information Act (5 U.S.C. 552) and the Privacy Act (5 U.S.C 552a). Records from this system of records may be disclosed to the Department of Justice to determine whether disclosure of these records is required by the Freedom of Information Act.
2. A record from this system of records may be disclosed, as a routine use, in the course of presenting evidence to a court, magistrate, or administrative tribunal, including disclosures to opposing counsel in the course of settlement negotiations.
3. A record in this system of records may be disclosed, as a routine use, to a Member of Congress submitting a request involving an individual, to whom the record pertains, when the individual has requested assistance from the Member with respect to the subject matter of the record.
4. A record in this system of records may be disclosed, as a routine use, to a contractor of the Agency having need for the information in order to perform a contract. Recipients of information shall be required to comply with the requirements of the Privacy Act of 1974, as amended, pursuant to 5 U.S.C. 552a(m).
5. A record related to an International Application filed under the Patent Cooperation Treaty in this system of records may be disclosed, as a routine use, to the International Bureau of the World Intellectual Property Organization, pursuant to the Patent Cooperation Treaty.
6. A record in this system of records may be disclosed, as a routine use, to another federal agency for purposes of National Security review (35 U.S.C. 181) and for review pursuant to the Atomic Energy Act (42 U.S.C. 218(c)).
7. A record from this system of records may be disclosed, as a routine use, to the Administrator, General Services, or his/her designee, during an inspection of records conducted by GSA as part of that agency's responsibility to recommend improvements in records management practices and programs, under authority of 44 U.S.C. 2904 and 2906. Such disclosure shall be made in accordance with the GSA regulations governing inspection of records for this purpose, and any other relevant (*i.e.*, GSA or Commerce) directive. Such disclosure shall not be used to make determinations about individuals.
8. A record from this system of records may be disclosed, as a routine use, to the public after either publication of the application pursuant to 35 U.S.C. 122(b) or issuance of a patent pursuant to 35 U.S.C. 151. Further, a record may be disclosed, subject to the limitations of 37 CFR 1.14, as a routine use, to the public if the record was filed in an application which became abandoned or in which the proceedings were terminated and which application is referenced by either a published application, an application open to public inspection or an issued patent.
9. A record from this system of records may be disclosed, as a routine use, to a Federal, State, or local law enforcement agency, if the USPTO becomes aware of a violation or potential violation of law or regulation.

# APPENDIX 18:
# REGULATORY REFERENCES TO THE
# FILING PROCESS

**Section 1.5 of Title 37 of the CFR:**

(a) No correspondence relating to an application should be filed prior to receipt of the application number from the Patent and Trademark Office. When a letter directed to the Patent and Trademark Office concerns a previously filed application for a patent, it must identify on the top page in a conspicuous location, the application number (consisting of the series code and the serial number; e.g., 07/123,456), or the serial number and filing date assigned to that application by the Patent and Trademark Office, or the international application number of the international application. Any correspondence not containing such identification will be returned to the sender where a return address is available. The returned correspondence will be accompanied with a cover letter which will indicate to the sender that if the returned correspondence is resubmitted to the Patent and Trademark Office within two weeks of the mail date on the cover letter; the original date of receipt of the correspondence will be considered by the Patent and Trademark Office as the date of receipt of the correspondence. Applicants may use either the Certificate of Mailing or Transmission procedure under § 1.8 or the Express Mail procedure under § 1.10 for resubmissions of returned correspondence if they desire to have the benefit of the date of deposit in the United States Postal Service. If the returned correspondence is not resubmitted within the two-week period, the date of receipt of the resubmission will be considered to be the date of receipt of the correspondence. The two-week period to resubmit the returned correspondence will not be extended. In addition to the application number, all letters directed to the Patent and Trademark Office concerning applications for patent should also state the name of the applicant, the title of the invention, the date of filing the same, and, if known, the group art unit or other unit within the Patent and Trademark Office responsible for considering the letter and the name of the examiner or other person to which it has been assigned.

(b) When the letter concerns a patent other than for purposes of paying a maintenance fee, it should state the number and date of issue of the patent, the name of the patentee, and the title of the invention. For letters concerning payment of a maintenance fee in a patent, see the provisions of § 1.366(c).

(c) [Reserved]

(d) A letter relating to a reexamination proceeding should identify it as such by the number of the patent undergoing reexamination, the reexamination request control number assigned to such proceeding, and, if known, the group art unit and name of the examiner to which it been assigned.

(e) [Reserved]

(f) When a paper concerns a provisional application, it should identify the application as such and include the application number.

**Section 1.33 of Title 37 of the CFR:**

(a) *Correspondence address and daytime telephone number.* When filing an application, a correspondence address must be set forth in either an application data sheet (§ 1.76), or elsewhere, in a clearly identifiable manner, in any paper submitted with an application filing. If no correspondence address is specified, the Office may treat the mailing address of the first named inventor (if provided, see §§ 1.76 (b)(1) and 1.63 (c)(2)) as the correspondence address. The Office will direct, or otherwise make available, all notices, official letters, and other communications relating to the application to the person associated with the correspondence address. For correspondence submitted via the Office's electronic filing system, however, an electronic acknowledgment receipt will be sent to the submitter. The Office will generally not engage in double correspondence with an applicant and a patent practitioner, or with more than one patent practitioner except as deemed necessary by the Director. If more than one correspondence address is specified in a single document, the Office will select one of the specified addresses for use as the correspondence address and, if given, will select the address associated with a Customer Number over a typed correspondence address. For the party to whom correspondence is to be addressed, a daytime telephone number should be supplied in a clearly identifiable manner and may be changed by any party who may change the correspondence address. The correspondence address may be changed as follows:

(1) Prior to filing of § 1.63 oath or declaration by any of the inventors. If a § 1.63 oath or declaration has not been filed by any of the inventors, the correspondence address may be changed by the party who filed the application. If the application was filed by a patent practitioner, any other patent practitioner named in the transmittal papers may also change the correspondence address. Thus, the inventor(s), any patent practitioner named in the transmittal papers accompanying the original application, or a party that will be the assignee who filed the application, may change the correspondence address in that application under this paragraph.

(2) *Where a § 1.63 oath or declaration has been filed by any of the inventors.* If a § 1.63 oath or declaration has been filed, or is filed concurrent with the filing of an application by any of the inventors, the correspondence address may be changed by the parties set forth in paragraph (b) of this section, except for paragraph (b)(2).

(b) *Amendments and other papers.* Amendments and other papers, except for written assertions pursuant to § 1.27(c)(2)(ii) of this part, filed in the application must be signed by:

(1) A patent practitioner of record appointed in compliance with § 1.32(b);

(2) A patent practitioner not of record who acts in a representative capacity under the provisions of § 1.34;

(3) An assignee as provided for under § 3.71(b) of this chapter; or

(4) All of the applicants (§ 1.41(b)) for patent, unless there is an assignee of the entire interest and such assignee has taken action in the application in accordance with § 3.71 of this chapter.

(c) All notices, official letters, and other communications for the patent owner or owners in a reexamination proceeding will be directed to the correspondence address. Amendments and other papers filed in a reexamination proceeding on behalf of the patent owner must be signed by the patent owner, or if there is more than one owner by all the owners, or by an attorney or agent of record in the patent file, or by a registered attorney or agent not of record who acts in a representative capacity under the provisions of § 1.34. Double correspondence with the patent owner or owners and the patent owner's attorney or agent, or with more than one attorney or agent, will not be undertaken.

(d) A "correspondence address" or change thereto may be filed with the Patent and Trademark Office during the enforceable life of the patent. The "correspondence address" will be used in any correspondence relating to maintenance fees unless a separate "fee address" has been specified. See § 1.363 for "fee address" used solely for maintenance fee purposes.

(e) A change of address filed in a patent application or patent does not change the address for a patent practitioner in the roster of patent attorneys and agents. See § 11.11 of this title.

### Section 1.54 of Title 37 of the CFR:

(a) It is desirable that all parts of the complete application be deposited in the Office together; otherwise, a letter must accompany each part, accurately and clearly connecting it with the other parts of the application. See § 1.53(f) and (g) with regard to completion of an application.

(b) Applicant will be informed of the application number and filing date by a filing receipt, unless the application is an application filed under § 1.53(d).

# APPENDIX 19:
# FEE TRANSMITTAL FORM

PTO/SB/17 (10-08)
Approved for use through 06/30/2010. OMB 0651-0032
U.S. Patent and Trademark Office; U.S. DEPARTMENT OF COMMERCE
Under the Paperwork Reduction Act of 1995 no persons are required to respond to a collection of information unless it displays a valid OMB control number

| | **Complete if Known** |
|---|---|
| *Effective on 12/08/2004.* Fees pursuant to the Consolidated Appropriations Act, 2005 (H.R. 4818). | |
| | Application Number |
| **FEE TRANSMITTAL** | Filing Date |
| **For FY 2009** | First Named Inventor |
| | Examiner Name |
| ☐ Applicant claims small entity status. See 37 CFR 1.27 | Art Unit |
| **TOTAL AMOUNT OF PAYMENT** ($) | Attorney Docket No. |

**METHOD OF PAYMENT** (check all that apply)

☐ Check ☐ Credit Card ☐ Money Order ☐ None ☐ Other (please identify): _____

☐ Deposit Account   Deposit Account Number: _____   Deposit Account Name: _____

For the above-identified deposit account, the Director is hereby authorized to: (check all that apply)

☐ Charge fee(s) indicated below            ☐ Charge fee(s) indicated below, **except for the filing fee**

☐ Charge any additional fee(s) or underpayments of fee(s)   ☐ Credit any overpayments
under 37 CFR 1.16 and 1.17

**WARNING: Information on this form may become public. Credit card information should not be included on this form. Provide credit card information and authorization on PTO-2038.**

**FEE CALCULATION**

**1. BASIC FILING, SEARCH, AND EXAMINATION FEES**

| | FILING FEES | | SEARCH FEES | | EXAMINATION FEES | | |
|---|---|---|---|---|---|---|---|
| **Application Type** | **Fee ($)** | **Small Entity Fee ($)** | **Fee ($)** | **Small Entity Fee ($)** | **Fee ($)** | **Small Entity Fee ($)** | **Fees Paid ($)** |
| Utility | 330 | 165 | 540 | 270 | 220 | 110 | _____ |
| Design | 220 | 110 | 100 | 50 | 140 | 70 | _____ |
| Plant | 220 | 110 | 330 | 165 | 170 | 85 | _____ |
| Reissue | 330 | 165 | 540 | 270 | 650 | 325 | _____ |
| Provisional | 220 | 110 | 0 | 0 | 0 | 0 | _____ |

**2. EXCESS CLAIM FEES**

| Fee Description | Fee ($) | Small Entity Fee ($) |
|---|---|---|
| Each claim over 20 (including Reissues) | 52 | 26 |
| Each independent claim over 3 (including Reissues) | 220 | 110 |
| Multiple dependent claims | 390 | 195 |

| **Total Claims** | **Extra Claims** | **Fee ($)** | **Fee Paid ($)** | **Multiple Dependent Claims** | |
|---|---|---|---|---|---|
| ____ - 20 or HP = | ____ x | ____ = | ____ | **Fee ($)** | **Fee Paid ($)** |

HP = highest number of total claims paid for, if greater than 20.

| **Indep. Claims** | **Extra Claims** | **Fee ($)** | **Fee Paid ($)** |
|---|---|---|---|
| ____ - 3 or HP = | ____ x | ____ = | ____ |

HP = highest number of independent claims paid for, if greater than 3.

**3. APPLICATION SIZE FEE**

If the specification and drawings exceed 100 sheets of paper (excluding electronically filed sequence or computer listings under 37 CFR 1.52(e)), the application size fee due is $270 ($135 for small entity) for each additional 50 sheets or fraction thereof. See 35 U.S.C. 41(a)(1)(G) and 37 CFR 1.16(s).

| **Total Sheets** | **Extra Sheets** | **Number of each additional 50 or fraction thereof** | **Fee ($)** | **Fee Paid ($)** |
|---|---|---|---|---|
| ____ - 100 = | ____ / 50 = | ____ (round **up** to a whole number) x | ____ = | ____ |

**4. OTHER FEE(S)**

Non-English Specification, $130 fee (no small entity discount)                                   **Fees Paid ($)** ____

Other (e.g., late filing surcharge): _____   ____

| **SUBMITTED BY** | | | |
|---|---|---|---|
| Signature | | Registration No. (Attorney/Agent) | Telephone |
| Name (Print/Type) | | | Date |

This collection of information is required by 37 CFR 1.136. The information is required to obtain or retain a benefit by the public which is to file (and by the USPTO to process) an application. Confidentiality is governed by 35 U.S.C. 122 and 37 CFR 1.14. This collection is estimated to take 30 minutes to complete, including gathering, preparing, and submitting the completed application form to the USPTO. Time will vary depending upon the individual case. Any comments on the amount of time you require to complete this form and/or suggestions for reducing this burden, should be sent to the Chief Information Officer, U.S. Patent and Trademark Office, U.S. Department of Commerce, P.O. Box 1450, Alexandria, VA 22313-1450. DO NOT SEND FEES OR COMPLETED FORMS TO THIS ADDRESS. **SEND TO: Commissioner for Patents, P.O. Box 1450, Alexandria, VA 22313-1450.**
*If you need assistance in completing the form, call 1-800-PTO-9199 and select option 2.*

## Privacy Act Statement

The **Privacy Act of 1974 (P.L. 93-579)** requires that you be given certain information in connection with your submission of the attached form related to a patent application or patent. Accordingly, pursuant to the requirements of the Act, please be advised that: (1) the general authority for the collection of this information is 35 U.S.C. 2(b)(2); (2) furnishing of the information solicited is voluntary; and (3) the principal purpose for which the information is used by the U.S. Patent and Trademark Office is to process and/or examine your submission related to a patent application or patent. If you do not furnish the requested information, the U.S. Patent and Trademark Office may not be able to process and/or examine your submission, which may result in termination of proceedings or abandonment of the application or expiration of the patent.

The information provided by you in this form will be subject to the following routine uses:

1. The information on this form will be treated confidentially to the extent allowed under the Freedom of Information Act (5 U.S.C. 552) and the Privacy Act (5 U.S.C 552a). Records from this system of records may be disclosed to the Department of Justice to determine whether disclosure of these records is required by the Freedom of Information Act.
2. A record from this system of records may be disclosed, as a routine use, in the course of presenting evidence to a court, magistrate, or administrative tribunal, including disclosures to opposing counsel in the course of settlement negotiations.
3. A record in this system of records may be disclosed, as a routine use, to a Member of Congress submitting a request involving an individual, to whom the record pertains, when the individual has requested assistance from the Member with respect to the subject matter of the record.
4. A record in this system of records may be disclosed, as a routine use, to a contractor of the Agency having need for the information in order to perform a contract. Recipients of information shall be required to comply with the requirements of the Privacy Act of 1974, as amended, pursuant to 5 U.S.C. 552a(m).
5. A record related to an International Application filed under the Patent Cooperation Treaty in this system of records may be disclosed, as a routine use, to the International Bureau of the World Intellectual Property Organization, pursuant to the Patent Cooperation Treaty.
6. A record in this system of records may be disclosed, as a routine use, to another federal agency for purposes of National Security review (35 U.S.C. 181) and for review pursuant to the Atomic Energy Act (42 U.S.C. 218(c)).
7. A record from this system of records may be disclosed, as a routine use, to the Administrator, General Services, or his/her designee, during an inspection of records conducted by GSA as part of that agency's responsibility to recommend improvements in records management practices and programs, under authority of 44 U.S.C. 2904 and 2906. Such disclosure shall be made in accordance with the GSA regulations governing inspection of records for this purpose, and any other relevant (*i.e.*, GSA or Commerce) directive. Such disclosure shall not be used to make determinations about individuals.
8. A record from this system of records may be disclosed, as a routine use, to the public after either publication of the application pursuant to 35 U.S.C. 122(b) or issuance of a patent pursuant to 35 U.S.C. 151. Further, a record may be disclosed, subject to the limitations of 37 CFR 1.14, as a routine use, to the public if the record was filed in an application which became abandoned or in which the proceedings were terminated and which application is referenced by either a published application, an application open to public inspection or an issued patent.
9. A record from this system of records may be disclosed, as a routine use, to a Federal, State, or local law enforcement agency, if the USPTO becomes aware of a violation or potential violation of law or regulation.

# APPENDIX 20:
# FEES

Section 607 of the MPEP:

## I. BASIC FILING, SEARCH, AND EXAMINATION FEES

The Consolidated Appropriations Act, 2005 (Consolidated Appropriations Act), effective December 8, 2004, provides for a separate filing fee, search fee, and examination fee during fiscal years 2005 and 2006. For nonprovisional applications filed under 35 U.S.C. 111(a) on or after December 8, 2004 (including reissue applications), the following fees are required: basic filing fee as set forth in 37 CFR 1.16(a)(1), (b)(1), (c)(1), or (e)(1); search fee as set forth in 37 CFR 1.16(k), (1), (m), or (n); examination fee as set forth in 37 CFR 1.16(o), (p), (q), or (r); application size fee, if applicable (see subsection II. below); and excess claims fees, if applicable (see subsection III. below).

For nonprovisional applications filed under 35 U.S.C. 111(a) before December 8, 2004 (including reissue applications), the following fees are required: basic filing fee as set forth in 37 CFR 1.16(a)(2), (b)(2), (c)(2), or (e)(2)); and excess claims fees, if applicable (see subsection III. below). No search and examination fees are required for nonprovisional applications filed under 35 U.S.C. 111(a) before December 8, 2004.

The basic filing, search and examination fees are due on filing of the nonprovisional application under 35 U.S.C. 111(a). These fees may be paid on a date later than the filing date of the application provided they are paid within the time period set forth in 37 CFR 1.53(f) and include the surcharge set forth in 37 CFR 1.16(f). For applications filed on or after December 8, 2004 but prior to July 1, 2005, which have been accorded a filing date under 37 CFR 1.53(b) or (d), if the search and/or examination fees are paid on a date later than the filing date of the application, the surcharge under 37 CFR 1.16(f) is not required. For applications filed on or after July 1, 2005, which have been accorded a filing date under 37 CFR 1.53(b) or (d), if any of the basic filing fee, the search fee, or the examination fee are paid on a date later than the filing date of the application, the surcharge under 37 CFR 1.16(f) is required.

For provisional applications filed under 35 U.S.C. 111(b), the basic filing fee set forth in 37 CFR 1.16(d) is required. The basic filing fee is due on filing of the provisional application but may be paid later if paid within the time period set forth in 37 CFR 1.53(g) and accompanied by payment of a surcharge as set forth in 37 CFR 1.16(g).

For international applications entering the national stage under 35 U.S.C. 371, see 37 CFR 1.492 for the required fees. See also MPEP § 1893.01(c).

See also MPEP § 1415 for reissue application fees.

## II. APPLICATION SIZE FEE

The Consolidated Appropriations Act also provides for an application size fee. 37 CFR 1.16(s) sets forth the application size fee for any application (including any provisional applications and any reissue applications) filed under 35 U.S.C. 111 on or after December 8, 2004, the specification (including claims) and drawings of which, excluding a sequence listing or computer program listing filed in an electronic medium in compliance with the rules (see 37 CFR 1.52(f)), exceed 100 sheets of paper. The application size fee does not apply to any applications filed before December 8, 2004. The application size fee applies for each additional 50 sheets or fraction thereof over 100 sheets of paper. Any sequence listing in an electronic medium in compliance with 37 CFR 1.52(e) and 37 CFR 1.821(c) or (e), and any computer program listing filed in an electronic medium in compliance with 37 CFR 1.52(e) and 1.96, will be excluded when determining the application size fee required by 37 CFR 1.16(s).

For purposes of determining the application size fee required by 37 CFR 1.16(s), for an application the specification (including claims) and drawings of which, excluding any sequence listing in compliance with 37 CFR 1.52(e) and 37 CFR 1.821(c) or (e), and any computer program listing filed in an electronic medium in compliance with 37 CFR 1.52(e) and 37 CFR 1.96, are submitted in whole or in part on an electronic medium other than the Office electronic filing system, each three kilobytes of content submitted on an electronic medium shall be counted as a sheet of paper. See 37 CFR 1.52(f)(1).

The paper size equivalent of the specification (including claims) and drawings of an application submitted via the Office electronic filing system will be considered to be seventy five percent of the number of sheets of paper present in the specification (including claims) and drawings of the application when entered into the Office file wrapper after being rendered by the Office electronic filing system for purposes of computing the application size fee required by 37 CFR 1.16(s). Any sequence listing in compliance with 37 CFR 1.821(c) or (e), and any computer program listing in compliance with 37 CFR 1.96, submitted via the Office electronic filing system will be excluded when determining the application size fee required by 37 CFR 1.16(s) if the listing is submitted in American Standard Code for Information Interchange (ASCII) text as part of an associated file of the application. See 37 CFR 1.52(f)(2). Sequence listings or computer program listings submitted via the Office electronic filing system in Portable Document Format (PDF) as part of the specification or as Tagg(ed) Image File Format (TIFF) drawing files would not be excluded when determining the application size fee required by 37 CFR 1.16(s).

For international applications entering the national stage where the basic national fee was not paid before December 8, 2004, see 37 CFR 1.492(j).

## III. EXCESS CLAIMS FEES

37 CFR 1.16(h) sets forth the excess claims fee for each independent claim in excess of three. 37 CFR 1.16(i) sets forth the excess claims fee for each claim (whether independent or dependent) in excess of twenty. The Consolidated Appropriations Act provides that the excess claims fees specified in 35 U.S.C. 41(a)(2) shall apply only as to those claims (independent or dependent) that, after taking into account any claims that have been canceled, are in excess of the number of claims for which the excess claims fee specified in 35 U.S.C. 41 was paid before December 8, 2004. Thus, the Office will charge the excess claims fees specified in 37 CFR 1.16(h) and (i) if an applicant in an application filed before and pending on or after December 8, 2004, adds a claim (independent or total) in excess of the number of claims (independent or total) for which the excess claims fee was previously paid (under the current or previous fee schedule). The excess claims fees specified in 37 CFR 1.16(h) and (i) apply to any excess claims fee paid on or after December 8, 2004, regardless of the filing date of the application and regardless of the date on which the claim necessitating the excess claims fee payment was added to the application.

The excess claims fees specified in 37 CFR 1.16(h) and (i) also apply to all reissue applications pending on or after December 8, 2004. Under 35 U.S.C. 41(a)(2) as amended by the Consolidated Appropriations Act, the claims in the original patent are not taken into account in determining the excess claims fee for a reissue application. The excess claims fees specified in 37 CFR 1.16(h) and (i) are required for each independent claim in excess of three that is presented in a reissue application on or after December 8, 2004, and for each claim (whether independent or dependent) in excess of twenty that is presented in a reissue application on or after December 8, 2004.

Fees for a proper multiple dependent claim are calculated based on the number of claims to which the multiple dependent claim refers, 37 CFR 1.75(c), and a separate fee is required in each application containing a proper multiple dependent claim. See 37 CFR 1.16(j). For an improper multiple dependent claim, the fee charged is that charged for a single dependent claim. See MPEP § 608.01(n) for multiple dependent claims.

Upon submission of an amendment (whether entered or not) affecting the claims, payment of fees for those claims in excess of the number previously paid for is required.

Amendments before the first action, or not filed in reply to an Office action, presenting additional claims in excess of the number already paid for, not accompanied by the full additional fee due, will not be entered in whole or in part and applicant will be so advised. Such amendments filed in reply to an Office action will be regarded as not responsive thereto and the practice set forth in MPEP § 714.03 will be followed.

The additional fees, if any, due with an amendment are calculated on the basis of the claims (total and independent) which would be present, if the amendment were entered. The amendment of a claim, unless it changes a dependent claim to an independent claim or adds to the number of claims referred to in a multiple dependent claim, and the replacement of a claim by a claim of the same type, unless it is a multiple dependent claim which refers to more prior claims, do not require any additional fees.

For purposes of determining the fee due the U.S. Patent and Trademark Office, a claim will be treated as dependent if it contains reference to one or more other claims in the application. A claim determined to be dependent by this test will be entered if the fee paid reflects this determination.

Any claim which is in dependent form but which is so worded that it, in fact, is not a proper dependent claim, as for example it does not include every limitation of the claim on which it depends, will be required to be canceled as not being a proper dependent claim; and cancellation of any further claim depending on such a dependent claim will be similarly required. The applicant may thereupon amend the claims to place them in proper dependent form, or may redraft them as independent claims, upon payment of any necessary additional fee.

After a requirement for restriction, nonelected claims will be included in determining the fees due in connection with a subsequent amendment unless such claims are canceled.

An amendment canceling claims accompanying the papers constituting the application will be effective to diminish the number of claims to be considered in calculating the filing fees to be paid. A preliminary amendment filed concurrently with a response to a Notice To File Missing Parts of Application that required the fees set forth in 37 CFR 1.16, which preliminary amendment cancels or adds claims, will be taken into account in determining the appropriate fees due in response to the Notice To File Missing Parts of Application. No refund will be made for claims being canceled in the responses that have already been paid for.

The additional fees, if any, due with an amendment are required prior to any consideration of the amendment by the examiner.

Money paid in connection with the filing of a proposed amendment will not be refunded by reason of the nonentry of the amendment. However, unentered claims will not be counted when calculating the fee due in subsequent amendments.

Amendments affecting the claims cannot serve as the basis for granting any refund. See MPEP § 607.02 subsection V for refund of excess claims fees.

Excess claims fees set forth in 37 CFR 1.20(c)(3) and (c)(4) apply to excess claims that are presented on or after December 8, 2004, during a reexamination proceeding.

### IV. APPLICANT DOES NOT SPECIFY FEES TO WHICH PAYMENT IS TO BE APPLIED

In situations in which a payment submitted for the fees due on filing in a nonprovisional application filed under 35 U.S.C. 111(a) is insufficient and the applicant has not specified the fees to which the payment is to be applied, the Office will apply the payment in the following order until the payment is expended:

(1) the basic filing fee (37 CFR 1.16(a), (b), (c), or (e));

(2) the application size fee (37 CFR 1.16(s));

(3) the late filing surcharge (37 CFR 1.16(f));

(4) the processing fee for an application filed in a language other than English (37 CFR 1.17(i));

(5) the search fee (37 CFR 1.16(k), (1), (m), or (n));

(6) the examination fee (37 CFR 1.16(o), (p), (q), or (r)); and

(7) the excess claims fee (37 CFR 1.16(h), (i), and (j)). In situations in which a payment submitted for the fees due on filing in a provisional application filed under 35 U.S.C. 111(b) is insufficient and the applicant has not specified the fees to which the payment is to be applied, the Office will apply the payment in the following order until the payment is expended:

(1) the basic filing fee (37 CFR 1.16(d));

(2) the application size fee (37 CFR 1.16(s)); and

(3) the late filing surcharge (37 CFR 1.16(g)).

See also MPEP § 509.

Since the basic filing fee, search fee, and examination fee under the new patent fee structure are often referred to as the "filing fee," the Office will treat a deposit account authorization to charge "the filing fee" as an authorization to charge the applicable fees under 37 CFR 1.16 (the basic filing fee, search fee, examination fee, any excess claims fee, and any application size fee) to the deposit account. The Office will also treat a deposit account authorization to charge "the basic filing fee" as an authorization to charge the applicable basic filing fee, search fee, and examination fee to the deposit account. Any deposit account authorization to charge the filing fee but not the search fee or examination fee must specifically limit the authorization by reference to one or more of paragraphs (a) through (e) of 37 CFR 1.16. See MPEP § 509.01.

### Section 1.27 of Title 37 of the CFR:

(a) *Definition of small entities.* A small entity as used in this chapter means any party (person, small business concern, or nonprofit organization) under paragraphs (a)(1) through (a)(3) of this section.

(1) *Person.* A person, as used in paragraph (c) of this section, means any inventor or other individual (e.g., an individual to

whom an inventor has transferred some rights in the invention) who has not assigned, granted, conveyed, or licensed, and is under no obligation under contract or law to assign, grant, convey, or license, any rights in the invention. An inventor or other individual who has transferred some rights in the invention to one or more parties, or is under an obligation to transfer some rights in the invention to one or more parties, can also qualify for small entity status if all the parties who have had rights in the invention transferred to them also qualify for small entity status either as a person, small business concern, or nonprofit organization under this section.

(2) *Small business concern.* A small business concern, as used in paragraph (c) of this section, means any business concern that:

(i) Has not assigned, granted, conveyed, or licensed, and is under no obligation under contract or law to assign, grant, convey, or license, any rights in the invention to any person, concern, or organization which would not qualify for small entity status as a person, small business concern, or nonprofit organization; and

(ii) Meets the size standards set forth in 13 CFR 121.801 through 121.805 to be eligible for reduced patent fees. Questions related to standards for a small business concern may be directed to: Small Business Administration, Size Standards Staff, 409 Third Street, SW., Washington, DC 20416.

(3) *Nonprofit Organization.* A nonprofit organization, as used in paragraph (c) of this section, means any nonprofit organization that:

(i) Has not assigned, granted, conveyed, or licensed, and is under no obligation under contract or law to assign, grant, convey, or license, any rights in the invention to any person, concern, or organization which would not qualify as a person, small business concern, or a nonprofit organization; and

(ii) Is either:

(A) A university or other institution of higher education located in any country;

(B) An organization of the type described in section 501(c) (3) of the Internal Revenue Code of 19 86 (26 U.S.C. 501(c) (3)) and exempt from taxation under section 501(a) of the Internal Revenue Code (26 U.S.C. 501(a));

(C) Any nonprofit scientific or educational organization qualified under a nonprofit organization statute of a state of this country (35 U.S.C. 201(i)); or

(D) Any nonprofit organization located in a foreign country which would qualify as a nonprofit organization under paragraphs (a)(3)(ii)(B) of this section or (a)(3)(ii)(C) of this section if it were located in this country.

(4) *License to a Federal agency.* (i) For persons under paragraph (a)(1) of this section, a license to the Government resulting from a rights determination under Executive Order 10096 does not constitute a license so as to prohibit claiming small entity status.

(ii) For small business concerns and nonprofit organizations under paragraphs (a)(2) and (a)(3) of this section, a license to a Federal agency resulting from a funding agreement with that agency pursuant to 35 U.S.C. 202 (c)(4) does not constitute a license for the purposes of paragraphs (a)(2)(i) and (a)(3)(i) of this section.

(5) *Security Interest.* A security interest does not involve an obligation to transfer rights in the invention for the purposes of paragraphs (a)(1) through (a)(3) of this section unless the security interest is defaulted upon.

(b) *Establishment of small entity status permits payment of reduced fees.*

(1) A small entity, as defined in paragraph (a) of this section, who has properly asserted entitlement to small entity status pursuant to paragraph (c) of this section will be accorded small entity status by the Office in the particular application or patent in which entitlement to small entity status was asserted. Establishment of small entity status allows the payment of certain reduced patent fees pursuant to 35 U.S.C. 41(h)(1).

(2) Submission of an original utility application in compliance with the Office electronic filing system by an applicant who has properly asserted entitlement to small entity status pursuant to paragraph (c) of this section in that application allows the payment of a reduced filing fee pursuant to 35 U.S.C. 41(h)(3).

(c) *Assertion of small entity status.* Any party (person, small business concern, or nonprofit organization) should make a determination, pursuant to paragraph (f) of this section, of entitlement to be accorded small entity status based on the definitions set forth in paragraph (a) of this section, and must, in order to establish small entity status for the purpose of paying small entity fees, actually make an assertion of entitlement to small entity status, in the manner set forth in paragraphs (c)(1) or (c)(3) of this section, in the application or patent in which such small entity fees are to be paid.

(1) *Assertion by writing.* Small entity status may be established by a written assertion of entitlement to small entity status. A written assertion must:

(i) Be clearly identifiable;

(ii) Be signed (see paragraph (c)(2) of this section); and

(iii) Convey the concept of entitlement to small entity status, such as by stating that applicant is a small entity, or that small entity status is entitled to be asserted for the application or patent. While no specific words or wording are required to assert small entity status, the intent to assert small entity status must be clearly indicated in order to comply with the assertion requirement.

(2) *Parties who can sign and file the written assertion.* The written assertion can be signed by:

(i) One of the parties identified in § 1.33(b) (e.g., an attorney or agent registered with the Office), § 3.73(b) of this chapter notwithstanding, who can also file the written assertion;

(ii) At least one of the individuals identified as an inventor (even though a § 1.63 executed oath or declaration has not been submitted), notwithstanding § 1.33(b)(4), who can also file the written assertion pursuant to the exception under § 1.33(b) of this part; or

(iii) An assignee of an undivided part interest, notwithstanding §§ 1.33(b)(3) and 3.73(b) of this chapter, but the partial assignee cannot file the assertion without resort to a party identified under § 1.33(b) of this part.

(3) *Assertion by payment of the small entity basic filing or basic national fee.* The payment, by any party, of the exact amount of one of the small entity basic filing fees set forth in §§ 1.16(a), 1.16(b), 1.16(c), 1.16(d), 1.16(e), or the small entity basic national fee set forth in § 1.492(a), will be treated as a written assertion of entitlement to small entity status even if the type of basic filing or basic national fee is inadvertently selected in error.

(i) If the Office accords small entity status based on payment of a small entity basic filing or basic national fee under paragraph (c)(3) of this section that is not applicable to that application, any balance of the small entity fee that is applicable to that application will be due along with the appropriate surcharge set forth in § 1.16(f) or § 1.16(g).

(ii) The payment of any small entity fee other than those set forth in paragraph (c)(3) of this section (whether in the exact fee amount or not) will not be treated as a written assertion of entitlement to small entity status and will not be sufficient to establish small entity status in an application or a patent.

(4) *Assertion required in related, continuing, and reissue applications.* Status as a small entity must be specifically established by an assertion in each related, continuing, and reissue application in which status is appropriate and desired. Status as a small entity in one application or patent does not affect the status of any other application or patent, regardless of the relationship of the applications or patents. The refiling of an application under § 1.53 as a continuation, divisional, or continuation-in-part application (including a continued prosecution application under § 1.53(d)), or the filing of a reissue application, requires a new assertion as to continued entitlement to small entity status for the continuing or reissue application.

(d) *When small entity fees can be paid.* Any fee, other than the small entity basic filing fees and the small entity national fees of paragraph (c)(3) of this section, can be paid in the small entity amount only if it is submitted with, or subsequent to, the submission of a written assertion of entitlement to small entity status, except when refunds are permitted by § 1.28(a).

(e) *Only one assertion required.*

(1) An assertion of small entity status need only be filed once in an application or patent. Small entity status, once established, remains in effect until changed pursuant to paragraph (g)(1) of this section. Where an assignment of rights or an obligation to assign rights to other parties who are small entities occurs subsequent to an assertion of small entity status, a second assertion is not required.

(2) Once small entity status is withdrawn pursuant to paragraph (g)(2) of this section, a new written assertion is required to again obtain small entity status.

(f) *Assertion requires a determination of entitlement to pay small entity fees.* Prior to submitting an assertion of entitlement to small entity status in an application, including a related, continuing, or reissue application, a determination of such entitlement should be made pursuant to the requirements of paragraph (a) of this section. It should be determined that all parties holding rights in the invention qualify for small entity status. The Office will generally not question any assertion of small entity status that is made in accordance with the requirements of this section, but note paragraph (h) of this section.

(g)(1) *New determination of entitlement to small entity status is needed when issue and maintenance fees are due.* Once status as a small entity has been established in an application or patent, fees as a small entity may thereafter be paid in that application or patent without regard to a change in status until the issue fee is due or any maintenance fee is due.

(2) *Notification of loss of entitlement to small entity status is required when issue and maintenance fees are due.* Notification of a loss of entitlement to small entity status must be filed in the application or patent prior to paying, or at the time of paying, the earliest of the issue fee or any maintenance fee due after the date on which status as a small entity as defined in paragraph (a) of this section is no longer appropriate. The notification that small entity status is no longer appropriate must be signed by a party identified in § 1.33(b). Payment of a fee in other than the small entity amount is not sufficient notification that small entity status is no longer appropriate.

(h) *Fraud attempted or practiced on the Office.*

(1) Any attempt to fraudulently establish status as a small entity, or pay fees as a small entity, shall be considered as a fraud practiced or attempted on the Office.

(2) Improperly, and with intent to deceive, establishing status as a small entity, or paying fees as a small entity, shall be considered as a fraud practiced or attempted on the Office.

# APPENDIX 21:
# APPLICATION DATA SHEET

PTO/SB/14 (07-07)
Approved for use through 06/30/2010. OMB 0651-0032
U.S. Patent and Trademark Office; U.S. DEPARTMENT OF COMMERCE
Under the Paperwork Reduction Act of 1995, no persons are required to respond to a collection of information unless it contains a valid OMB control number.

| Application Data Sheet 37 CFR 1.76 | Attorney Docket Number | |
| | Application Number | |
| Title of Invention | | |

## Publication Information:

☐ Request Early Publication (Fee required at time of Request 37 CFR 1.219)

☐ **Request Not to Publish.** I hereby request that the attached application not be published under 35 U.S. C. 122(b) and certify that the invention disclosed in the attached application **has not and will not** be the subject of an application filed in another country, or under a multilateral international agreement, that requires publication at eighteen months after filing.

## Representative Information:

Representative information should be provided for all practitioners having a power of attorney in the application. Providing this information in the Application Data Sheet does not constitute a power of attorney in the application (see 37 CFR 1.32). Enter either Customer Number or complete the Representative Name section below. If both sections are completed the Customer Number will be used for the Representative Information during processing.

| Please Select One: | ● Customer Number | ○ US Patent Practitioner | ○ Limited Recognition (37 CFR 11.9) |
| Customer Number | | | |

## Domestic Benefit/National Stage Information:

This section allows for the applicant to either claim benefit under 35 U.S.C. 119(e), 120, 121, or 365(c) or indicate National Stage entry from a PCT application. Providing this information in the application data sheet constitutes the specific reference required by 35 U.S.C. 119(e) or 120, and 37 CFR 1.78(a)(2) or CFR 1.78(a)(4), and need not otherwise be made part of the specification.

| Prior Application Status | | | Remove |
| Application Number | Continuity Type | Prior Application Number | Filing Date (YYYY-MM-DD) |
| | | | |

Additional Domestic Benefit/National Stage Data may be generated within this form by selecting the **Add** button.     Add

## Foreign Priority Information:

This section allows for the applicant to claim benefit of foreign priority and to identify any prior foreign application for which priority is not claimed. Providing this information in the application data sheet constitutes the claim for priority as required by 35 U.S.C. 119(b) and 37 CFR 1.55(a).

| | | | Remove |
| Application Number | Country i | Parent Filing Date (YYYY-MM-DD) | Priority Claimed |
| | | | ● Yes ○ No |

Additional Foreign Priority Data may be generated within this form by selecting the **Add** button.     Add

## Assignee Information:

Providing this information in the application data sheet does not substitute for compliance with any requirement of part 3 of Title 37 of the CFR to have an assignment recorded in the Office.

| Assignee 1 | Remove |

EFS Web 2.2.2

---

PTO/SB/14 (07-07)
Approved for use through 06/30/2010. OMB 0651-0032
U.S. Patent and Trademark Office; U.S. DEPARTMENT OF COMMERCE
Under the Paperwork Reduction Act of 1995, no persons are required to respond to a collection of information unless it contains a valid OMB control number.

| Application Data Sheet 37 CFR 1.76 | Attorney Docket Number | |
| | Application Number | |
| Title of Invention | | |

The application data sheet is part of the provisional or nonprovisional application for which it is being submitted. The following form contains the bibliographic data arranged in a format specified by the United States Patent and Trademark Office as outlined in 37 CFR 1.76.
This document may be completed electronically and submitted to the Office in electronic format using the Electronic Filing System (EFS) or the document may be printed and included in a paper filed application.

## Secrecy Order 37 CFR 5.2

☐ Portions or all of the application associated with this Application Data Sheet may fall under a Secrecy Order pursuant to 37 CFR 5.2 (Paper filers only. Applications that fall under Secrecy Order may not be filed electronically.)

## Applicant Information:

**Applicant 1** [Remove]

| Applicant Authority ◉ Inventor | ○ Legal Representative under 35 U.S.C. 117 | | ○ Party of Interest under 35 U.S.C. 118 | |
| Prefix | Given Name | Middle Name | Family Name | Suffix |
| | | | | |

| Residence Information (Select One) ◉ US Residency ○ Non US Residency ○ Active US Military Service | | | |
| City | | State/Province | Country of Residence i |
| Citizenship under 37 CFR 1.41(b) i | | | |
| Mailing Address of Applicant: | | | |
| Address 1 | | | |
| Address 2 | | | |
| City | | State/Province | |
| Postal Code | | Countryi | |

All Inventors Must Be Listed - Additional Inventor Information blocks may be generated within this form by selecting the **Add** button.     [Add]

## Correspondence Information:

Enter either Customer Number or complete the Correspondence Information section below.
For further information see 37 CFR 1.33(a).

☐ An Address is being provided for the correspondence Information of this application.

| Customer Number | | |
| Email Address | | [Add Email] [Remove Email] |

## Application Information:

| Title of the Invention | | | |
| Attorney Docket Number | | Small Entity Status Claimed ☐ | |
| Application Type | | | |
| Subject Matter | | | |
| Suggested Class (if any) | | Sub Class (if any) | |
| Suggested Technology Center (if any) | | | |
| Total Number of Drawing Sheets (if any) | | Suggested Figure for Publication (if any) | |

EFS Web 2.2.2

PTO/SB/14 (07-07)
Approved for use through 06/30/2010. OMB 0651-0032
U.S. Patent and Trademark Office; U.S. DEPARTMENT OF COMMERCE
Under the Paperwork Reduction Act of 1995, no persons are required to respond to a collection of information unless it contains a valid OMB control number.

| Application Data Sheet 37 CFR 1.76 | Attorney Docket Number | |
| | Application Number | |

| Title of Invention | |

If the Assignee is an Organization check here. ☐

| Prefix | Given Name | Middle Name | Family Name | Suffix |
|---|---|---|---|---|
| | | | | |

**Mailing Address Information:**

| Address 1 | |
| Address 2 | |

| City | | State/Province | |
| Country i | | Postal Code | |
| Phone Number | | Fax Number | |
| Email Address | |

Additional Assignee Data may be generated within this form by selecting the **Add** button.    [ Add ]

## Signature:

A signature of the applicant or representative is required in accordance with 37 CFR 1.33 and 10.18. Please see 37 CFR 1.4(d) for the form of the signature.

| Signature | | | Date (YYYY-MM-DD) | |
| First Name | | Last Name | Registration Number | |

EFS Web 2.2.2

# Privacy Act Statement

The Privacy Act of 1974 (P.L. 93-579) requires that you be given certain information in connection with your submission of the attached form related to a patent application or patent. Accordingly, pursuant to the requirements of the Act, please be advised that: (1) the general authority for the collection of this information is 35 U.S.C. 2(b)(2); (2) furnishing of the information solicited is voluntary; and (3) the principal purpose for which the information is used by the U.S. Patent and Trademark Office is to process and/or examine your submission related to a patent application or patent. If you do not furnish the requested information, the U.S. Patent and Trademark Office may not be able to process and/or examine your submission, which may result in termination of proceedings or abandonment of the application or expiration of the patent.

The information provided by you in this form will be subject to the following routine uses:

1.  The information on this form will be treated confidentially to the extent allowed under the Freedom of Information Act (5 U.S.C. 552) and the Privacy Act (5 U.S.C. 552a). Records from this system of records may be disclosed to the Department of Justice to determine whether the Freedom of Information Act requires disclosure of these records.

2.  A record from this system of records may be disclosed, as a routine use, in the course of presenting evidence to a court, magistrate, or administrative tribunal, including disclosures to opposing counsel in the course of settlement negotiations.

3.  A record in this system of records may be disclosed, as a routine use, to a Member of Congress submitting a request involving an individual, to whom the record pertains, when the individual has requested assistance from the Member with respect to the subject matter of the record.

4.  A record in this system of records may be disclosed, as a routine use, to a contractor of the Agency having need for the information in order to perform a contract. Recipients of information shall be required to comply with the requirements of the Privacy Act of 1974, as amended, pursuant to 5 U.S.C. 552a(m).

5.  A record related to an International Application filed under the Patent Cooperation Treaty in this system of records may be disclosed, as a routine use, to the International Bureau of the World Intellectual Property Organization, pursuant to the Patent Cooperation Treaty.

6.  A record in this system of records may be disclosed, as a routine use, to another federal agency for purposes of National Security review (35 U.S.C. 181) and for review pursuant to the Atomic Energy Act (42 U.S.C. 218(c)).

7.  A record from this system of records may be disclosed, as a routine use, to the Administrator, General Services, or his/her designee, during an inspection of records conducted by GSA as part of that agency's responsibility to recommend improvements in records management practices and programs, under authority of 44 U.S.C. 2904 and 2906. Such disclosure shall be made in accordance with the GSA regulations governing inspection of records for this purpose, and any other relevant (i.e., GSA or Commerce) directive. Such disclosure shall not be used to make determinations about individuals.

8.  A record from this system of records may be disclosed, as a routine use, to the public after either publication of the application pursuant to 35 U.S.C. 122(b) or issuance of a patent pursuant to 35 U.S.C. 151. Further, a record may be disclosed, subject to the limitations of 37 CFR 1.14, as a routine use, to the public if the record was filed in an application which became abandoned or in which the proceedings were terminated and which application is referenced by either a published application, an application open to public inspections or an issued patent.

9.  A record from this system of records may be disclosed, as a routine use, to a Federal, State, or local law enforcement agency, if the USPTO becomes aware of a violation or potential violation of law or regulation.

EFS Web 2.2.2

# APPENDIX 22:
# APPLICATION DATA SHEET
# REQUIREMENTS

**Section 1.76 of Title 37 of the CFR:**

(a) *Application data sheet.* An application data sheet is a sheet or sheets that may be voluntarily submitted in either provisional or nonprovisional applications, which contains bibliographic data, arranged in a format specified by the Office. An application data sheet must be titled "Application Data Sheet" and must contain all of the section headings listed in paragraph (b) of this section, with any appropriate data for each section heading. If an application data sheet is provided, the application data sheet is part of the provisional or nonprovisional application for which it has been submitted.

(b) *Bibliographic data.* Bibliographic data as used in paragraph (a) of this section includes:

(1) *Applicant information.* This information includes the name, residence, mailing address, and citizenship of each applicant (§ 1.41(b)). The name of each applicant must include the family name and at least one given name without abbreviation together with any other given name or initial. If the applicant is not an inventor, this information also includes the applicant's authority (§§ 1.42, 1.43, and 1.47) to apply for the patent on behalf of the inventor.

(2) *Correspondence information.* This information includes the correspondence address, which may be indicated by reference to a customer number, to which correspondence is to be directed (see § 1.33(a)).

(3) *Application information.* This information includes the title of the invention, a suggested classification, by class and subclass,

the Technology Center to which the subject matter of the invention is assigned, the total number of drawing sheets, a suggested drawing figure for publication (in a nonprovisional application), any docket number assigned to the application, the type of application (e.g., utility, plant, design, reissue, provisional), whether the application discloses any significant part of the subject matter of an application under a secrecy order pursuant to § 5.2 of this chapter (see § 5.2(c)), and, for plant applications, the Latin name of the genus and species of the plant claimed, as well as the variety denomination. The suggested classification and Technology Center information should be supplied for provisional applications whether or not claims are present. If claims are not present in a provisional application, the suggested classification and Technology Center should be based upon the disclosure.

(4) *Representative information.* This information includes the registration number of each practitioner having a power of attorney in the application (preferably by reference to a customer number). Providing this information in the application data sheet does not constitute a power of attorney in the application (see § 1.32).

(5) *Domestic priority information.* This information includes the application number, the filing date, the status (including patent number if available), and relationship of each application for which a benefit is claimed under 35 U.S.C. 119(e), 120, 121, or 365(c). Providing this information in the application data sheet constitutes the specific reference required by 35 U.S.C. 119(e) or 120, and § 1.78(a)(2) or § 1.78(a)(5), and need not otherwise be made part of the specification.

(6) *Foreign priority information.* This information includes the application number, country, and filing date of each foreign application for which priority is claimed, as well as any foreign application having a filing date before that of the application for which priority is claimed. Providing this information in the application data sheet constitutes the claim for priority as required by 35 U.S.C. 119(b) and § 1.55(a).

(7) *Assignee information.* This information includes the name (either person or juristic entity) and address of the assignee of the entire right, title, and interest in an application. Providing this information in the application data sheet does not substitute for compliance with any requirement of part 3 of this chapter to have an assignment recorded by the Office.

(c) *Supplemental application data sheets.* Supplemental application data sheets:

(1) May be subsequently supplied prior to payment of the issue fee either to correct or update information in a previously submitted application data sheet, or an oath or declaration under § 1.63 or § 1.67, except that inventorship changes are governed by § 1.48, correspondence changes are governed by § 1.33(a), and citizenship changes are governed by § 1.63 or § 1.67; and

(2) Must be titled "Supplemental Application Data Sheet," include all of the section headings listed in paragraph (b) of this section, include all appropriate data for each section heading, and must identify the information that is being changed, preferably with underlining for insertions, and strike-through or brackets for text removed.

(d) *Inconsistencies between application data sheet and other documents.* For inconsistencies between information that is supplied by both an application data sheet under this section and other documents.

(1) The latest submitted information will govern notwithstanding whether supplied by an application data sheet, an amendment to the specification, a designation of a correspondence address, or by a § 1.63 or § 1.67 oath or declaration, except as provided by paragraph (d)(3) of this section;

(2) The information in the application data sheet will govern when the inconsistent information is supplied at the same time by an amendment to the specification, a designation of correspondence address, or a § 1.63 or § 1.67 oath or declaration, except as provided by paragraph (d)(3) of this section;

(3) The oath or declaration under § 1.63 or § 1.67 governs inconsistencies with the application data sheet in the naming of inventors (§ 1.41 (a)(1)) and setting forth their citizenship (35 U.S.C. 115);

(4) The Office will capture bibliographic information from the application data sheet (notwithstanding whether an oath or declaration governs the information). Thus, the Office shall generally, for example, not look to an oath or declaration under § 1.63 to see if the bibliographic information contained therein is consistent with the bibliographic information captured from an application data sheet (whether the oath or declaration is submitted prior to or subsequent to the application data sheet). Captured bibliographic information derived from an application data sheet containing errors may be corrected if applicant submits a request therefor and a supplemental application data sheet.

# APPENDIX 23: STATUTORY AND REGULATORY REFERENCES REGARDING PATENT SPECIFICATIONS

**Excerpt from Section 112 of the Patent Act:**

The specification shall contain a written description of the invention, and of the manner and process of making and using it, in such full, clear, concise, and exact terms as to enable any person skilled in the art to which it pertains, or with which it is most nearly connected, to make and use the same, and shall set forth the best mode contemplated by the inventor of carrying out his invention.

The specification shall conclude with one or more claims particularly pointing out and distinctly claiming the subject matter which the applicant regards as his invention.

**Excerpt from Section 1.77 of Title 37 of the CFR:**

(b) The specification should include the following sections in order:

(1) Title of the invention, which may be accompanied by an introductory portion stating the name, citizenship, and residence of the applicant (unless included in the application data sheet).

(2) Cross-reference to related applications (unless included in the application data sheet).

(3) Statement regarding federally sponsored research or development.

(4) The names of the parties to a joint research agreement.

(5) Reference to a "Sequence Listing," a table, or a computer program listing an appendix, submitted on a compact disc and an incorporation-by-reference of the material on the compact disc (see § 1.52(e)(5)). The total number of compact discs including duplicates and the files on each compact disc shall be specified.

(6) Background of the invention.

(7) Brief summary of the invention.

(8) Brief description of the several views of the drawing.

(9) Detailed description of the invention.

(10) A claim or claims.

(11) Abstract of the disclosure.

(12) "Sequence Listing," if on paper (see §§ 1.821 through 1.825).

(c) The text of the specification sections defined in paragraphs (b)(1) through (b)(12) of this section, if applicable, should be preceded by a section heading in uppercase and without underlining or bold type.

# APPENDIX 24:
# TITLE OF THE INVENTION

**Excerpt from Section 1.72 of Title 37 of the CFR:**

(a) The title of the invention may not exceed 500 characters in length and must be as short and specific as possible. Characters that cannot be captured and recorded in the Office's automated information systems may not be reflected in the Office's records in such systems or in documents created by the Office. Unless the title is supplied in an application data sheet (§ 1.76), the title of the invention should appear as a heading on the first page of the specification.

**Excerpt from Section 606 of the MPEP:**

The title of the invention should be placed at the top of the first page of the specification unless it is provided in the application data sheet (see 37 CFR 1.76). The title should be brief but technically accurate and descriptive and should contain fewer than 500 characters. Inasmuch as the words "new," "improved," "improvement of," and "improvement in" are not considered as part of the title of an invention, these words should not be included at the beginning of the title of the invention and will be deleted when the Office enters the title into the Office's computer records and when any patent issues. Similarly, the articles "a," "an," and "the" should not be included as the first words of the title of the invention and will be deleted when the Office enters the title into the Office's computer records and when any patent issues.

**Excerpt from Section 606.01 of the MPEP:**

Where the title is not descriptive of the invention claimed, the examiner should require the substitution of a new title that is clearly indicative of the invention to which the claims are directed.

# APPENDIX 25:
# CREATE ACT PROVISIONS

**Section 103(c) of the Patent Act, Constituting the CREATE Act:**

(c)(1) Subject matter developed by another person, which qualifies as prior art only under one or more of subsections (e), (f), and (g) of section 102 of this title, shall not preclude patentability under this section where the subject matter and the claimed invention were, at the time the claimed invention was made, owned by the same person or subject to an obligation of assignment to the same person.

(2) For purposes of this subsection, subject matter developed by another person and a claimed invention shall be deemed to have been owned by the same person or subject to an obligation of assignment to the same person if—

(A) the claimed invention was made by or on behalf of parties to a joint research agreement that was in effect on or before the date the claimed invention was made;

(B) the claimed invention was made as a result of activities undertaken within the scope of the joint research agreement; and

(C) the application for patent for the claimed invention discloses or is amended to disclose the names of the parties to the joint research agreement.

(3) For purposes of paragraph (2), the term "joint research agreement" means a written contract, grant, or cooperative agreement entered into by two or more persons or entities for the performance of experimental, developmental, or research work in the field of the claimed invention.

# APPENDIX 26:
# LISTINGS ON COMPACT DISC

**Excerpt from Section 1.52 of Title 37 of the CFR:**

(e) *Electronic documents that are to become part of the permanent United States Patent and Trademark Office records in the file of a patent application or reexamination proceeding.*

(1) The following documents may be submitted to the Office on a compact disc in compliance with this paragraph:

(i) A computer program listing (see § 1.96);

(ii) A "Sequence Listing" (submitted under § 1.821(c)); or

(iii) Any individual table (see § 1.58) if the table is more than 50 pages in length, or if the total number of pages of all of the tables in an application exceeds 100 pages in length, where a table page is a page printed on paper in conformance with paragraph (b) of this section and § 1.58(c).

(2) A compact disc as used in this part means a Compact Disc-Read Only Memory (CD-ROM) or a Compact Disc-Recordable (CD-R) in compliance with this paragraph. A CD-ROM is a "read-only" medium on which the data is pressed into the disc so that it cannot be changed or erased. A CD-R is a "write once" medium on which once the data is recorded, is permanent, and cannot be changed or erased.

(3)(i) Each compact disc must conform to the International Standards Organization (ISO) 9660 standard, and the contents of each compact disc must be in compliance with the American Standard Code for Information Interchange (ASCII). CD-R discs must be finalized so that they are closed to further writing to the CD-R.

(ii) Each compact disc must be enclosed in a hard compact disc case within an unsealed padded and protective mailing envelope and accompanied by a transmittal letter on paper in accordance with paragraph (a) of this section. The transmittal letter must list for each compact disc the machine format (e.g., IBM-PC, Macintosh); the operating system compatibility (e.g., MS-DOS, MS-Windows, Macintosh, Unix); a list of files contained on the compact disc including their names, sizes in bytes, and dates of creation; plus any other special information that is necessary to identify, maintain, and interpret (e.g., tables in landscape orientation should be identified as landscape orientation or be identified when inquired about) the information on the compact disc. Compact discs submitted to the Office will not be returned to the applicant.

(4) Any compact disc must be submitted in duplicate unless it contains only the "Sequence Listing" in computer readable form required by § 1.821(e). The compact disc and duplicate copy must be labeled "Copy 1" and "Copy 2," respectively. The transmittal letter which accompanies the compact disc must include a statement that the two compact discs are identical. In the event that the two compact discs are not identical, the Office will use the compact disc labeled "Copy 1" for further processing. Any amendment to the information on a compact disc must be by way of a replacement compact disc in compliance with this paragraph containing the substitute information and must be accompanied by a statement that the replacement compact disc contains no new matter. The compact disc and copy must be labeled "COPY 1 REPLACEMENT MM/DD/YYYY" (with the month, day, and year of creation indicated), and "COPY 2 REPLACEMENT MM/DD/YYYY," respectively.

(5) The specification must contain an incorporation-by-reference of the material on the compact disc in a separate paragraph (§ 1.77(b) (5)), identifying each compact disc by the names of the files contained on each of the compact discs, their date of creation, and their sizes in bytes. The Office may require the applicant to amend the specification to include in the paper portion any part of the specification previously submitted on compact disc.

(6) A compact disc must also be labeled with the following information:

(i) The name of each inventor (if known);

(ii) Title of the invention;

(iii) The docket number, or application number if known, used by the person filing the application to identify the application; and

(iv) A creation date of the compact disc.

(v) If multiple compact discs are submitted, the label shall indicate their order (e.g., "1 of X").

(vi) An indication that the disk is "Copy 1" or "Copy 2" of the submission. See paragraph (b)(4) of this section.

(7) If a file is unreadable on both copies of the disc, the unreadable file will be treated as not having been submitted. A file is unreadable if, for example, it is of a format that does not comply with the requirements of paragraph (e)(3) of this section, it is corrupted by a computer virus, or it is written onto a defective compact disc.

(f)(1)Any sequence listing in an electronic medium in compliance with §§ 1.52(e) and 1.821(c) or (e), and any computer program listing filed in an electronic medium in compliance with §§ 1.52(e) and 1.96 will be excluded when determining the application size fee required by § 1.16(s) or § 1.492(j). For purposes of determining the application size fee required by § 1.16(s) or § 1.492(j), the specification and drawings of which, excluding any sequence listing in compliance with § 1.821(c) or (e), and any computer program listing filed in an electronic medium in compliance with §§ 1.52(e) and 1.96, are submitted in whole or in part on an electronic medium other than the Office electronic filing system, each three kilobytes of content submitted on an electronic medium shall be counted as a sheet of paper.

(2) Except as otherwise provided in this paragraph, the paper size equivalent of the specification and drawings of an application submitted via the Office electronic filing system will be considered to be seventy-five percent of the number of sheets of paper present in the specification and drawings of the application when entered into the Office file wrapper after being rendered by the Office electronic filing system for purposes of determining the application size fee required by § 1.16(s). Any sequence listing in compliance with § 1.821(c) or (e), and any computer program listing in compliance with § 1.96, submitted via the Office electronic filing system will be excluded when determining the application size fee required by § 1.16(s) if the listing is submitted in ASCII text as part of an associated file.

### Section 1.58 of Title 37 of the CFR:

(a) The specification, including the claims, may contain chemical and mathematical formulae but shall not contain drawings or flow diagrams. The description portion of the specification may contain tables, but the same tables may only be included in both the drawings and description portion of the specification if the application was filed under 35 U.S.C. 371. Claims may contain tables either if necessary to conform to 35 U.S.C. 112 or if otherwise found to be desirable.

(b) Tables that are submitted in electronic form (§§ 1.96(c) and 1.821(c)) must maintain the spatial relationships (e.g., alignment of columns and rows) of the table elements when displayed so as to visually preserve the relational information they convey. Chemical and mathematical formulae must be encoded to maintain the proper positioning of their characters when displayed in order to preserve their intended meaning.

(c) Chemical and mathematical formulae and tables must be presented in compliance with § 1.52(a) and (b), except that chemical and mathematical formulae or tables may be placed in a landscape orientation if they cannot be presented satisfactorily in a portrait orientation. Typewritten characters used in such formulae and tables must be chosen from a block (nonscript) type font or lettering style having capital letters which should be at least 0.422 cm. (0.166 inch) high (e.g., preferably Arial, Times Roman, or Courier with a font size of 12) but may be no smaller than 0.21 cm. (0.08 inch) high (e.g., a font size of 6). A space at least 0.64 cm. (1/4 inch) high should be provided between complex formulae and tables and the text. Tables should have the lines and columns of data closely spaced to conserve space, consistent with a high degree of legibility.

### Section 1.96 of Title 37 of the CFR:

(a) *General:*

Descriptions of the operation and general content of computer program listings should appear in the description portion of the specification. A computer program listing for the purpose of this section is defined as a printout that lists in appropriate sequence the instructions, routines, and other contents of a program for a computer. The program listing may be either in machine or machine-independent (object or source) language which will cause a computer to perform a desired procedure or task such as solve a problem, regulate the flow of work in a computer, or control or monitor events. Computer program listings may be submitted in patent applications as set forth in paragraphs (b) and (c) of this section.

(b) *Material which will be printed in the patent:*

If the computer program listing is contained in 300 lines or fewer, with each line of 72 characters or fewer, it may be submitted either as drawings or as part of the specification.

(1) *Drawings.* If the listing is submitted as drawings, it must be submitted in the manner and complying with the requirements for drawings as provided in § 1.84. At least one figure numeral is required on each sheet of drawing.

(2) *Specification.*

(i) If the listing is submitted as part of the specification, it must be submitted in accordance with the provisions of § 1.52.

(ii) Any listing having more than 60 lines of code that is submitted as part of the specification must be positioned at the end of the description but before the claims. Any amendment must be made by way of submission of a substitute sheet.

(c) *As an appendix which will not be printed:*

Any computer program listing may, and any computer program listing having over 300 lines (up to 72 characters per line), must be submitted on a compact disc in compliance with § 1.52(e). A compact disc containing such a computer program listing is to be referred to as a "computer program listing appendix." The "computer program listing appendix" will not be part of the printed patent. The specification must include a reference to the "computer program listing appendix" at the location indicated in § 1.77(b)(5).

(1) Multiple computer program listings for a single application may be placed on a single compact disc. Multiple compact discs may be submitted for a single application if necessary. A separate compact disc is required for each application containing a computer program listing that must be submitted on a "computer program listing appendix."

(2) The "computer program listing appendix" must be submitted on a compact disc that complies with § 1.52(e) and the following specifications (no other format shall be allowed):

(i) Computer Compatibility: IBM PC/XT/ AT, or compatibles, or Apple Macintosh;

(ii) Operating System Compatibility: MSDOS, MS-Windows, Unix, or Macintosh;

(iii) Line Terminator: ASCII Carriage Return plus ASCII Line Feed;

(iv) Control Codes: the data must not be dependent on control characters or codes which are not defined in the ASCII character set; and

(v) Compression: uncompressed data.

## SECTIONS 1.821–1.825 OF TITLE 37 OF THE CFR:

### Section 1.821:

(a) Nucleotide and/or amino acid sequences as used in §§ 1.821 through 1.825 are interpreted to mean an unbranched sequence of four or more amino acids or an unbranched sequence of ten or more nucleotides. Branched sequences are specifically excluded from this definition. Sequences with fewer than four specifically defined nucleotides or amino acids are specifically excluded from this section. "Specifically defined" means those amino acids other than "Xaa" and those nucleotide bases other than "n" defined in accordance with the World Intellectual Property Organization (WIPO) Handbook on Industrial Property Information and Documentation, Standard ST.25: Standard for the Presentation of Nucleotide and Amino Acid Sequence Listings in Patent Applications (1998), including Tables 1 through 6 in Appendix 2, herein incorporated by reference. (Hereinafter "WIPO Standard ST.25 (1998)".) This incorporation by reference was approved by the Director of the Federal Register in accordance with 5 U.S.C. 552(a) and 1 CFR part 51. Copies of WIPO Standard ST.25 (1998) may be obtained from the World Intellectual Property Organization; 34 chemin des Colombettes; 1211 Geneva 20 Switzerland. Copies may also be inspected at the National Archives and Records Administration (NARA). For information on the availability of this material at NARA, call 202–741–6030, or go to http:// www.archives.gov/federal_register/code_of_federal_regulations/ ibr_locations.html. Nucleotides and amino acids are further defined as follows:

(1) *Nucleotides:* Nucleotides are intended to embrace only those nucleotides that can be represented using the symbols set forth in WIPO Standard ST.25 (1998), Appendix 2, Table 1. Modifications, e.g., methylated bases, may be described as set forth in WIPO Standard ST.25 (1998), Appendix 2, Table 2, but shall not be shown explicitly in the nucleotide sequence.

(2) *Amino acids:* Amino acids are those Lamino acids commonly found in naturally occurring proteins and are listed in WIPO Standard ST.25 (1998), Appendix 2, Table 3. Those amino acid

sequences containing D-amino acids are not intended to be embraced by this definition. Any amino acid sequence that contains post-translationally modified amino acids may be described as the amino acid sequence that is initially translated using the symbols shown in WIPO Standard ST.25 (1998), Appendix 2, Table 3 with the modified positions; e.g., hydroxylations or glycosylations, being described as set forth in WIPO Standard ST.25 (1998), Appendix 2, Table 4, but these modifications shall not be shown explicitly in the amino acid sequence. Any peptide or protein that can be expressed as a sequence using the symbols in WIPO Standard ST.25 (1998), Appendix 2, Table 3 in conjunction with a description in the Feature section to describe, for example, modified linkages, cross links and end caps, non-peptidyl bonds, etc., is embraced by this definition.

(b) Patent applications which contain disclosures of nucleotide and/or amino acid sequences, in accordance with the definition in paragraph (a) of this section, shall, with regard to the manner in which the nucleotide and/or amino acid sequences are presented and described, conform exclusively to the requirements of §§ 1.821 through 1.825.

(c) Patent applications which contain disclosures of nucleotide and/ or amino acid sequences must contain, as a separate part of the disclosure, a paper or compact disc copy (see § 1.52(e)) disclosing the nucleotide and/or amino acid sequences and associated information using the symbols and format in accordance with the requirements of §§ 1.822 and 1.823. This paper or compact disc copy is referred to elsewhere in this subpart as the "Sequence Listing." Each sequence disclosed must appear separately in the "Sequence Listing." Each sequence set forth in the "Sequence Listing" must be assigned a separate sequence identifier. The sequence identifiers must begin with 1 and increase sequentially by integers. If no sequence is present for a sequence identifier, the code "000" must be used in place of the sequence. The response for the numeric identifier <160> must include the total number of SEQ ID NOs, whether followed by a sequence or by the code "000."

(d) Where the description or claims of a patent application discuss a sequence that is set forth in the "Sequence Listing" in accordance with paragraph (c) of this section, reference must be made to the sequence by use of the sequence identifier, preceded by "SEQ ID NO:" in the text of the description or claims, even if the sequence is also embedded in the text of the description or claims of the patent application.

(e) A copy of the "Sequence Listing" referred to in paragraph (c) of this section must also be submitted in computer readable form (CRF) in accordance with the requirements of § 1.824. The computer readable form must be a copy of the "Sequence Listing" and may not be retained as a part of the patent application file. If the computer readable form of a new application is to be identical with the computer readable form of another application of the applicant on file in the Office, reference may be made to the other application and computer readable form in lieu of filing a duplicate computer readable form in the new application if the computer readable form in the other application was compliant with all of the requirements of this subpart. The new application must be accompanied by a letter making such reference to the other application and computer readable form, both of which shall be completely identified. In the new application, applicant must also request the use of the compliant computer readable "Sequence Listing" that is already on file for the other application and must state that the paper or compact disc copy of the "Sequence Listing" in the new application is identical to the computer readable copy filed for the other application.

(f) In addition to the paper or compact disc copy required by paragraph (c) of this section and the computer readable form required by paragraph (e) of this section, a statement that the "Sequence Listing" content of the paper or compact disc copy and the computer readable copy are the same must be submitted with the computer readable form, e.g., a statement that "the sequence listing information recorded in computer readable form is identical to the written (on paper or compact disc) sequence listing."

(g) If any of the requirements of paragraphs (b) through (f) of this section are not satisfied at the time of filing under 35 U.S.C. 111(a) or at the time of entering the national stage under 35 U.S.C. 371, applicant will be notified and given a period of time within which to comply with such requirements in order to prevent abandonment of the application. Any submission in reply to a requirement under this paragraph must be accompanied by a statement that the submission includes no new matter.

(h) If any of the requirements of paragraphs (b) through (f) of this section are not satisfied at the time of filing an international application under the Patent Cooperation Treaty (PCT), which application is to be searched by the United States International Searching Authority or examined by the United States International Preliminary Examining Authority, applicant will be sent a notice necessitating compliance with the requirements within a prescribed time period.

Any submission in reply to a requirement under this paragraph must be accompanied by a statement that the submission does not include matter which goes beyond the disclosure in the international application as filed. If applicant fails to timely provide the required computer readable form, the United States International Searching Authority shall search only to the extent that a meaningful search can be performed without the computer readable form and the United States International Preliminary Examining Authority shall examine only to the extent that a meaningful examination can be performed without the computer readable form.

Section 1.822:

(a) The symbols and format to be used for nucleotide and/or amino acid sequence data shall conform to the requirements of paragraphs (b) through (e) of this section.

(b) The code for representing the nucleotide and/or amino acid sequence characters shall conform to the code set forth in the tables in WIPO Standard ST.25 (1998), Appendix 2, Tables 1 and 3. This incorporation by reference was approved by the Director of the Federal Register in accordance with 5 U.S.C. 552(a) and 1 CFR part 51. Copies of ST.25 may be obtained from the World Intellectual Property Organization; 34 chemin des Colombettes; 1211 Geneva 20 Switzerland. Copies may also be inspected at the National Archives and Records Administration (NARA). For information on the availability of this material at NARA, call 202–741–6030, or go to http://www.archives. gov/federal_register/ code_of_federal_regulations/ibr_locations.html. No code other than that specified in these sections shall be used in nucleotide and amino acid sequences. A modified base or modified or unusual amino acid may be presented in a given sequence as the corresponding unmodified base or amino acid if the modified base or modified or unusual amino acid is one of those listed in WIPO Standard ST.25 (1998), Appendix 2, Tables 2 and 4, and the modification is also set forth in the Feature section. Otherwise, each occurrence of a base or amino acid not appearing in WIPO Standard ST.25 (1998), Appendix 2, Tables 1 and 3, shall be listed in a given sequence as "n" or "Xaa," respectively, with further information, as appropriate, given in the Feature section, preferably by including one or more feature keys listed in WIPO Standard ST.25 (1998), Appendix 2, Tables 5 and 6.

(c) *Format representation of nucleotides.* (1) A nucleotide sequence shall be listed using the lowercase letter for representing the one-letter code for the nucleotide bases set forth in WIPO Standard ST.25 (1998), Appendix 2, Table 1.

(2) The bases in a nucleotide sequence (including introns) shall be listed in groups of 10 bases except in the coding parts of the sequence. Leftover bases, fewer than 10 in number, at the end of noncoding parts of a sequence shall be grouped together and separated from adjacent groups of 10 or 3 bases by a space.

(3) The bases in the coding parts of a nucleotide sequence shall be listed as triplets (codons). The amino acids corresponding to the codons in the coding parts of a nucleotide sequence shall be typed immediately below the corresponding codons. Where a codon spans an intron, the amino acid symbol shall be typed below the portion of the codon containing two nucleotides.

(4) A nucleotide sequence shall be listed with a maximum of 16 codons or 60 bases per line, with a space provided between each codon or group of 10 bases.

(5) A nucleotide sequence shall be presented, only by a single strand, in the 5 to 3 direction, from left to right.

(6) The enumeration of nucleotide bases shall start at the first base of the sequence with number 1. The enumeration shall be continuous through the whole sequence in the direction 5 to 3. The enumeration shall be marked in the right margin, next to the line containing the one-letter codes for the bases, and giving the number of the last base of that line.

(7) For those nucleotide sequences that are circular in configuration, the enumeration method set forth in paragraph (c)(6) of this section remains applicable with the exception that the designation of the first base of the nucleotide sequence may be made at the option of the applicant.

(d) *Representation of amino acids.* (1) The amino acids in a protein or peptide sequence shall be listed using the three-letter abbreviation with the first letter as an upper case character, as in WIPO Standard ST.25 (1998), Appendix 2, Table 3.

(2) A protein or peptide sequence shall be listed with a maximum of 16 amino acids per line, with a space provided between each amino acid.

(3) An amino acid sequence shall be presented in the amino to carboxy direction, from left to right, and the amino and carboxy groups shall not be presented in the sequence.

(4) The enumeration of amino acids may start at the first amino acid of the first mature protein, with the number 1. When presented,

the amino acids preceding the mature protein, e.g., pre-sequences, pro-sequences, pre-pro-sequences, and signal sequences, shall have negative numbers, counting backwards starting with the amino acid next to number 1. Otherwise, the enumeration of amino acids shall start at the first amino acid at the amino terminal as number 1. It shall be marked below the sequence every 5 amino acids. The enumeration method for amino acid sequences that is set forth in this section remains applicable for amino acid sequences that are circular in configuration, with the exception that the designation of the first amino acid of the sequence may be made at the option of the applicant.

(5) An amino acid sequence that contains internal terminator symbols (e.g., "Ter," "*," or ".," etc.) may not be represented as a single amino acid sequence but shall be presented as separate amino acid sequences.

(e) A sequence with a gap or gaps shall be presented as a plurality of separate sequences, with separate sequence identifiers, with the number of separate sequences being equal in number to the number of continuous strings of sequence data. A sequence that is made up of one or more noncontiguous segments of a larger sequence or segments from different sequences shall be presented as a separate sequence.

**Excerpt from Section 1.823:**

(a)(1) If the "Sequence Listing" required by § 1.821(c) is submitted on paper: The "Sequence Listing," setting forth the nucleotide and/or amino acid sequence and associated information in accordance with paragraph (b) of this section, must begin on a new page and must be titled "Sequence Listing." The pages of the "Sequence Listing" preferably should be numbered independently of the numbering of the remainder of the application. Each page of the "Sequence Listing" shall contain no more than 66 lines and each line shall contain no more than 72 characters. The sheet or sheets presenting a sequence listing may not include material other than part of the sequence listing. A fixed-width font should be used exclusively throughout the "Sequence Listing."

(2) If the "Sequence Listing" required by § 1.821(c) is submitted on compact disc: The "Sequence Listing" must be submitted on a compact disc in compliance with § 1.52(e). The compact disc may also contain table information if the application contains table information that may be submitted on a compact disc (§ 1.52(e)(1)(iii)). The specification must contain an incorporation-by-reference of the Sequence Listing as required by § 1.52(e)(5). The presentation of the "Sequence

Listing" and other materials on compact disc under § 1.821(c) does not substitute for the Computer Readable Form that must be submitted on disk, compact disc, or tape in accordance with § 1.824.

(b) The "Sequence Listing" shall, except as otherwise indicated, include the actual nucleotide and/or amino acid sequence, the numeric identifiers and their accompanying information as shown in the following table. The numeric identifier shall be used only in the "Sequence Listing." The order and presentation of the items of information in the "Sequence Listing" shall conform to the arrangement given below. Each item of information shall begin on a new line and shall begin with the numeric identifier enclosed in angle brackets as shown. The submission of those items of information designated with an "M" is mandatory. The submission of those items of information designated with an "O" is optional. Numeric identifiers <110> through <170> shall only be set forth at the beginning of the "Sequence Listing."

### Excerpt from Section 1.824:

(a) The computer readable form required by § 1.821(e) shall meet the following requirements:

(1) The computer readable form shall contain a single "Sequence Listing" as either a diskette, series of diskettes, or other permissible media outlined in paragraph (c) of this section.

(2) The "Sequence Listing" in paragraph (a)(1) of this section shall be submitted in American Standard Code for Information Interchange (ASCII) text. No other formats shall be allowed.

(3) The computer readable form may be created by any means, such as word processors, nucleotide/amino acid sequence editors' or other custom computer programs; however, it shall conform to all requirements detailed in this section.

(4) File compression is acceptable when using diskette media, so long as the compressed file is in a self-extracting format that will decompress on one of the systems described in paragraph (b) of this section.

(5) Page numbering must not appear within the computer readable form version of the "Sequence Listing" file.

(6) All computer readable forms must have a label permanently affixed thereto on which has been hand-printed or typed: the name of the applicant, the title of the invention, the date on which the

data were recorded on the computer readable form, the operating system used, a reference number, and an application number and filing date, if known. If multiple diskettes are submitted, the diskette labels must indicate their order (e.g., "1 of X").

(b) Computer readable form submissions must meet these format requirements:

(1) Computer Compatibility: IBM PC/XT/AT or Apple Macintosh;

(2) Operating System Compatibility: MSDOS, MS-Windows, Unix, or Macintosh;

(3) Line Terminator: ASCII Carriage Return plus ASCII Line Feed; and

(4) Pagination: Continuous file (no "hard page break" codes permitted).

**Section 1.825:**

(a) Any amendment to a paper copy of the "Sequence Listing" (§ 1.821(c)) must be made by the submission of substitute sheets and include a statement that the substitute sheets include no new matter. Any amendment to a compact disc copy of the "Sequence Listing" (§ 1.821(c)) must be made by the submission of a replacement compact disc (2 copies) in compliance with § 1.52(e). Amendments must also be accompanied by a statement that indicates support for the amendment in the application, as filed, and a statement that the replacement compact disc includes no new matter.

(b) Any amendment to the paper or compact disc copy of the "Sequence Listing," in accordance with paragraph (a) of this section, must be accompanied by a substitute copy of the computer readable form (§ 1.821(e)) including all previously submitted data with the amendment incorporated therein, accompanied by a statement that the copy in computer readable form is the same as the substitute copy of the "Sequence Listing."

(c) Any appropriate amendments to the "Sequence Listing" in a patent; e.g., by reason of reissue or certificate of correction, must comply with the requirements of paragraphs (a) and (b) of this section.

(d) If, upon receipt, the computer readable form is found to be damaged or unreadable, applicant must provide, within such time as set by the Director, a substitute copy of the data in computer readable form accompanied by a statement that the substitute data is identical to that originally filed.

# APPENDIX 27:
# BACKGROUND OF THE INVENTION

**Section 608.01(c) of the MPEP:**

The Background of the Invention ordinarily comprises two parts:

(1) Field of the Invention: A statement of the field of art to which the invention pertains. This statement may include a paraphrasing of the applicable U.S. patent classification definitions. The statement should be directed to the subject matter of the claimed invention.

(2) Description of the related art including information disclosed under 37 CFR 1.97 and 37 CFR 1.98: A paragraph(s) describing to the extent practical the state of the prior art or other information disclosed known to the applicant, including references to specific prior art or other information where appropriate. Where applicable, the problems involved in the prior art or other information disclosed which are solved by the applicant's invention should be indicated.

**Section 1.97 of Title 37 of the CFR:**

(a) In order for an applicant for a patent or for a reissue of a patent to have an information disclosure statement in compliance with § 1.98 considered by the Office during the pendency of the application, the information disclosure statement must satisfy one of paragraphs (b), (c), or (d) of this section.

(b) An information disclosure statement shall be considered by the Office if filed by the applicant within any one of the following time periods:

(1) Within three months of the filing date of a national application other than a continued prosecution application under § 1.53(d);

(2) Within three months of the date of entry of the national stage as set forth in § 1.491 in an international application;

---

(3) Before the mailing of a first Office action on the merits; or

(4) Before the mailing of a first Office action after the filing of a request for continued examination under § 1.114.

(c) An information disclosure statement shall be considered by the Office if filed after the period specified in paragraph (b) of this section, provided that the information disclosure statement is filed before the mailing date of any of a final action under § 1.113, a notice of allowance under § 1.311, or an action that otherwise closes prosecution in the application, and it is accompanied by one of:

(1) The statement specified in paragraph (e) of this section; or

(2) The fee set forth in § 1.17(p).

(d) An information disclosure statement shall be considered by the Office if filed by the applicant after the period specified in paragraph (c) of this section, provided that the information disclosure statement is filed on or before payment of the issue fee and is accompanied by:

(1) The statement specified in paragraph (e) of this section; and

(2) The fee set forth in § 1.17(p).

(e) A statement under this section must state either:

(1) That each item of information contained in the information disclosure statement was first cited in any communication from a foreign patent office in a counterpart foreign application not more than three months prior to the filing of the information disclosure statement; or

(2) That no item of information contained in the information disclosure statement was cited in a communication from a foreign patent office in a counterpart foreign application, and, to the knowledge of the person signing the certification after making reasonable inquiry, no item of information contained in the information disclosure statement was known to any individual designated in § 1.56(c) more than three months prior to the filing of the information disclosure statement.

(f) No extensions of time for filing an information disclosure statement are permitted under § 1.136. If a *bona fide* attempt is made to comply with § 1.98, but part of the required content is inadvertently omitted, additional time may be given to enable full compliance.

(g) An information disclosure statement filed in accordance with this section shall not be construed as a representation that a search has been made.

(h) The filing of an information disclosure statement shall not be construed to be an admission that the information cited in the statement is, or is considered to be, material to patentability as defined in § 1.56(b).

(i) If an information disclosure statement does not comply with either this section or § 1.98, it will be placed in the file but will not be considered by the Office.

### Section 1.98 of Title 37 of the CFR:

(a) Any information disclosure statement filed under § 1.97 shall include the items listed in paragraphs (a)(1), (a)(2), and (a)(3) of this section.

(1) A list of all patents, publications, applications, or other information submitted for consideration by the Office. U.S. patents and U.S. patent application publications must be listed in a section separately from citations of other documents. Each page of the list must include:

(i) The application number of the application in which the information disclosure statement is being submitted;

(ii) A column that provides a space, next to each document to be considered, for the examiner's initials; and

(iii) A heading that clearly indicates that the list is an information disclosure statement.

(2) A legible copy of:

(i) Each foreign patent;

(ii) Each publication or that portion which caused it to be listed, other than U.S. patents and U.S. patent application publications unless required by the Office;

(iii) For each cited pending unpublished U.S. application, the application specification including the claims, and any drawing of the application, or that portion of the application which caused it to be listed including any claims directed to that portion; and

(iv) All other information or that portion which caused it to be listed.

(3)(i) A concise explanation of the relevance, as it is presently understood by the individual designated in § 1.56(c) most knowledgeable about the content of the information, of each patent, publication, or other information listed that is not in the

English language. The concise explanation may be either separate from applicant's specification or incorporated therein.

(ii) A copy of the translation if a written English-language translation of a non-English-language document, or portion thereof, is within the possession, custody, or control of, or is readily available to any individual designated in § 1.56(c).

(b)(1) Each U.S. patent listed in an information disclosure statement must be identified by inventor, patent number, and issue date.

(2) Each U.S. patent application publication listed in an information disclosure statement shall be identified by applicant, patent application publication number, and publication date.

(3) Each U.S. application listed in an information disclosure statement must be identified by the inventor, application number, and filing date.

(4) Each foreign patent or published foreign patent application listed in an information disclosure statement must be identified by the country or patent office which issued the patent or published the application, an appropriate document number, and the publication date indicated on the patent or published application.

(5) Each publication listed in an information disclosure statement must be identified by publisher, author (if any), title, relevant pages of the publication, date, and place of publication.

(c) When the disclosures of two or more patents or publications listed in an information disclosure statement are substantively cumulative, a copy of one of the patents or publications as specified in paragraph (a) of this section may be submitted without copies of the other patents or publications, provided that it is stated that these other patents or publications are cumulative.

(d) A copy of any patent, publication, pending U.S. application or other information, as specified in paragraph (a) of this section, listed in an information disclosure statement is required to be provided, even if the patent, publication, pending U.S. application or other information was previously submitted to, or cited by, the Office in an earlier application, unless:

(1) The earlier application is properly identified in the information disclosure statement and is relied on for an earlier effective filing date under 35 U.S.C. 120; and

(2) The information disclosure statement submitted in the earlier application complies with paragraphs (a) through (c) of this section.

# APPENDIX 28:
# INFORMATION DISCLOSURE STATEMENTS

PTO/SB/08a (07-09)
Approved for use through 07/31/2012. OMB 0651-0031
U.S. Patent and Trademark Office; U.S. DEPARTMENT OF COMMERCE
Under the Paperwork Reduction Act of 1995, no persons are required to respond to a collection of information unless it contains a valid OMB control number.

Substitute for form 1449/PTO

## INFORMATION DISCLOSURE
## STATEMENT BY APPLICANT
*(Use as many sheets as necessary)*

Sheet _____ of _____

**Complete if Known**

| | |
|---|---|
| Application Number | |
| Filing Date | |
| First Named Inventor | |
| Art Unit | |
| Examiner Name | |
| Attorney Docket Number | |

### U. S. PATENT DOCUMENTS

| Examiner Initials* | Cite No.[1] | Document Number<br>Number-Kind Code[2] *(if known)* | Publication Date MM-DD-YYYY | Name of Patentee or Applicant of Cited Document | Pages, Columns, Lines, Where Relevant Passages or Relevant Figures Appear |
|---|---|---|---|---|---|
| | | US- | | | |
| | | US- | | | |
| | | US- | | | |
| | | US- | | | |
| | | US- | | | |
| | | US- | | | |
| | | US- | | | |
| | | US- | | | |
| | | US- | | | |
| | | US- | | | |
| | | US- | | | |
| | | US- | | | |
| | | US- | | | |
| | | US- | | | |
| | | US- | | | |
| | | US- | | | |

### FOREIGN PATENT DOCUMENTS

| Examiner Initials* | Cite No.[1] | Foreign Patent Document<br>Country Code[3] Number[4] Kind Code[5] *(if known)* | Publication Date MM-DD-YYYY | Name of Patentee or Applicant of Cited Document | Pages, Columns, Lines, Where Relevant Passages Or Relevant Figures Appear | T[6] |
|---|---|---|---|---|---|---|
| | | | | | | |
| | | | | | | |
| | | | | | | |
| | | | | | | |
| | | | | | | |
| | | | | | | |

| Examiner Signature | | Date Considered | |
|---|---|---|---|

*EXAMINER: Initial if reference considered, whether or not citation is in conformance with MPEP 609. Draw line through citation if not in conformance and not considered. Include copy of this form with next communication to applicant. [1] Applicant's unique citation designation number (optional). [2] See Kinds Codes of USPTO Patent Documents at www.uspto.gov or MPEP 901.04. [3] Enter Office that issued the document, by the two-letter code (WIPO Standard ST.3). [4] For Japanese patent documents, the indication of the year of the reign of the Emperor must precede the serial number of the patent document. [5] Kind of document by the appropriate symbols as indicated on the document under WIPO Standard ST.16 if possible. [6] Applicant is to place a check mark here if English language Translation is attached.

This collection of information is required by 37 CFR 1.97 and 1.98. The information is required to obtain or retain a benefit by the public which is to file (and by the USPTO to process) an application. Confidentiality is governed by 35 U.S.C. 122 and 37 CFR 1.14. This collection is estimated to take 2 hours to complete, including gathering, preparing, and submitting the completed application form to the USPTO. Time will vary depending upon the individual case. Any comments on the amount of time you require to complete this form and/or suggestions for reducing this burden, should be sent to the Chief Information Officer, U.S. Patent and Trademark Office, P.O. Box 1450, Alexandria, VA 22313-1450. DO NOT SEND FEES OR COMPLETED FORMS TO THIS ADDRESS. **SEND TO: Commissioner for Patents, P.O. Box 1450, Alexandria, VA 22313-1450.**

*If you need assistance in completing the form, call 1-800-PTO-9199 (1-800-786-9199) and select option 2.*

# Privacy Act Statement

**The Privacy Act of 1974 (P.L. 93-579)** requires that you be given certain information in connection with your submission of the attached form related to a patent application or patent. Accordingly, pursuant to the requirements of the Act, please be advised that: (1) the general authority for the collection of this information is 35 U.S.C. 2(b)(2); (2) furnishing of the information solicited is voluntary; and (3) the principal purpose for which the information is used by the U.S. Patent and Trademark Office is to process and/or examine your submission related to a patent application or patent. If you do not furnish the requested information, the U.S. Patent and Trademark Office may not be able to process and/or examine your submission, which may result in termination of proceedings or abandonment of the application or expiration of the patent.

The information provided by you in this form will be subject to the following routine uses:

1. The information on this form will be treated confidentially to the extent allowed under the Freedom of Information Act (5 U.S.C. 552) and the Privacy Act (5 U.S.C 552a). Records from this system of records may be disclosed to the Department of Justice to determine whether disclosure of these records is required by the Freedom of Information Act.
2. A record from this system of records may be disclosed, as a routine use, in the course of presenting evidence to a court, magistrate, or administrative tribunal, including disclosures to opposing counsel in the course of settlement negotiations.
3. A record in this system of records may be disclosed, as a routine use, to a Member of Congress submitting a request involving an individual, to whom the record pertains, when the individual has requested assistance from the Member with respect to the subject matter of the record.
4. A record in this system of records may be disclosed, as a routine use, to a contractor of the Agency having need for the information in order to perform a contract. Recipients of information shall be required to comply with the requirements of the Privacy Act of 1974, as amended, pursuant to 5 U.S.C. 552a(m).
5. A record related to an International Application filed under the Patent Cooperation Treaty in this system of records may be disclosed, as a routine use, to the International Bureau of the World Intellectual Property Organization, pursuant to the Patent Cooperation Treaty.
6. A record in this system of records may be disclosed, as a routine use, to another federal agency for purposes of National Security review (35 U.S.C. 181) and for review pursuant to the Atomic Energy Act (42 U.S.C. 218(c)).
7. A record from this system of records may be disclosed, as a routine use, to the Administrator, General Services, or his/her designee, during an inspection of records conducted by GSA as part of that agency's responsibility to recommend improvements in records management practices and programs, under authority of 44 U.S.C. 2904 and 2906. Such disclosure shall be made in accordance with the GSA regulations governing inspection of records for this purpose, and any other relevant (i.e., GSA or Commerce) directive. Such disclosure shall not be used to make determinations about individuals.
8. A record from this system of records may be disclosed, as a routine use, to the public after either publication of the application pursuant to 35 U.S.C. 122(b) or issuance of a patent pursuant to 35 U.S.C. 151. Further, a record may be disclosed, subject to the limitations of 37 CFR 1.14, as a routine use, to the public if the record was filed in an application which became abandoned or in which the proceedings were terminated and which application is referenced by either a published application, an application open to public inspection or an issued patent.
9. A record from this system of records may be disclosed, as a routine use, to a Federal, State, or local law enforcement agency, if the USPTO becomes aware of a violation or potential violation of law or regulation.

PTO/SB/08b (07-09)
Approved for use through 07/31/2012. OMB 0651-0031
U.S. Patent and Trademark Office; U.S. DEPARTMENT OF COMMERCE
Under the Paperwork Reduction Act of 1995, no persons are required to respond to a collection of information unless it contains a valid OMB control number.

| Substitute for form 1449/PTO | *Complete if Known* | |
|---|---|---|
| **INFORMATION DISCLOSURE STATEMENT BY APPLICANT** *(Use as many sheets as necessary)* | Application Number | |
| | Filing Date | |
| | First Named Inventor | |
| | Art Unit | |
| | Examiner Name | |
| Sheet | of | Attorney Docket Number | |

## NON PATENT LITERATURE DOCUMENTS

| Examiner Initials* | Cite No.[1] | Include name of the author (in CAPITAL LETTERS), title of the article (when appropriate), title of the item (book, magazine, journal, serial, symposium, catalog, etc.), date, page(s), volume-issue number(s), publisher, city and/or country where published. | T[2] |
|---|---|---|---|
| | | | |
| | | | |
| | | | |
| | | | |
| | | | |
| | | | |
| | | | |
| | | | |
| | | | |

| Examiner Signature | | Date Considered | |
|---|---|---|---|

*EXAMINER: Initial if reference considered, whether or not citation is in conformance with MPEP 609. Draw line through citation if not in conformance and not considered. Include copy of this form with next communication to applicant.
1 Applicant's unique citation designation number (optional). 2 Applicant is to place a check mark here if English language Translation is attached.
This collection of information is required by 37 CFR 1.98. The information is required to obtain or retain a benefit by the public which is to file (and by the USPTO to process) an application. Confidentiality is governed by 35 U.S.C. 122 and 37 CFR 1.14. This collection is estimated to take 2 hours to complete, including gathering, preparing, and submitting the completed application form to the USPTO. Time will vary depending upon the individual case. Any comments on the amount of time you require to complete this form and/or suggestions for reducing this burden, should be sent to the Chief Information Officer, U.S. Patent and Trademark Office, P.O. Box 1450, Alexandria, VA 22313-1450. DO NOT SEND FEES OR COMPLETED FORMS TO THIS ADDRESS. **SEND TO: Commissioner for Patents, P.O. Box 1450, Alexandria, VA 22313-1450.**

*If you need assistance in completing the form, call 1-800-PTO-9199 (1-800-786-9199) and select option 2.*

## Privacy Act Statement

The **Privacy Act of 1974 (P.L. 93-579)** requires that you be given certain information in connection with your submission of the attached form related to a patent application or patent. Accordingly, pursuant to the requirements of the Act, please be advised that: (1) the general authority for the collection of this information is 35 U.S.C. 2(b)(2); (2) furnishing of the information solicited is voluntary; and (3) the principal purpose for which the information is used by the U.S. Patent and Trademark Office is to process and/or examine your submission related to a patent application or patent. If you do not furnish the requested information, the U.S. Patent and Trademark Office may not be able to process and/or examine your submission, which may result in termination of proceedings or abandonment of the application or expiration of the patent.

The information provided by you in this form will be subject to the following routine uses:

1. The information on this form will be treated confidentially to the extent allowed under the Freedom of Information Act (5 U.S.C. 552) and the Privacy Act (5 U.S.C 552a). Records from this system of records may be disclosed to the Department of Justice to determine whether disclosure of these records is required by the Freedom of Information Act.
2. A record from this system of records may be disclosed, as a routine use, in the course of presenting evidence to a court, magistrate, or administrative tribunal, including disclosures to opposing counsel in the course of settlement negotiations.
3. A record in this system of records may be disclosed, as a routine use, to a Member of Congress submitting a request involving an individual, to whom the record pertains, when the individual has requested assistance from the Member with respect to the subject matter of the record.
4. A record in this system of records may be disclosed, as a routine use, to a contractor of the Agency having need for the information in order to perform a contract. Recipients of information shall be required to comply with the requirements of the Privacy Act of 1974, as amended, pursuant to 5 U.S.C. 552a(m).
5. A record related to an International Application filed under the Patent Cooperation Treaty in this system of records may be disclosed, as a routine use, to the International Bureau of the World Intellectual Property Organization, pursuant to the Patent Cooperation Treaty.
6. A record in this system of records may be disclosed, as a routine use, to another federal agency for purposes of National Security review (35 U.S.C. 181) and for review pursuant to the Atomic Energy Act (42 U.S.C. 218(c)).
7. A record from this system of records may be disclosed, as a routine use, to the Administrator, General Services, or his/her designee, during an inspection of records conducted by GSA as part of that agency's responsibility to recommend improvements in records management practices and programs, under authority of 44 U.S.C. 2904 and 2906. Such disclosure shall be made in accordance with the GSA regulations governing inspection of records for this purpose, and any other relevant (*i.e.*, GSA or Commerce) directive. Such disclosure shall not be used to make determinations about individuals.
8. A record from this system of records may be disclosed, as a routine use, to the public after either publication of the application pursuant to 35 U.S.C. 122(b) or issuance of a patent pursuant to 35 U.S.C. 151. Further, a record may be disclosed, subject to the limitations of 37 CFR 1.14, as a routine use, to the public if the record was filed in an application which became abandoned or in which the proceedings were terminated and which application is referenced by either a published application, an application open to public inspection or an issued patent.
9. A record from this system of records may be disclosed, as a routine use, to a Federal, State, or local law enforcement agency, if the USPTO becomes aware of a violation or potential violation of law or regulation.

**Understanding Patent Law: A Beginner's Guide**

# APPENDIX 29:
# SUMMARY OF THE INVENTION

**Section 1.73 of Title 37 of the CFR:**

A brief summary of the invention indicating its nature and substance, which may include a statement of the object of the invention, should precede the detailed description. Such summary should, when set forth, be commensurate with the invention as claimed, and any object recited should be that of the invention as claimed.

**Section 608.01(d) of the MPEP:**

Since the purpose of the brief summary of invention is to apprise the public, and more especially those interested in the particular art to which the invention relates, of the nature of the invention, the summary should be directed to the specific invention being claimed, in contradistinction to mere generalities which would be equally applicable to numerous preceding patents. That is, the subject matter of the invention should be described in one or more clear, concise sentences or paragraphs. Stereotyped general statements that would fit one application as well as another serve no useful purpose and may well be required to be canceled as surplusage, and, in the absence of any illuminating statement, replaced by statements that are directly on point as applicable exclusively to the case at hand.

The brief summary, if properly written to set out the exact nature, operation, and purpose of the invention, will be of material assistance in aiding ready understanding of the patent in future searches. The brief summary should be more than a mere statement of the objects of the invention, which statement is also permissible under 37 CFR 1.73.

The brief summary of invention should be consistent with the subject matter of the claims.

---

# APPENDIX 30:
# BEST MODE OF THE INVENTION

## SECTION 1.71(B) OF TITLE 37 OF THE CFR

(b) The specification must set forth the precise invention for which a patent is solicited, in such manner as to distinguish it from other inventions and from what is old. It must describe completely a specific embodiment of the process, machine, manufacture, composition of matter or improvement invented, and must explain the mode of operation or principle whenever applicable. The best mode contemplated by the inventor of carrying out his invention must be set forth.

## SECTION 608.01(H) OF THE MPEP

The best mode contemplated by the inventor of carrying out his or her invention must be set forth in the description. See 35 U.S.C. 112. There is no statutory requirement for the disclosure of a specific example. A patent specification is not intended nor required to be a production specification. *Spectra-Physics, Inc. v. Coherent, Inc.*, 827 F.2d 1524, 1536, 3 USPQ2d 1737, 1745 (Fed. Cir. 1987); *In re Gay*, 309 F.2d 769, 135 USPQ 311 (CCPA 1962). The absence of a specific working example is not necessarily evidence that the best mode has not been disclosed, nor is the presence of one evidence that it has. *In re Honn*, 364 F.2d 454, 150 USPQ 652 (CCPA 1966). In determining the adequacy of a best mode disclosure, only evidence of concealment (accidental or intentional) is to be considered. That evidence must tend to show that the quality of an applicant's best mode disclosure is so poor as to effectively result in concealment. *Spectra-Physics, Inc. v. Coherent, Inc.*, 827 F.2d 1524, 1536, 3 USPQ2d 1737, 1745 (Fed. Cir. 1987); *In re Sherwood*, 613 F.2d 809, 204 USPQ 537 (CCPA 1980).

The question of whether an inventor has or has not disclosed what he or she feels is his or her best mode is a question separate and distinct from the question of sufficiency of the disclosure. *Spectra-Physics, Inc. v. Coherent, Inc.,* 827 F.2d 1524, 1532, 3 USPQ2d 1737, 1742 (Fed. Cir. 1987); *In re Glass,* 492 F.2d 1228, 181 USPQ 31 (CCPA 1974); *In re Gay,* 309 F.2d 769, 135 USPQ 311 (CCPA 1962). See 35 U.S.C. 112 and 37 CFR 1.71(b).

If the best mode contemplated by the inventor at the time of filing the application is not disclosed, such defect cannot be cured by submitting an amendment seeking to put into the specification something required to be there when the application was originally filed. *In re Hay,* 534 F.2d 917, 189 USPQ 790 (CCPA 1976). Any proposed amendment of this type should be treated as new matter.

Patents have been held invalid in cases where the patentee did not disclose the best mode known to him or her. See *Chemcast Corp. v. Arco Indus. Corp.,* 913 F.2d 923. 16 USPQ2d 1033 (Fed. Cir. 1990); *Dana Corp. v. IPC Ltd. Partnership,* 860 F.2d 415, 8 USPQ2d 1692 (Fed. Cir. 1988); *Spectra-Physics, Inc. v. Coherent, Inc.,* 821 F.2d 1524, 3 USPQ2d 1737 (Fed. Cir. 1987).

### SECTIONS 2165–2165.04 OF THE MPEP

Section 2165:

"The best mode requirement creates a statutory bargained-for-exchange by which a patentee obtains the right to exclude others from practicing the claimed invention for a certain time period, and the public receives knowledge of the preferred embodiments for practicing the claimed invention." *Eli Lilly & Co. v. Barr Laboratories Inc.,* 251 F.3d 955, 963, 58 USPQ2d 1865, 1874 (Fed. Cir. 2001).

The best mode requirement is a safeguard against the desire on the part of some people to obtain patent protection without making a full disclosure as required by the statute. The requirement does not permit inventors to disclose only what they know to be their second-best embodiment, while retaining the best for themselves. *In re Nelson,* 280 F.2d 172, 126 USPQ 242 (CCPA 1960).

Determining compliance with the best mode requirement requires a two-prong inquiry. First, it must be determined whether, at the time the application was filed, the inventor possessed a best mode for practicing the invention. This is a subjective inquiry which focuses on the inventor's state of mind at the time of filing. Second, if the inventor did possess a best mode, it must be determined whether the written description disclosed the best mode such that a person skilled in the art could practice it. This is an objective inquiry, focusing on the scope of the claimed invention and the level of skill in the art. *Eli Lilly & Co. v. Barr Laboratories Inc.*, 251 F.3d 955, 963, 58 USPQ2d 1865, 1874 (Fed. Cir. 2001).

The failure to disclose a better method will not invalidate a patent if the inventor, at the time of filing the application, did not know of the better method *OR* did not appreciate that it was the best method. All applicants are required to disclose for the claimed subject matter the best mode contemplated by the inventor even though applicant may not have been the discoverer of that mode. *Benger Labs. Ltd. v. R.K. Laros Co.*, 209 F. Supp. 639, 135 USPQ 11 (E.D. Pa. 1962).

ACTIVE CONCEALMENT OR GROSSLY INEQUITABLE CONDUCT IS NOT REQUIRED TO ESTABLISH FAILURE TO DISCLOSE THE BEST MODE

Failure to disclose the best mode need not rise to the level of active concealment or grossly inequitable conduct in order to support a rejection or invalidate a patent. Where an inventor knows of a specific material that will make possible the successful reproduction of the effects claimed by the patent, but does not disclose it, speaking instead in terms of broad categories, the best mode requirement has not been satisfied. *Union Carbide Corp. v. Borg-Warner*, 550 F.2d 555, 193 USPQ 1 (6th Cir. 1977).

If the failure to set forth the best mode in a patent disclosure is the result of inequitable conduct (e.g., where the patent specification omitted crucial ingredients and disclosed a fictitious and inoperable slurry as Example 1), not only is that patent in danger of being held unenforceable, but other patents dealing with the same technology that are sought to be enforced in the same cause of action are subject to being held unenforceable. *Consolidated Aluminum Corp. v. Foseco Inc.*, 910 F.2d 804, 15 USPQ2d 1481 (Fed. Cir. 1990).

**Section 2165.01:**

2165.01 Considerations Relevant to Best Mode

**I. DETERMINE WHAT IS THE INVENTION**

Determine what the invention is—the invention is defined in the claims. The specification need not set forth details not relating to the essence of the invention. *In re Bosy*, 360 F.2d 972, 149 USPQ 789 (CCPA 1966). See also *Northern Telecom Ltd. v. Samsung Electronics Co.*, 215 F.3d 1281, 55 USPQ2d 1065 (Fed. Cir. 2000) (Unclaimed matter that is unrelated to the operation of the claimed invention does not trigger the best mode requirement); *Eli Lilly & Co. v. Barr Laboratories Inc.,* 251 F.3d 955, 966, 58 USPQ2d 1865, 1877 (Fed. Cir. 2001) ("[P]atentee's failure to disclose an unclaimed preferred mode for accomplishing a routine detail does not violate the best mode requirement because one skilled in the art is aware of alternative means for accomplishing the routine detail that would still produce the best mode of the claimed invention.").

## II. SPECIFIC EXAMPLE IS NOT REQUIRED

There is no statutory requirement for the disclosure of a specific example—a patent specification is not intended nor required to be a production specification. *In re Gay,* 309 F.2d 768, 135 USPQ 311 (CCPA 1962).

The absence of a specific working example is not necessarily evidence that the best mode has not been disclosed, nor is the presence of one evidence that it has. Best mode may be represented by a preferred range of conditions or group of reactants. *In re Honn,* 364 F.2d 454, 150 USPQ 652 (CCPA 1966).

## III. DESIGNATION AS BEST MODE IS NOT REQUIRED

There is no requirement in the statute that applicants point out which of their embodiments they consider to be their best; that the disclosure includes the best mode contemplated by applicants is enough to satisfy the statute. *Ernsthausen v. Nakayama,* 1 USPQ2d 1539 (Bd. Pat. App. & Inter. 1985).

## IV. UPDATING BEST MODE IS NOT REQUIRED

There is no requirement to update in the context of a foreign priority application under 35 U.S.C. 119, *Standard Oil Co. v. Montedison, S.p.A.,* 494 F.Supp. 370, 206 USPQ 676 (D.Del. 1980) (better catalyst developed between Italian priority and U.S. filing dates), and continuing applications claiming the benefit of an earlier filing date under 35 U.S.C. 120; *Transco Products, Inc. v. Performance Contracting Inc.,* 38 F.3d 551, 32 USPQ2d 1077 (Fed. Cir. 1994) (continuation under former 37 CFR 1.60); *Sylgab Steel and Wire Corp. v. Imoco-Gateway Corp.,* 357 F.Supp. 657, 178 USPQ 22 (N.D. Ill. 1973) (continuation); *Johns-Manville Corp. v. Guardian Industries Corp.,* 586 F. Supp. 1034, 221 USPQ 319 (E.D. Mich. 1983) (continuation and CIP). In the last cited case, the court stated that applicant would have been obliged to disclose an updated refinement if it were essential to the successful practice of the invention *and* it related to amendments to the CIP that were not present in the parent application. In *Carter-Wallace, Inc. v. Riverton Labs., Inc.,* 433 F.2d 1034, 167 USPQ 656 (2d Cir. 1970), the court assumed, but did not decide, that an applicant must update the best mode when filing a CIP application.

## V. DEFECT IN BEST MODE CANNOT BE CURED BY NEW MATTER

If the best mode contemplated by the inventor at the time of filing the application is not disclosed, such a defect cannot be cured by submitting an amendment seeking to put into the specification something required to be there when the patent application was originally filed. *In re Hay,* 534 F.2d 917, 189 USPQ 790 (CCPA 1976).

Any proposed amendment of this type (adding a specific mode of practicing the invention not described in the application as filed) should be treated as new matter. New matter under 35 U.S.C. 132 and 251 should be objected to and coupled with a requirement to cancel the new matter.

**Section 2165.02:**

2165.02 Best Mode Requirement Compared to Enablement Requirement

The best mode requirement is a separate and distinct requirement from the enablement requirement of the first paragraph of 35 U.S.C. 112. *In re Newton,* 414 F.2d 1400, 163 USPQ 34 (CCPA 1969).

The best mode provision of 35 U.S.C. 112 is not directed to a situation where the application fails to set forth any mode—such failure is equivalent to nonenablement. *In re Glass,* 492 F.2d 1228, 181 USPQ 31 (CCPA 1974).

The enablement requirement looks to placing the subject matter of the claims generally in the possession of the public. If, however, the applicant develops specific instrumentalities or techniques which are recognized by the applicant at the time of filing as the best way of carrying out the invention, then the best mode requirement imposes an obligation to disclose that information to the public as well. *Spectra-Physics, Inc. v. Coherent, Inc.,* 827 F.2d 1524, 3 USPQ 2d 1737 (Fed. Cir.), cert. denied, 484 U.S. 954 (1987).

**Section 2165.03:**

2165.03 Requirements for Rejection for Lack of Best Mode

ASSUME BEST MODE IS DISCLOSED UNLESS THERE IS EVIDENCE TO THE CONTRARY

The examiner should assume that the best mode is disclosed in the application, unless evidence is presented that is inconsistent with that assumption. It is extremely rare that a best mode rejection properly would be made in *ex parte* prosecution. The information that is necessary to form the basis for a rejection based on the failure to set forth the best mode is rarely accessible to the examiner, but is generally uncovered during discovery procedures in interference, litigation, or other *inter partes* proceedings.

EXAMINER MUST DETERMINE WHETHER THE INVENTOR KNEW THAT ONE MODE WAS BETTER THAN ANOTHER, AND IF SO, WHETHER THE DISCLOSURE IS ADEQUATE TO ENABLE ONE OF ORDINARY SKILL IN THE ART TO PRACTICE THE BEST MODE

According to the approach used by the court in *Chemcast Corp. v. Arco Industries,* 913 F.2d 923, 16 USPQ2d 1033 (Fed. Cir. 1990), a proper best mode analysis has two components:

(A) Determine whether, at the time the application was filed, the inventor knew of a mode of practicing the claimed invention that the inventor considered to be better than any other. The first component is a subjective inquiry because it focuses on the inventor's state of mind at the time the application was filed. Unless the examiner has evidence that the inventors had information in their possession

(1) at the time the application was filed

(2) that a mode was considered to be better than any others by the inventors, there is no reason to address the second component and there is no proper basis for a best mode rejection. If the facts satisfy the first component, then, and only then, is the following second component analyzed:

(B) Compare what was known in (A) with what was disclosed—is the disclosure adequate to enable one skilled in the art to practice the best mode?

Assessing the adequacy of the disclosure in this regard is largely an objective inquiry that depends on the level of skill in the art. Is the information contained in the specification disclosure sufficient to enable a person skilled in the relevant art to make and use the best mode?

A best mode rejection is proper only when the first inquiry can be answered in the affirmative, and the second inquiry answered in the negative with reasons to support the conclusion that the specification is nonenabling with respect to the best mode.

**Section 2165.04:**

2165.04 Examples of Evidence of Concealment

In determining the adequacy of a best mode disclosure, only evidence of concealment (accidental or intentional) is to be considered. That evidence must tend to show that the *quality* of an applicant's best mode disclosure is so poor as to effectively result in concealment.

## I. EXAMPLES—BEST MODE REQUIREMENT SATISFIED

In one case, even though the inventor had more information in his possession concerning the contemplated best mode than was disclosed (a known computer program), the specification was held to delineate the best mode in a manner sufficient to require only the application of routine skill to produce a workable digital computer program. *In re Sherwood,* 613 F.2d 809, 204 USPQ 537 (CCPA 1980).

In another case, the claimed subject matter was a time controlled thermostat, but the application did not disclose the specific Quartzmatic motor which was used in a commercial embodiment. The Court concluded that failure to disclose the commercial motor did not amount to concealment since similar clock motors were widely available and widely advertised. There was no evidence that the specific Quartzmatic motor was superior except possibly in price. *Honeywell v. Diamond,* 208 USPQ 452 (D.D.C. 1980).

There was held to be no violation of the best mode requirement even though the inventor did not disclose the only mode of calculating the stretch rate for plastic rods that he used because that mode would have been employed by those of ordinary skill in the art at the time the application was filed. *W.L. Gore & Assoc., Inc. v. Garlock Inc.,* 721 F.2d 1540, 220 USPQ 303 (Fed. Cir. 1983).

There was no best mode violation where the patentee failed to disclose in the specification "[k]nown ways to perform a known operation" to practice the claimed invention. "Known ways of performing a known operation cannot be deemed intentionally concealed absent evidence of intent to deliberately withhold that information." *High Concrete Structures Inc. v. New Enter. Stone & Lime Co.,* 377 F.3d 1379, 1384, 71 USPQ2d 1948, 1951 (Fed. Cir. 2004). The unintentional failure to disclose in the specification the use of a crane to support the patented frame in order to carry out the method of loading and tilting the frame was held not to defeat the best mode requirement because one of ordinary skill in the art would understand and use a crane to move heavy loads. Id. "The best mode requirement of [35 U.S.C.] § 112 is not violated by unintentional omission of information that would be readily known to persons in the field of the invention." Id.

There was no best mode violation where there was no evidence that the monoclonal antibodies used by the inventors differed from those obtainable according to the processes described in the specification. It was not disputed that the inventors obtained the antibodies used in the invention by following the procedures in the specification, that these were the inventors' preferred procedures, and that the data reported in the specification was for the antibody that the inventors had actually used. *Scripps Clinic and Research Foundation v. Genentech, Inc.,* 927 F.2d 1565, 18 USPQ 2d 1001 (Fed. Cir. 1991).

Where an organism was created by the insertion of genetic material into a cell obtained from generally available sources, all that was required to satisfy the best mode requirement was an adequate description of the means for carrying out the invention, not deposit of the cells. As to the observation that no scientist could ever duplicate exactly the cell used by applicants, the court observed that the issue is whether the disclosure is adequate, not that an exact duplication is necessary. *Amgen, Inc. v. Chugai Pharmaceutical Co.,* 927 F.2d 1200, 18 USPQ 2d 1016 (Fed. Cir. 1991).

There was held to be no violation of the best mode requirement where the Solicitor argued that concealment could be inferred from the disclosure in a specification that each analog is "surprisingly and unexpectedly more useful than one of the corresponding prostaglandins . . . for at least one of the pharmacological purposes." It was argued that appellant must have had test results to substantiate this statement and this data should have been disclosed. The court concluded that no withholding could be inferred from general statements of increased selectivity and narrower spectrum of potency for these novel analogs, conclusions which could be drawn from the elementary pharmacological testing of the analogs. *In re Bundy,* 642 F.2d 430, 435, 209 USPQ 48, 52 (CCPA 1981).

## II. EXAMPLES—BEST MODE REQUIREMENT NOT SATISFIED

The best mode requirement was held to be violated where inventors of a laser failed to disclose details of their preferred TiCuSil brazing method which were not contained in the prior art and were contrary to criteria for the use of TiCuSil as contained in the literature. *Spectra-Physics, Inc. v. Coherent, Inc.,* 827 F.2d 1524, 3 USPQ 2d 1737 (Fed. Cir. 1987).

The best mode requirement was violated because an inventor failed to disclose whether to use a specific surface treatment that he knew was necessary to the satisfactory performance of his invention, even though how to perform the treatment itself was known in the art. The argument that the best mode requirement may be met solely by reference to what was known in the prior art was rejected as incorrect. *Dana Corp. v. IPC Ltd. Partnership,* 860 F.2d 415, 8 USPQ2d 1692 (Fed. Cir. 1988).

# APPENDIX 31:
# CLAIMS

**Excerpt from Section 112 of the Patent Act:**

The specification shall conclude with one or more claims particularly pointing out and distinctly claiming the subject matter which the applicant regards as his invention.

A claim may be written in independent or, if the nature of the case admits, in dependent or multiple dependent form.

Subject to the following paragraph, a claim in dependent form shall contain a reference to a claim previously set forth and then specify a further limitation of the subject matter claimed. A claim in dependent form shall be construed to incorporate by reference all the limitations of the claim to which it refers.

A claim in multiple dependent form shall contain a reference, in the alternative only, to more than one claim previously set forth and then specify a further limitation of the subject matter claimed. A multiple dependent claim shall not serve as a basis for any other multiple dependent claim. A multiple dependent claim shall be construed to incorporate by reference all the limitations of the particular claim in relation to which it is being considered.

An element in a claim for a combination may be expressed as a means or step for performing a specified function without the recital of structure, material, or acts in support thereof, and such claim shall be construed to cover the corresponding structure, material, or acts described in the specification and equivalents thereof.

**Section 1.75 of Title 37 of the CFR:**

(a) The specification must conclude with a claim particularly pointing out and distinctly claiming the subject matter which the applicant regards as his invention or discovery.

(b) More than one claim may be presented, provided they differ substantially from each other and are not unduly multiplied.

(c) One or more claims may be presented in dependent form, referring back to and further limiting another claim or claims in the same application. Any dependent claim which refers to more than one other claim ("multiple dependent claim") shall refer to such other claims in the alternative only. A multiple dependent claim shall not serve as a basis for any other multiple dependent claim. For fee calculation purposes under § 1.16, a multiple dependent claim will be considered to be that number of claims to which direct reference is made therein. For fee calculation purposes also, any claim depending from a multiple dependent claim will be considered to be that number of claims to which direct reference is made in that multiple dependent claim. In addition to the other filing fees, any original application which is filed with, or is amended to include, multiple dependent claims must have paid therein the fee set forth in § 1.16(j). Claims in dependent form shall be construed to include all the limitations of the claim incorporated by reference into the dependent claim. A multiple dependent claim shall be construed to incorporate by reference all the limitations of each of the particular claims in relation to which it is being considered.

(d)(1) The claim or claims must conform to the invention as set forth in the remainder of the specification and the terms and phrases used in the claims must find clear support or antecedent basis in the description so that the meaning of the terms in the claims may be ascertainable by reference to the description. (See § 1.58(a)).

(2) See §§ 1.141 to 1.146 as to claiming different inventions in one application.

(e) Where the nature of the case admits, as in the case of an improvement, any independent claim should contain in the following order:

(1) A preamble comprising a general description of all the elements or steps of the claimed combination which are conventional or known,

(2) A phrase such as "wherein the improvement comprises," and

(3) Those elements, steps, and/or relationships which constitute that portion of the claimed combination which the applicant considers as the new or improved portion.

(f) If there are several claims, they shall be numbered consecutively in Arabic numerals.

(g) The least restrictive claim should be presented as claim number 1, and all dependent claims should be grouped together with the claim or claims to which they refer to the extent practicable.

(h) The claim or claims must commence on a separate physical sheet or electronic page. Any sheet including a claim or portion of a claim may not contain any other parts of the application or other material.

(i) Where a claim sets forth a plurality of elements or steps, each element or step of the claim should be separated by a line indentation.

**Excerpts from Section 608.01 of the MPEP:**

608.01(m) Form of Claims

The claim or claims must commence on a separate physical sheet or electronic page and should appear after the detailed description of the invention. Any sheet including a claim or portion of a claim may not contain any other parts of the application or other material. While there is no set statutory form for claims, the present Office practice is to insist that each claim must be the object of a sentence starting with "I (or we) claim," "The invention claimed is" (or the equivalent). If, at the time of allowance, the quoted terminology is not present, it is inserted by the Office of Data Management. Each claim begins with a capital letter and ends with a period. Periods may not be used elsewhere in the claims except for abbreviations. See *Fressola v. Manbeck,* 36 USPQ2d 1211 (D.D.C. 1995). Where a claim sets forth a plurality of elements or steps, each element or step of the claim should be separated by a line indentation, 37 CFR 1.75(i).

There may be plural indentations to further segregate subcombinations or related steps. In general, the printed patent copies will follow the format used but printing difficulties or expense may prevent the duplication of unduly complex claim formats.

Reference characters corresponding to elements recited in the detailed description and the drawings may be used in conjunction with the recitation of the same element or group of elements in the claims. The reference characters, however, should be enclosed within parentheses so as to avoid confusion with other numbers or characters which may appear in the claims. The use of reference characters is to be considered as having no effect on the scope of the claims.

Many of the difficulties encountered in the prosecution of patent applications after final rejection may be alleviated if each applicant includes, at the time of filing or no later than the first reply, claims varying from the broadest to which he or she believes he or she is entitled to the most detailed that he or she is willing to accept.

Claims should preferably be arranged in order of scope so that the first claim presented is the least restrictive. All dependent claims should be grouped together with the claim or claims to which they refer to the extent practicable. Where separate species are claimed, the claims of like species should be grouped together where possible. Similarly, product and process claims should be separately grouped. Such arrangements are for the purpose of facilitating classification and examination.

608.01(o) Basis for Claim Terminology in Description

The meaning of every term used in any of the claims should be apparent from the descriptive portion of the specification with clear disclosure as to its import; and in mechanical cases, it should be identified in the descriptive portion of the specification by reference to the drawing, designating the part or parts therein to which the term applies. A term used in the claims may be given a special meaning in the description.

Usually the terminology of the original claims follows the nomenclature of the specification, but sometimes in amending the claims or in adding new claims, new terms are introduced that do not appear in the specification. The use of a confusing variety of terms for the same thing should not be permitted.

New claims and amendments to the claims already in the application should be scrutinized not only for new matter but also for new terminology. While an applicant is not limited to the nomenclature used in the application as filed, he or she should make appropriate amendment of the specification whenever this nomenclature is departed from by amendment of the claims so as to have clear support or antecedent basis in the specification for the new terms appearing in the claims. This is necessary in order to insure certainty in construing the claims in the light of the specification, Ex parte *Kotler,* 1901 C.D. 62, 95 O.G. 2684 (Comm'r Pat. 1901). See 37 CFR 1.75, MPEP § 608.01(i) and § 1302.01. Note that examiners should ensure that the terms and phrases used in claims presented late in prosecution of the application (including claims amended via an examiner's amendment) find clear support or antecedent basis in the description so that the meaning of the terms in the claims may be ascertainable by reference to the description; see 37 CFR 1.75(d)(1). If the examiner determines that the claims presented late in prosecution do not comply with 37 CFR 1.75(d)(1), applicant will be required to make appropriate amendment to the description to provide clear support or antecedent basis for the terms appearing in the claims provided no new matter is introduced.

# APPENDIX 32:
# ABSTRACT OF THE DISCLOSURE

## Section 1.72(b) of Title 37 of the CFR:

(b) A brief abstract of the technical disclosure in the specification must commence on a separate sheet, preferably following the claims, under the heading "Abstract" or "Abstract of the Disclosure." The sheet or sheets presenting the abstract may not include other parts of the application or other material. The abstract in an application filed under 35 U.S.C. 111 may not exceed 150 words in length. The purpose of the abstract is to enable the United States Patent and Trademark Office and the public generally to determine quickly from a cursory inspection the nature and gist of the technical disclosure.

## Section 608.01(b) of the MPEP:

The Office of Patent Application Processing (OPAP) will review all applications filed under 35 U.S.C. 111(a) for compliance with 37 CFR 1.72 and will require an abstract, if one has not been filed. In all other applications which lack an abstract, the examiner in the first Office action should require the submission of an abstract directed to the technical disclosure in the specification. See Form Paragraph 6.12 (below). Applicants may use either "Abstract" or "Abstract of the Disclosure" as a heading.

If the abstract contained in the application does not comply with the guidelines, the examiner should point out the defect to the applicant in the first Office action, or at the earliest point in the prosecution that the defect is noted, and require compliance with the guidelines. Since the abstract of the disclosure has been interpreted to be a part of the specification for the purpose of compliance with paragraph 1 of 35 U.S.C. 112 (*In re Armbruster,* 512 F.2d 676, 678–79, 185 USPQ 152, 154 (CCPA 1975)), it would ordinarily be preferable that the applicant make the necessary changes to the abstract to bring it into compliance with the guidelines.

Replies to such actions requiring either a new abstract or amendment to bring the abstract into compliance with the guidelines should be treated under 37 CFR 1.111(b) practice like any other formal matter. Any submission of a new abstract or amendment to an existing abstract should be carefully reviewed for introduction of new matter, 35 U.S.C. 132, MPEP § 608.04.

Upon passing the application to issue, the examiner should make certain that the abstract is an adequate and clear statement of the contents of the disclosure and generally in line with the guidelines. If the application is otherwise in condition for allowance except that the abstract does not comply with the guidelines, the examiner generally should make any necessary revisions by a formal examiner's amendment after obtaining applicant's authorization (see MPEP § 1302.04 rather than issuing an Ex parte *Quayle* action requiring applicant to make the necessary revisions.

Under current practice, in all instances where the application contains an abstract when sent to issue, the abstract will be printed on the patent.

## GUIDELINES FOR THE PREPARATION OF PATENT ABSTRACTS

A. Background

The Rules of Practice in Patent Cases require that each application for patent include an abstract of the disclosure, 37 CFR 1.72(b).

The content of a patent abstract should be such as to enable the reader thereof, regardless of his or her degree of familiarity with patent documents, to determine quickly from a cursory inspection of the nature and gist of the technical disclosure and should include that which is new in the art to which the invention pertains.

B. Content

A patent abstract is a concise statement of the technical disclosure of the patent and should include that which is new in the art to which the invention pertains.

If the patent is of a basic nature, the entire technical disclosure may be new in the art, and the abstract should be directed to the entire disclosure.

If the patent is in the nature of an improvement in old apparatus, process, product, or composition, the abstract should include the technical disclosure of the improvement.

In certain patents, particularly those for compounds and compositions, wherein the process for making and/or the use thereof are not obvious, the abstract should set forth a process for making and/or a use thereof.

If the new technical disclosure involves modifications or alternatives, the abstract should mention by way of example the preferred modification or alternative.

The abstract should not refer to purported merits or speculative applications of the invention and should not compare the invention with the prior art.

Where applicable, the abstract should include the following: (1) if a machine or apparatus, its organization and operation; (2) if an article, its method of making; (3) if a chemical compound, its identity and use; (4) if a mixture, its ingredients; (5) if a process, the steps. Extensive mechanical and design details of apparatus should not be given.

With regard particularly to chemical patents, for compounds or compositions, the general nature of the compound or composition should be given as well as the use thereof, e.g., "The compounds are of the class of alkyl benzene sulfonyl ureas, useful as oral anti-diabetics." Exemplification of a species could be illustrative of members of the class. For processes, the type reaction, reagents, and process conditions should be stated, generally illustrated by a single example unless variations are necessary.

C. Language and Format

The abstract must commence on a separate sheet, preferably following the claims, under the heading "Abstract" or "Abstract of the Disclosure." The sheet or sheets presenting the abstract may not include other parts of the application or other material. Form paragraph 6.16.01 (below) may be used if the abstract does not commence on a separate sheet. Note that the abstract for a national stage application filed under 35 U.S.C. 371 may be found on the front page of the Patent Cooperation Treaty publication (i.e., pamphlet). See MPEP § 1893.03(e).

The abstract should be in narrative form and generally limited to a single paragraph within the range of 50 to 150 words. The abstract should not exceed 15 lines of text. Abstracts exceeding 15 lines of text should be checked to see that it does not exceed 150 words in length since the space provided for the abstract on the computer tape by the printer is limited. If the abstract cannot be placed on the computer tape because of its excessive length, the application will be returned to the examiner for preparation of a shorter abstract. The form and legal phraseology often used in patent claims, such as "means" and "said," should be avoided. The abstract should sufficiently describe the disclosure to assist readers in deciding whether there is a need for consulting the full patent text for details.

The language should be clear and concise and should not repeat information given in the title. It should avoid using phrases which can be implied, such as, "This disclosure concerns," "The disclosure defined by this invention," "This disclosure describes," etc.

D. Responsibility

Preparation of the abstract is the responsibility of the applicant. Background knowledge of the art and an appreciation of the applicant's contribution to the art are most important in the preparation of the abstract. The review of the abstract for compliance with these guidelines, with any necessary editing and revision on allowance of the application, is the responsibility of the examiner.

E. Sample Abstracts

(1) A heart valve which has an annular valve body defining an orifice and a plurality of struts forming a pair of cages on opposite sides of the orifice. A spherical closure member is captively held within the cages and is moved by blood flow between open and closed positions in check valve fashion. A slight leak or backflow is provided in the closed position by making the orifice slightly larger than the closure member. Blood flow is maximized in the open position of the valve by providing an inwardly convex contour on the orifice-defining surfaces of the body. An annular rib is formed in a channel around the periphery of the valve body to anchor a suture ring used to secure the valve within a heart.

(2) A method for sealing whereby heat is applied to seal, overlapping closure panels of a folding box made from paperboard having an extremely thin coating of moisture-proofing thermoplastic material on opposite surfaces. Heated air is directed at the surfaces to be bonded, the temperature of the air at the point of impact on the surfaces being above the char point of the board. The duration of application of heat is made so brief, by a corresponding high rate of advance of the boxes through the air stream, that the coating on the reverse side of the panels remains substantially non-tacky. The bond is formed immediately after heating within a period of time for any one surface point less than the total time of exposure to heated air of that point. Under such conditions the heat applied to soften the thermoplastic coating is dissipated after completion of the bond by

absorption into the board acting as a heat sink without the need for cooling devices.

(3) Amides are produced by reacting an ester of a carbonized acid with an amine, using as catalyst a dioxide of an alkali metal. The ester is first heated to at least 75°C under a pressure of no more than 500 mm. of mercury to remove moisture and acid gases which would prevent the reaction, and then converted to an amide without heating to initiate the reaction.

# APPENDIX 33:
# DRAWINGS

## SECTION 113 OF THE PATENT ACT

The applicant shall furnish a drawing where necessary for the understanding of the subject matter sought to be patented. When the nature of such subject matter admits of illustration by a drawing and the applicant has not furnished such a drawing, the Director may require its submission within a time period of not less than two months from the sending of a notice thereof. Drawings submitted after the filing date of the application may not be used (i) to overcome any insufficiency of the specification due to lack of an enabling disclosure or otherwise inadequate disclosure therein, or (ii) to supplement the original disclosure thereof for the purpose of interpretation of the scope of any claim.

## SECTIONS 1.74, 1.81, 1.83, 1.84, AND 1.85 OF TITLE 37 OF THE CFR

### Section 1.74:

When there are drawings, there shall be a brief description of the several views of the drawings and the detailed description of the invention shall refer to the different views by specifying the numbers of the figures and to the different parts by use of reference letters or numerals (preferably the latter).

### Section 1.81:

(a) The applicant for a patent is required to furnish a drawing of his or her invention where necessary for the understanding of the subject matter sought to be patented; this drawing, or a high quality copy thereof, must be filed with the application. Since corrections are the responsibility of the applicant, the original drawing(s) should be retained by the applicant for any necessary future correction.

(b) Drawings may include illustrations which facilitate an understanding of the invention (for example, flow sheets in cases of processes, and diagrammatic views).

(c) Whenever the nature of the subject matter sought to be patented admits of illustration by a drawing without its being necessary for the understanding of the subject matter and the applicant has not furnished such a drawing, the examiner will require its submission within a time period of not less than two months from the date of the sending of a notice thereof.

(d) Drawings submitted after the filing date of the application may not be used to overcome any insufficiency of the specification due to lack of an enabling disclosure or otherwise inadequate disclosure therein, or to supplement the original disclosure thereof for the purpose of interpretation of the scope of any claim.

**Section 1.83:**

(a) The drawing in a nonprovisional application must show every feature of the invention specified in the claims. However, conventional features disclosed in the description and claims, where their detailed illustration is not essential for a proper understanding of the invention, should be illustrated in the drawing in the form of a graphical drawing symbol or a labeled representation (e.g., a labeled rectangular box). In addition, tables and sequence listings that are included in the specification are, except for applications filed under 35 U.S.C. 371, not permitted to be included in the drawings.

(b) When the invention consists of an improvement on an old machine the drawing must when possible exhibit, in one or more views, the improved portion itself, disconnected from the old structure, and also in another view, so much only of the old structure as will suffice to show the connection of the invention therewith.

(c) Where the drawings in a nonprovisional application do not comply with the requirements of paragraphs (a) and (b) of this section, the examiner shall require such additional illustration within a time period of not less than two months from the date of the sending of a notice thereof. Such corrections are subject to the requirements of § 1.81(d).

**Section 1.84:**

(a) *Drawings.* There are two acceptable categories for presenting drawings in utility and design patent applications.

    (1) *Black ink.* Black and white drawings are normally required. India ink, or its equivalent that secures solid black lines, must be used for drawings; or

(2) *Color.* On rare occasions, color drawings may be necessary as the only practical medium by which to disclose the subject matter sought to be patented in a utility or design patent application or the subject matter of a statutory invention registration. The color drawings must be of sufficient quality such that all details in the drawings are reproducible in black and white in the printed patent. Color drawings are not permitted in international applications (see PCT Rule 11.13), or in an application, or copy thereof, submitted under the Office electronic filing system. The Office will accept color drawings in utility or design patent applications and statutory invention registrations only after granting a petition filed under this paragraph explaining why the color drawings are necessary. Any such petition must include the following:

(i) The fee set forth in § 1.17(h);

(ii) Three (3) sets of color drawings;

(iii) An amendment to the specification to insert (unless the specification contains or has been previously amended to contain) the following language as the first paragraph of the brief description of the drawings: The patent or application file contains at least one drawing executed in color. Copies of this patent or patent application publication with color drawing(s) will be provided by the Office upon request and payment of the necessary fee.

(b) *Photographs—*

(1) *Black and white.* Photographs, including photocopies of photographs, are not ordinarily permitted in utility and design patent applications. The Office will accept photographs in utility and design patent applications, however, if photographs are the only practicable medium for illustrating the claimed invention. For example, photographs or photomicrographs of: electrophoresis gels, blots (e.g., immunological, Western, Southern, and Northern), autoradiographs, cell cultures (stained and unstained), histological tissue cross sections (stained and unstained), animals, plants, in vivo imaging, thin layer chromatography plates, crystalline structures, and, in a design patent application, ornamental effects, are acceptable. If the subject matter of the application admits of illustration by a drawing, the examiner may require a drawing in place of the photograph. The photographs must be of sufficient quality so that all details in the photographs are reproducible in the printed patent.

(2) *Color photographs.* Color photographs will be accepted in utility and design patent applications if the conditions for accepting color drawings and black and white photographs have been satisfied. See paragraphs (a)(2) and (b)(1) of this section.

(c) *Identification of drawings.* Identifying indicia should be provided, and if provided, should include the title of the invention, inventor's name, and application number, or docket number (if any) if an application number has not been assigned to the application. If this information is provided, it must be placed on the front of each sheet within the top margin. Each drawing sheet submitted after the filing date of an application must be identified as either "Replacement Sheet" or "New Sheet" pursuant to § 1.121(d). If a marked-up copy of any amended drawing figure including annotations indicating the changes made is filed, such marked-up copy must be clearly labeled as "Annotated Sheet" pursuant to § 1.121(d)(1).

(d) *Graphic forms in drawings.* Chemical or mathematical formulae, tables, and waveforms may be submitted as drawings and are subject to the same requirements as drawings. Each chemical or mathematical formula must be labeled as a separate figure, using brackets when necessary, to show that information is properly integrated. Each group of waveforms must be presented as a single figure, using a common vertical axis with time extending along the horizontal axis. Each individual waveform discussed in the specification must be identified with a separate letter designation adjacent to the vertical axis.

(e) *Type of paper.* Drawings submitted to the Office must be made on paper which is flexible, strong, white, smooth, non-shiny, and durable. All sheets must be reasonably free from cracks, creases, and folds. Only one side of the sheet may be used for the drawing. Each sheet must be reasonably free from erasures and must be free from alterations, overwritings, and interlineations. Photographs must be developed on paper meeting the sheet-size requirements of paragraph (f) of this section and the margin requirements of paragraph (g) of this section. See paragraph (b) of this section for other requirements for photographs.

(f) *Size of paper.* All drawing sheets in an application must be the same size. One of the shorter sides of the sheet is regarded as its top. The size of the sheets on which drawings are made must be:

(1) 21.0 cm. by 29.7 cm. (DIN size A4), or

(2) 21.6 cm. by 27.9 cm. (8 1/2 by 11 inches).

(g) *Margins.* The sheets must not contain frames around the sight (i.e., the usable surface), but should have scan target points (i.e., crosshairs) printed on two cater-corner margin corners. Each sheet must include a top margin of at least 2.5 cm. (1 inch), a left side margin of at least 2.5 cm. (1 inch), a right side margin of at least 1.5 cm. (5/8 inch), and a bottom margin of at least 1.0 cm. (3/8 inch), thereby leaving a sight no greater than 17.0 cm. by 26.2 cm. on 21.0 cm. by 29.7 cm. (DIN size A4) drawing sheets, and a sight no greater than 17.6 cm. by 24.4 cm. (6 15/16 by 9 5/8 inches) on 21.6 cm. by 27.9 cm. (8 1/2 by 11 inch) drawing sheets.

(h) *Views.* The drawing must contain as many views as necessary to show the invention. The views may be plan, elevation, section, or perspective views. Detail views of portions of elements, on a larger scale if necessary, may also be used. All views of the drawing must be grouped together and arranged on the sheet(s) without wasting space, preferably in an upright position, clearly separated from one another, and must not be included in the sheets containing the specifications, claims, or abstract. Views must not be connected by projection lines and must not contain center lines. Waveforms of electrical signals may be connected by dashed lines to show the relative timing of the waveforms.

(1) *Exploded views.* Exploded views, with the separated parts embraced by a bracket, to show the relationship or order of assembly of various parts are permissible. When an exploded view is shown in a figure which is on the same sheet as another figure, the exploded view should be placed in brackets.

(2) *Partial views.* When necessary, a view of a large machine or device in its entirety may be broken into partial views on a single sheet, or extended over several sheets if there is no loss in facility of understanding the view. Partial views drawn on separate sheets must always be capable of being linked edge to edge so that no partial view contains parts of another partial view. A smaller scale view should be included showing the whole formed by the partial views and indicating the positions of the parts shown. When a portion of a view is enlarged for magnification purposes, the view and the enlarged view must each be labeled as separate views.

(i) Where views on two or more sheets form, in effect, a single complete view, the views on the several sheets must be so arranged that the complete figure can be assembled without concealing any part of any of the views appearing on the various sheets.

(ii) A very long view may be divided into several parts placed one above the other on a single sheet. However, the relationship between the different parts must be clear and unambiguous.

(3) *Sectional views.* The plane upon which a sectional view is taken should be indicated on the view from which the section is cut by a broken line. The ends of the broken line should be designated by Arabic or Roman numerals corresponding to the view number of the sectional view and should have arrows to indicate the direction of sight. Hatching must be used to indicate section portions of an object and must be made by regularly spaced oblique parallel lines spaced sufficiently apart to enable the lines to be distinguished without difficulty. Hatching should not impede the clear reading of the reference characters and lead lines. If it is not possible to place reference characters outside the hatched area, the hatching may be broken off wherever reference characters are inserted. Hatching must be at a substantial angle to the surrounding axes or principal lines, preferably $45°$. A cross section must be set out and drawn to show all of the materials as they are shown in the view from which the cross section was taken. The parts in cross section must show proper material(s) by hatching with regularly spaced parallel oblique strokes, the space between strokes being chosen on the basis of the total area to be hatched. The various parts of a cross section of the same item should be hatched in the same manner and should accurately and graphically indicate the nature of the material(s) that is illustrated in the cross section. The hatching of juxtaposed different elements must be angled in a different way. In the case of large areas, hatching may be confined to an edging drawn around the entire inside of the outline of the area to be hatched. Different types of hatching should have different conventional meanings as regards the nature of a material seen in cross section.

(4) *Alternate position.* A moved position may be shown by a broken line superimposed upon a suitable view if this can be done without crowding; otherwise, a separate view must be used for this purpose.

(5) *Modified forms.* Modified forms of construction must be shown in separate views.

(i) *Arrangement of views.* One view must not be placed upon another or within the outline of another. All views on the same sheet should stand in the same direction and, if possible, stand so that they can be read with the sheet held in an upright position. If views wider than the width of the sheet are necessary for the clearest illustration of the invention, the sheet may be turned on its side so that the top of the sheet, with the appropriate top margin to be used as the heading space, is on the right-hand side. Words must appear in a horizontal, left-to-right fashion when the page is either upright or turned so that the top becomes the right side, except for graphs utilizing standard scientific convention to denote the axis of abscissas (of X) and the axis of ordinates (of Y).

(j) *Front page view.* The drawing must contain as many views as necessary to show the invention. One of the views should be suitable for inclusion on the front page of the patent application publication and patent as the illustration of the invention. Views must not be connected by projection lines and must not contain center lines. Applicant may suggest a single view (by figure number) for inclusion on the front page of the patent application publication and patent.

(k) *Scale.* The scale to which a drawing is made must be large enough to show the mechanism without crowding when the drawing is reduced in size to two-thirds in reproduction. Indications such as "actual size" or "scale 1/2" on the drawings are not permitted since these lose their meaning with reproduction in a different format.

(l) *Character of lines, numbers, and letters.* All drawings must be made by a process which will give them satisfactory reproduction characteristics. Every line, number, and letter must be durable, clean, black (except for color drawings), sufficiently dense and dark, and uniformly thick and well defined. The weight of all lines and letters must be heavy enough to permit adequate reproduction. This requirement applies to all lines however fine, to shading, and to lines representing cut surfaces in sectional views. Lines and strokes of different thicknesses may be used in the same drawing where different thicknesses have a different meaning.

(m) *Shading.* The use of shading in views is encouraged if it aids in understanding the invention and if it does not reduce legibility. Shading is used to indicate the surface or shape of spherical, cylindrical, and conical elements of an object. Flat parts may also be lightly shaded. Such shading is preferred in the case of parts shown in perspective, but not for cross sections. See paragraph (h)(3) of this section. Spaced lines for shading are preferred. These lines must be thin, as few in number as practicable, and must contrast with the rest of the drawings. As a substitute for shading, heavy lines on the shade side of objects can be used except where they superimpose on each other or obscure reference characters. Light should come from the upper left corner at an angle of 45°. Surface delineations should preferably be shown by proper shading. Solid black shading areas are not permitted, except when used to represent bar graphs or color.

(n) *Symbols.* Graphical drawing symbols may be used for conventional elements when appropriate. The elements for which such symbols and labeled representations are used must be adequately identified in the specification. Known devices should be illustrated by symbols which have a universally recognized conventional meaning and are generally accepted in the art. Other symbols which are not universally recognized may be used, subject to approval by the Office, if they are not likely to be confused with existing conventional symbols and if they are readily identifiable.

(o) *Legends.* Suitable descriptive legends may be used subject to approval by the Office, or may be required by the examiner where necessary for understanding of the drawing. They should contain as few words as possible.

(p) *Numbers, letters, and reference characters.*

(1) Reference characters (numerals are preferred), sheet numbers, and view numbers must be plain and legible, and must not be used in association with brackets or inverted commas, or enclosed within outlines, e.g., encircled. They must be oriented in the same direction as the view so as to avoid having to rotate the sheet. Reference characters should be arranged to follow the profile of the object depicted.

(2) The English alphabet must be used for letters, except where another alphabet is customarily used, such as the Greek alphabet to indicate angles, wavelengths, and mathematical formulas.

(3) Numbers, letters, and reference characters must measure at least .32 cm. (1/8 inch) in height. They should not be placed in the drawing so as to interfere with its comprehension. Therefore, they should not cross or mingle with the lines. They should not be placed upon hatched or shaded surfaces. When necessary, such as indicating a surface or cross section, a reference character may be underlined and a blank space may be left in the hatching or shading where the character occurs so that it appears distinct.

(4) The same part of an invention appearing in more than one view of the drawing must always be designated by the same

reference character, and the same reference character must never be used to designate different parts.

(5) Reference characters not mentioned in the description shall not appear in the drawings. Reference characters mentioned in the description must appear in the drawings.

(q) *Lead lines.* Lead lines are those lines between the reference characters and the details referred to. Such lines may be straight or curved and should be as short as possible. They must originate in the immediate proximity of the reference character and extend to the feature indicated. Lead lines must not cross each other. Lead lines are required for each reference character except for those which indicate the surface or cross section on which they are placed. Such a reference character must be underlined to make it clear that a lead line has not been left out by mistake. Lead lines must be executed in the same way as lines in the drawing. See paragraph (1) of this section.

(r) *Arrows.* Arrows may be used at the ends of lines, provided that their meaning is clear, as follows:

(1) On a lead line, a freestanding arrow to indicate the entire section towards which it points;

(2) On a lead line, an arrow touching a line to indicate the surface shown by the line looking along the direction of the arrow; or

(3) To show the direction of movement.

(s) *Copyright or Mask Work Notice.* A copyright or mask work notice may appear in the drawing, but must be placed within the sight of the drawing immediately below the figure representing the copyright or mask work material and be limited to letters having a print size of 32 cm. to 64 cm. (1/8 to 1/4 inches) high. The content of the notice must be limited to only those elements provided for by law. For example, "©1983 John Doe" (17 U.S.C. 401) and "*M* John Doe" (17 U.S.C. 909) would be properly limited and, under current statutes, legally sufficient notices of copyright and mask work, respectively. Inclusion of a copyright or mask work notice will be permitted only if the authorization language set forth in § 1.71(e) is included at the beginning (preferably as the first paragraph) of the specification.

(t) *Numbering of sheets of drawings.* The sheets of drawings should be numbered in consecutive Arabic numerals, starting with 1, within the sight as defined in paragraph (g) of this section. These numbers, if present, must be placed in the middle of the top of the sheet, but not in the margin. The numbers can be placed on the right-hand side if the drawing extends too close to the middle of the top edge of the usable surface. The drawing sheet numbering must be clear and larger than the numbers used as reference characters to avoid confusion. The number of each sheet should be shown by two Arabic numerals placed on either side of an oblique line, with the first being the sheet number and the second being the total number of sheets of drawings, with no other marking.

(u) *Numbering of views.*

(1) The different views must be numbered in consecutive Arabic numerals, starting with 1, independent of the numbering of the sheets and, if possible, in the order in which they appear on the drawing sheet(s). Partial views intended to form one complete view, on one or several sheets, must be identified by the same number followed by a capital letter. View numbers must be preceded by the abbreviation "FIG." Where only a single view is used in an application to illustrate the claimed invention, it must not be numbered and the abbreviation "FIG." must not appear.

(2) Numbers and letters identifying the views must be simple and clear and must not be used in association with brackets, circles, or inverted commas. The view numbers must be larger than the numbers used for reference characters.

(v) *Security markings.* Authorized security markings may be placed on the drawings provided they are outside the sight, preferably centered in the top margin.

(w) *Corrections.* Any corrections on drawings submitted to the Office must be durable and permanent.

(x) *Holes.* No holes should be made by applicant in the drawing sheets.

(y) *Types of drawings.* See § 1.152 for design drawings, § 1.165 for plant drawings, and § 1.173(a)(2) for reissue drawings.

## Section 1.85:

(a) A utility or plant application will not be placed on the files for examination until objections to the drawings have been corrected. Except as provided in § 1.215(c), any patent application publication will not include drawings filed after the application has been placed on the files for examination. Unless applicant is otherwise notified in an Office action, objections to the drawings in a utility or plant application will not be held in abeyance, and a request to hold objections to the drawings in abeyance will not be considered a *bona fide* attempt to advance the application to final action (§ 1.135(c)). If a drawing in a design application meets the requirements of § 1.84(e), (f), and (g) and is suitable for reproduction, but is not otherwise in compliance with § 1.84, the drawing may be admitted for examination.

(b) The Office will not release drawings for purposes of correction. If corrections are necessary, new corrected drawings must be submitted within the time set by the Office.

(c) If a corrected drawing is required or if a drawing does not comply with § 1.84 at the time an application is allowed, the Office may notify the applicant and set a three-month period of time from the mail date of the notice of allowability within which the applicant must file a corrected drawing in compliance with § 1.84 to avoid abandonment. This time period is not extendable under § 1.136(a) or § 1.136(b).

# APPENDIX 34:
# INVENTORS; OATH OR DECLARATION

## SECTIONS 115–118 OF THE PATENT ACT

### Section 115:

The applicant shall make oath that he believes himself to be the original and first inventor of the process, machine, manufacture, or composition of matter, or improvement thereof, for which he solicits a patent; and shall state of what country he is a citizen. Such oath may be made before any person within the United States authorized by law to administer oaths, or, when made in a foreign country, before any diplomatic or consular officer of the United States authorized to administer oaths, or before any officer having an official seal and authorized to administer oaths in the foreign country in which the applicant may be, whose authority is proved by certificate of a diplomatic or consular officer of the United States, or apostille of an official designated by a foreign country which, by treaty or convention, accords like effect to apostilles of designated officials in the United States. Such oath is valid if it complies with the laws of the state or country where made. When the application is made as provided in this title by a person other than the inventor, the oath may be so varied in form that it can be made by him. For purposes of this section, a consular officer shall include any United States citizen serving overseas, authorized to perform notarial functions pursuant to section 1750 of the Revised Statutes, as amended (22 U.S.C. 4221).

### Section 116:

When an invention is made by two or more persons jointly, they shall apply for patent jointly and each make the required oath, except as otherwise provided in this title. Inventors may apply for a patent jointly even though (1) they did not physically work together or at the same time, (2) each did not make the same type or amount of contribution, or (3) each did not make a contribution to the subject matter of every claim of the patent.

If a joint inventor refuses to join in an application for patent or cannot be found or reached after diligent effort, the application may be made by the other inventor on behalf of himself and the omitted inventor. The Director, on proof of the pertinent facts and after such notice to the omitted inventor as he prescribes, may grant a patent to the inventor making the application, subject to the same rights which the omitted inventor would have had if he had been joined. The omitted inventor may subsequently join in the application.

Whenever through error a person is named in an application for patent as the inventor, or through an error an inventor is not named in an application, and such error arose without any deceptive intention on his part, the Director may permit the application to be amended accordingly, under such terms as he prescribes.

Section 117:

Legal representatives of deceased inventors and of those under legal incapacity may make application for patent upon compliance with the requirements and on the same terms and conditions applicable to the inventor.

Section 118:

Whenever an inventor refuses to execute an application for patent, or cannot be found or reached after diligent effort, a person to whom the inventor has assigned or agreed in writing to assign the invention or who otherwise shows sufficient proprietary interest in the matter justifying such action, may make application for patent on behalf of and as agent for the inventor on proof of the pertinent facts and a showing that such action is necessary to preserve the rights of the parties or to prevent irreparable damage; and the Director may grant a patent to such inventor upon such notice to him as the Director deems sufficient, and on compliance with such regulations as he prescribes.

## SECTIONS 1.47 AND 1.48 OF TITLE 37 OF THE CFR

Section 1.47:

(a) If a joint inventor refuses to join in an application for patent or cannot be found or reached after diligent effort, the application may be made by the other inventor on behalf of himself or herself and the nonsigning inventor. The oath or declaration in such an application must be accompanied by a petition including proof of the pertinent facts, the fee set forth in § 1.17(g), and the last known address of the nonsigning inventor. The nonsigning inventor may subsequently join in the application by filing an oath or declaration complying with § 1.63.

(b) Whenever all of the inventors refuse to execute an application for patent, or cannot be found or reached after diligent effort, a person to whom an inventor has assigned or agreed in writing to assign the invention, or who otherwise shows sufficient proprietary interest in the matter justifying such action, may make application for patent on behalf of and as agent for all the inventors. The oath or declaration in such an application must be accompanied by a petition including proof of the pertinent facts, a showing that such action is necessary to preserve the rights of the parties or to prevent irreparable damage, the fee set forth in § 1.17(g), and the last known address of all of the inventors. An inventor may subsequently join in the application by filing an oath or declaration complying with § 1.63.

(c) The Office will send notice of the filing of the application to all inventors who have not joined in the application at the address(es) provided in the petition under this section, and publish notice of the filing of the application in the *Official Gazette.* The Office may dispense with this notice provision in a continuation or divisional application, if notice regarding the filing of the prior application was given to the nonsigning inventor(s).

## Section 1.48:

(a) *Nonprovisional application after oath/declaration filed.* If the inventive entity is set forth in error in an executed § 1.63 oath or declaration in a nonprovisional application, and such error arose without any deceptive intention on the part of the person named as an inventor in error or on the part of the person who through error was not named as an inventor, the inventorship of the nonprovisional application may be amended to name only the actual inventor or inventors. Amendment of the inventorship requires:

(1) A request to correct the inventorship that sets forth the desired inventorship change;

(2) A statement from each person being added as an inventor and from each person being deleted as an inventor that the error in inventorship occurred without deceptive intention on his or her part;

(3) An oath or declaration by the actual inventor or inventors as required by § 1.63 or as permitted by §§ 1.42, 1.43, or § 1.47;

(4) The processing fee set forth in § 1.17(i); and

(5) If an assignment has been executed by any of the original named inventors, the written consent of the assignee (see § 3.73(b) of this chapter).

(b) *Nonprovisional application—fewer inventors due to amendment or cancellation of claims.* If the correct inventors are named in a nonprovisional application, and the prosecution of the nonprovisional application results in the amendment or cancellation of claims so that fewer than all of the currently named inventors are the actual inventors of the invention being claimed in the nonprovisional application, an amendment must be filed requesting deletion of the name or names of the person or persons who are not inventors of the invention being claimed. Amendment of the inventorship requires:

(1) A request, signed by a party set forth in § 1.33(b), to correct the inventorship that identifies the named inventor or inventors being deleted and acknowledges that the inventor's invention is no longer being claimed in the nonprovisional application; and

(2) The processing fee set forth in § 1.17(i).

(c) *Nonprovisional application—inventors added for claims to previously unclaimed subject matter.* If a nonprovisional application discloses unclaimed subject matter by an inventor or inventors not named in the application, the application may be amended to add claims to the subject matter and name the correct inventors for the application. Amendment of the inventorship requires:

(1) A request to correct the inventorship that sets forth the desired inventorship change;

(2) A statement from each person being added as an inventor that the addition is necessitated by amendment of the claims and that the inventorship error occurred without deceptive intention on his or her part;

(3) An oath or declaration by the actual inventors as required by § 1.63 or as permitted by §§ 1.42, 1.43, or § 1.47;

(4) The processing fee set forth in § 1.17(i); and

(5) If an assignment has been executed by any of the original named inventors, the written consent of the assignee (see § 3.73(b) of this chapter).

(d) *Provisional application—adding omitted inventors.* If the name or names of an inventor or inventors were omitted in a provisional application through error without any deceptive intention on the part of the omitted inventor or inventors, the provisional application may be amended to add the name or names of the omitted inventor or inventors. Amendment of the inventorship requires:

(1) A request, signed by a party set forth in § 1.33(b), to correct the inventorship that identifies the inventor or inventors being added and states that the inventorship error occurred without deceptive intention on the part of the omitted inventor or inventors; and

(2) The processing fee set forth in § 1.17(q).

(e) *Provisional application—deleting the name or names of the inventor or inventors.* If a person or persons were named as an inventor or inventors in a provisional application through error without any deceptive intention on the part of such person or persons, an amendment may be filed in the provisional application deleting the name or names of the person or persons who were erroneously named. Amendment of the inventorship requires:

(1) A request to correct the inventorship that sets forth the desired inventorship change;

(2) A statement by the person or persons whose name or names are being deleted that the inventorship error occurred without deceptive intention on the part of such person or persons;

(3) The processing fee set forth in § 1.17(q); and

(4) If an assignment has been executed by any of the original named inventors, the written consent of the assignee (see § 3.73(b) of this chapter).

(f)(1) *Nonprovisional application—filing executed oath/declaration corrects inventorship.* If the correct inventor or inventors are not named on filing a nonprovisional application under § 1.53(b) without an executed oath or declaration under § 1.63 by any of the inventors, the first submission of an executed oath or declaration under § 1.63 by any of the inventors during the pendency of the application will act to correct the earlier identification of inventorship. See §§ 1.41(a) (4) and 1.497(d) and (f) for submission of an executed oath or declaration to enter the national stage under 35 U.S.C. 371 naming an inventive entity different from the inventive entity set forth in the international stage.

(2) *Provisional application filing cover sheet corrects inventorship.* If the correct inventor or inventors are not named on filing a provisional application without a cover sheet under § 1.51(c)(1), the later submission of a cover sheet under § 1.51(c)(1) during the pendency of the application will act to correct the earlier identification of inventorship.

(g) *Additional information may be required.* The Office may require such other information as may be deemed appropriate under the particular circumstances surrounding the correction of inventorship.

(h) *Reissue applications not covered.* The provisions of this section do not apply to reissue applications. See §§ 1.171 and 1.175 for correction of inventorship in a patent via a reissue application.

(i) *Correction of inventorship in patent.* See § 1.324 for correction of inventorship in a patent.

(j) *Correction of inventorship in a contested case before the Board of Patent Appeals and Interferences.*

In a contested case under part 41, subpart D, of this title, a request for correction of an application must be in the form of a motion under § 41.121(a)(2) of this title and must comply with the requirements of this section.

# APPENDIX 35:
# DECLARATION FORMS

Doc Code: Oath
Document Description: Oath or declaration filed

PTO/SB/01 (04-09)
Approved for use through 06/30/2010. OMB 0651-0032
U.S. Patent and Trademark Office; U.S. DEPARTMENT OF COMMERCE
Under the Paperwork Reduction Act of 1995, no persons are required to respond to a collection of information unless it contains a valid OMB control number.

| **DECLARATION FOR UTILITY OR DESIGN PATENT APPLICATION (37 CFR 1.63)** | Attorney Docket Number | |
|---|---|---|
| | First Named Inventor | |
| | *COMPLETE IF KNOWN* | |
| ☐ Declaration Submitted With Initial Filing  **OR**  ☐ Declaration Submitted After Initial Filing (surcharge (37 CFR 1.16(f)) required) | Application Number | |
| | Filing Date | |
| | Art Unit | |
| | Examiner Name | |

I hereby declare that: (1) Each inventor's residence, mailing address, and citizenship are as stated below next to their name; and (2) I believe the inventor(s) named below to be the original and first inventor(s) of the subject matter which is claimed and for which a patent is sought on the invention titled:

*(Title of the Invention)*

the application of which

☐ is attached hereto

OR

☐ was filed on (MM/DD/YYYY)_____ as United States Application Number or PCT International

Application Number _____ and was amended on (MM/DD/YYYY)_____ (if applicable).

I hereby state that I have reviewed and understand the contents of the above identified application, including the claims, as amended by any amendment specifically referred to above.

I acknowledge the duty to disclose information which is material to patentability as defined in 37 CFR 1.56, including for continuation-in-part applications, material information which became available between the filing date of the prior application and the national or PCT international filing date of the continuation-in-part application.

## Authorization To Permit Access To Application by Participating Offices

☐ If checked, the undersigned hereby grants the USPTO authority to provide the European Patent Office (EPO), the Japan Patent Office (JPO), the Korean Intellectual Property Office (KIPO), the World Intellectual Property Office (WIPO), and any other intellectual property offices in which a foreign application claiming priority to the above-identified patent application is filed access to the above-identified patent application. See 37 CFR 1.14(c) and (h). This box should not be checked if the applicant does not wish the EPO, JPO, KIPO, WIPO, or other intellectual property office in which a foreign application claiming priority to the above-identified patent application is filed to have access to the above-identified patent application.

In accordance with 37 CFR 1.14(h)(3), access will be provided to a copy of the above-identified patent application with respect to: 1) the above-identified patent application-as-filed; 2) any foreign application to which the above-identified patent application claims priority under 35 U.S.C. 119(a)-(d) if a copy of the foreign application that satisfies the certified copy requirement of 37 CFR 1.55 has been filed in the above-identified patent application; and 3) any U.S. application-as-filed from which benefit is sought in the above-identified patent application.

In accordance with 37 CFR 1.14(c), access may be provided to information concerning the date of filing the Authorization to Permit Access to Application by Participating Offices.

[Page 1 of 3]

PTO/SB/01 (04-09)
Approved for use through 06/30/2010. OMB 0651-0032
U.S. Patent and Trademark Office; U.S. DEPARTMENT OF COMMERCE
Under the Paperwork Reduction Act of 1995, no persons are required to respond to a collection of information unless it contains a valid OMB control number.

## DECLARATION — Utility or Design Patent Application

### Claim of Foreign Priority Benefits

I hereby claim foreign priority benefits under 35 U.S.C. 119(a)-(d) or (f), or 365(b) of any foreign application(s) for patent, inventor's or plant breeder's rights certificate(s), or 365(a) of any PCT international application which designated at least one country other than the United States of America, listed below and have also identified below, by checking the box, any foreign application for patent, inventor's or plant breeder's rights certificate(s), or any PCT international application having a filing date before that of the application on which priority is claimed.

| Prior Foreign Application Number(s) | Country | Foreign Filing Date (MM/DD/YYYY) | Priority Not Claimed | Certified Copy Attached? YES | NO |
|---|---|---|---|---|---|
| | | | ☐ | ☐ | ☐ |
| | | | ☐ | ☐ | ☐ |
| | | | ☐ | ☐ | ☐ |
| | | | ☐ | ☐ | ☐ |

☐ Additional foreign application number(s) are listed on a supplemental priority data sheet PTO/SB/02B attached hereto.

[Page 2 of 3]

PTO/SB/01 (04-09)
Approved for use through 06/30/2010. OMB 0651-0032
U.S. Patent and Trademark Office; U.S. DEPARTMENT OF COMMERCE
Under the Paperwork Reduction Act of 1995, no persons are required to respond to a collection of information unless it contains a valid OMB control number.

## DECLARATION — Utility or Design Patent Application

| Direct all correspondence to: | ☐ | The address associated with Customer Number: | | OR | ☐ | Correspondence address below |
|---|---|---|---|---|---|---|

| Name |
|---|
| |

| Address |
|---|
| |

| City | State | Zip |
|---|---|---|
| | | |

| Country | Telephone | Email |
|---|---|---|
| | | |

### WARNING:

Petitioner/applicant is cautioned to avoid submitting personal information in documents filed in a patent application that may contribute to identity theft. Personal information such as social security numbers, bank account numbers, or credit card numbers (other than a check or credit card authorization form PTO-2038 submitted for payment purposes) is never required by the USPTO to support a petition or an application. If this type of personal information is included in documents submitted to the USPTO, petitioners/applicants should consider redacting such personal information from the documents before submitting them to the USPTO. Petitioner/applicant is advised that the record of a patent application is available to the public after publication of the application (unless a non-publication request in compliance with 37 CFR 1.213(a) is made in the application) or issuance of a patent. Furthermore, the record from an abandoned application may also be available to the public if the application is referenced in a published application or an issued patent (see 37 CFR 1.14). Checks and credit card authorization forms PTO-2038 submitted for payment purposes are not retained in the application file and therefore are not publicly available. Petitioner/applicant is advised that documents which form the record of a patent application (such as the PTO/SB/01) are placed into the Privacy Act system of records DEPARTMENT OF COMMERCE, COMMERCE-PAT-7, System name: *Patent Application Files*. Documents not retained in an application file (such as the PTO-2038) are placed into the Privacy Act system of COMMERCE/PAT-TM-10, System name: *Deposit Accounts and Electronic Funds Transfer Profiles*.

I hereby declare that all statements made herein of my own knowledge are true and that all statements made on information and belief are believed to be true; and further that these statements were made with the knowledge that willful false statements and the like so made are punishable by fine or imprisonment, or both, under 18 U.S.C. 1001 and that such willful false statements may jeopardize the validity of the application or any patent issued thereon.

| NAME OF SOLE OR FIRST INVENTOR: | ☐ A petition has been filed for this unsigned inventor | |
|---|---|---|
| Given Name (first and middle [if any]) | Family Name or Surname | |

| Inventor's Signature | Date |
|---|---|
| | |

| Residence: City | State | Country | Citizenship |
|---|---|---|---|
| | | | |

| Mailing Address |
|---|
| |

| City | State | Zip | Country |
|---|---|---|---|
| | | | |

☐ Additional inventors or a legal representative are being named on the _____ supplemental sheet(s) PTO/SB/02A or 02LR attached hereto

[Page 3 of 3]

# Privacy Act Statement

**The Privacy Act of 1974 (P.L. 93-579)** requires that you be given certain information in connection with your submission of the attached form related to a patent application or patent. Accordingly, pursuant to the requirements of the Act, please be advised that: (1) the general authority for the collection of this information is 35 U.S.C. 2(b)(2); (2) furnishing of the information solicited is voluntary; and (3) the principal purpose for which the information is used by the U.S. Patent and Trademark Office is to process and/or examine your submission related to a patent application or patent. If you do not furnish the requested information, the U.S. Patent and Trademark Office may not be able to process and/or examine your submission, which may result in termination of proceedings or abandonment of the application or expiration of the patent.

The information provided by you in this form will be subject to the following routine uses:

1. The information on this form will be treated confidentially to the extent allowed under the Freedom of Information Act (5 U.S.C. 552) and the Privacy Act (5 U.S.C 552a). Records from this system of records may be disclosed to the Department of Justice to determine whether disclosure of these records is required by the Freedom of Information Act.
2. A record from this system of records may be disclosed, as a routine use, in the course of presenting evidence to a court, magistrate, or administrative tribunal, including disclosures to opposing counsel in the course of settlement negotiations.
3. A record in this system of records may be disclosed, as a routine use, to a Member of Congress submitting a request involving an individual, to whom the record pertains, when the individual has requested assistance from the Member with respect to the subject matter of the record.
4. A record in this system of records may be disclosed, as a routine use, to a contractor of the Agency having need for the information in order to perform a contract. Recipients of information shall be required to comply with the requirements of the Privacy Act of 1974, as amended, pursuant to 5 U.S.C. 552a(m).
5. A record related to an International Application filed under the Patent Cooperation Treaty in this system of records may be disclosed, as a routine use, to the International Bureau of the World Intellectual Property Organization, pursuant to the Patent Cooperation Treaty.
6. A record in this system of records may be disclosed, as a routine use, to another federal agency for purposes of National Security review (35 U.S.C. 181) and for review pursuant to the Atomic Energy Act (42 U.S.C. 218(c)).
7. A record from this system of records may be disclosed, as a routine use, to the Administrator, General Services, or his/her designee, during an inspection of records conducted by GSA as part of that agency's responsibility to recommend improvements in records management practices and programs, under authority of 44 U.S.C. 2904 and 2906. Such disclosure shall be made in accordance with the GSA regulations governing inspection of records for this purpose, and any other relevant (i.e., GSA or Commerce) directive. Such disclosure shall not be used to make determinations about individuals.
8. A record from this system of records may be disclosed, as a routine use, to the public after either publication of the application pursuant to 35 U.S.C. 122(b) or issuance of a patent pursuant to 35 U.S.C. 151. Further, a record may be disclosed, subject to the limitations of 37 CFR 1.14, as a routine use, to the public if the record was filed in an application which became abandoned or in which the proceedings were terminated and which application is referenced by either a published application, an application open to public inspection or an issued patent.
9. A record from this system of records may be disclosed, as a routine use, to a Federal, State, or local law enforcement agency, if the USPTO becomes aware of a violation or potential violation of law or regulation.

PTO/SB/01A (01-09)
Approved for use through 06/30/2010.  OMB 0651-0032
U.S. Patent and Trademark Office; U.S. DEPARTMENT OF COMMERCE
Under the Paperwork Reduction Act of 1995, no persons are required to respond to a collection of information unless it displays a valid OMB control number.

## DECLARATION (37 CFR 1.63) FOR UTILITY OR DESIGN APPLICATION USING AN APPLICATION DATA SHEET (37 CFR 1.76)

| Title of Invention | |
|---|---|

As the below named inventor(s), I/we declare that:

This declaration is directed to:

☐ The attached application, or

☐ Application No. _____ filed on _____

☐ As amended on _____ (if applicable);

I/we believe that I/we am/are the original and first inventor(s) of the subject matter which is claimed and for which a patent is sought;

I/we have reviewed and understand the contents of the above-identified application, including the claims, as amended by any amendment specifically referred to above;

I/we acknowledge the duty to disclose to the United States Patent and Trademark Office all information known to me/us to be material to patentability as defined in 37 CFR 1.56, including for continuation-in-part applications, material information which became available between the filing date of the prior application and the national or PCT International filing date of the continuation-in-part application.

### WARNING:

Petitioner/applicant is cautioned to avoid submitting personal information in documents filed in a patent application that may contribute to identity theft.  Personal information such as social security numbers, bank account numbers, or credit card numbers (other than a check or credit card authorization form PTO-2038 submitted for payment purposes) is never required by the USPTO to support a petition or an application.  If this type of personal information is included in documents submitted to the USPTO, petitioners/applicants should consider redacting such personal information from the documents before submitting them to the USPTO.  Petitioner/applicant is advised that the record of a patent application is available to the public after publication of the application (unless a non-publication request in compliance with 37 CFR 1.213(a) is made in the application)  or issuance of a patent.  Furthermore, the record from an abandoned application may also be available to the public if the  application is referenced in a published application or an issued patent (see 37 CFR  1.14).  Checks and credit card  authorization forms PTO-2038 submitted for payment purposes are not retained in the application file and therefore are not  publicly available.

All statements made herein of my/our own knowledge are true, all statements made herein on information and belief are believed to be true, and further that these statements were made with the knowledge that willful false statements and the like are  punishable by fine or imprisonment, or both, under 18 U.S.C. 1001, and may jeopardize the validity of the application or any patent issuing thereon.

FULL NAME OF INVENTOR(S)

Inventor one: _____ Date: _____

Signature: _____ Citizen of: _____

Inventor two: _____ Date: _____

Signature: _____ Citizen of: _____

☐ Additional inventors or a legal representative are being named on _____ additional form(s) attached hereto.

## Privacy Act Statement

The **Privacy Act of 1974 (P.L. 93-579)** requires that you be given certain information in connection with your submission of the attached form related to a patent application or patent. Accordingly, pursuant to the requirements of the Act, please be advised that: (1) the general authority for the collection of this information is 35 U.S.C. 2(b)(2); (2) furnishing of the information solicited is voluntary; and (3) the principal purpose for which the information is used by the U.S. Patent and Trademark Office is to process and/or examine your submission related to a patent application or patent. If you do not furnish the requested information, the U.S. Patent and Trademark Office may not be able to process and/or examine your submission, which may result in termination of proceedings or abandonment of the application or expiration of the patent.

The information provided by you in this form will be subject to the following routine uses:

1. The information on this form will be treated confidentially to the extent allowed under the Freedom of Information Act (5 U.S.C. 552) and the Privacy Act (5 U.S.C 552a). Records from this system of records may be disclosed to the Department of Justice to determine whether disclosure of these records is required by the Freedom of Information Act.
2. A record from this system of records may be disclosed, as a routine use, in the course of presenting evidence to a court, magistrate, or administrative tribunal, including disclosures to opposing counsel in the course of settlement negotiations.
3. A record in this system of records may be disclosed, as a routine use, to a Member of Congress submitting a request involving an individual, to whom the record pertains, when the individual has requested assistance from the Member with respect to the subject matter of the record.
4. A record in this system of records may be disclosed, as a routine use, to a contractor of the Agency having need for the information in order to perform a contract. Recipients of information shall be required to comply with the requirements of the Privacy Act of 1974, as amended, pursuant to 5 U.S.C. 552a(m).
5. A record related to an International Application filed under the Patent Cooperation Treaty in this system of records may be disclosed, as a routine use, to the International Bureau of the World Intellectual Property Organization, pursuant to the Patent Cooperation Treaty.
6. A record in this system of records may be disclosed, as a routine use, to another federal agency for purposes of National Security review (35 U.S.C. 181) and for review pursuant to the Atomic Energy Act (42 U.S.C. 218(c)).
7. A record from this system of records may be disclosed, as a routine use, to the Administrator, General Services, or his/her designee, during an inspection of records conducted by GSA as part of that agency's responsibility to recommend improvements in records management practices and programs, under authority of 44 U.S.C. 2904 and 2906. Such disclosure shall be made in accordance with the GSA regulations governing inspection of records for this purpose, and any other relevant (*i.e.*, GSA or Commerce) directive. Such disclosure shall not be used to make determinations about individuals.
8. A record from this system of records may be disclosed, as a routine use, to the public after either publication of the application pursuant to 35 U.S.C. 122(b) or issuance of a patent pursuant to 35 U.S.C. 151. Further, a record may be disclosed, subject to the limitations of 37 CFR 1.14, as a routine use, to the public if the record was filed in an application which became abandoned or in which the proceedings were terminated and which application is referenced by either a published application, an application open to public inspection or an issued patent.
9. A record from this system of records may be disclosed, as a routine use, to a Federal, State, or local law enforcement agency, if the USPTO becomes aware of a violation or potential violation of law or regulation.

# APPENDIX 36:
# MODELS, SPECIMENS, AND EXHIBITS

### SECTION 114 OF THE PATENT ACT

The Director may require the applicant to furnish a model of convenient size to exhibit advantageously the several parts of his invention.

When the invention relates to a composition of matter, the Director may require the applicant to furnish specimens or ingredients for the purpose of inspection or experiment.

### SECTIONS 1.91 AND 1.94 OF TITLE 37 OF THE CFR

**Section 1.91:**

(a) A model or exhibit will not be admitted as part of the record of an application unless it:

(1) Substantially conforms to the requirements of § 1.52 or § 1.84;

(2) Is specifically required by the Office; or

(3) Is filed with a petition under this section including:

(i) The fee set forth in § 1.17(h); and

(ii) An explanation of why entry of the model or exhibit in the file record is necessary to demonstrate patentability.

(b) Notwithstanding the provisions of paragraph (a) of this section, a model, working model, or other physical exhibit may be required by the Office if deemed necessary for any purpose in examination of the application.

(c) Unless the model or exhibit substantially conforms to the requirements of § 1.52 or § 1.84 under paragraph (a)(1) of this section, it must be accompanied by photographs that show multiple views of the material features of the model or exhibit and that substantially conform to the requirements of § 1.84.

**Section 1.94:**

(a) Models, exhibits, or specimens may be returned to the applicant if no longer necessary for the conduct of business before the Office. When applicant is notified that a model, exhibit, or specimen is no longer necessary for the conduct of business before the Office and will be returned, applicant must arrange for the return of the model, exhibit, or specimen at the applicant's expense. The Office will dispose of perishables without notice to applicant unless applicant notifies the Office upon submission of the model, exhibit, or specimen that a return is desired and makes arrangements for its return promptly upon notification by the Office that the model, exhibit, or specimen is no longer necessary for the conduct of business before the Office.

(b) Applicant is responsible for retaining the actual model, exhibit, or specimen for the enforceable life of any patent resulting from the application. The provisions of this paragraph do not apply to a model or exhibit that substantially conforms to the requirements of § 1.52 or § 1.84, where the model or exhibit has been described by photographs that substantially conform to § 1.84, or where the model, exhibit, or specimen is perishable.

(c) Where applicant is notified, pursuant to paragraph (a) of this section, of the need to arrange for return of a model, exhibit or specimen, applicant must arrange for the return within the period set in such notice, to avoid disposal of the model, exhibit, or specimen by the Office. Extensions of time are available under § 1.136, except in the case of perishables. Failure to establish that the return of the item has been arranged for within the period set or failure to have the item removed from Office storage within a reasonable amount of time notwithstanding any arrangement for return, will permit the Office to dispose of the model, exhibit, or specimen.

# APPENDIX 37:
# POWER OF ATTORNEY

PTO/SB/81 (01-09)
Approved for use through 11/30/2011. OMB 0651-0035
U.S. Patent and Trademark Office; U.S. DEPARTMENT OF COMMERCE
Under the Paperwork Reduction Act of 1995, no persons are required to respond to a collection of information unless it displays a valid OMB control number.

| POWER OF ATTORNEY OR REVOCATION OF POWER OF ATTORNEY WITH A NEW POWER OF ATTORNEY AND CHANGE OF CORRESPONDENCE ADDRESS | |
|---|---|
| | Application Number | |
| | Filing Date | |
| | First Named Inventor | |
| | Title | |
| | Art Unit | |
| | Examiner Name | |
| | Attorney Docket Number | |

I hereby revoke all previous powers of attorney given in the above-identified application.

☐ A Power of Attorney is submitted herewith.

OR

☐ I hereby appoint Practitioner(s) associated with the following Customer Number as my/our attorney(s) or agent(s) to prosecute the application identified above, and to transact all business in the United States Patent and Trademark Office connected therewith:

OR

☐ I hereby appoint Practitioner(s) named below as my/our attorney(s) or agent(s) to prosecute the application identified above, and to transact all business in the United States Patent and Trademark Office connected therewith:

| Practitioner(s) Name | Registration Number |
|---|---|
| | |
| | |
| | |

Please recognize or change the correspondence address for the above-identified application to:

☐ The address associated with the above-mentioned Customer Number.

OR

☐ The address associated with Customer Number:

OR

| Firm or Individual Name | |
|---|---|
| Address | |
| City | | State | | Zip | |
| Country | |
| Telephone | | Email | |

I am the:

☐ Applicant/Inventor.

OR

☐ Assignee of record of the entire interest. See 37 CFR 3.71.
Statement under 37 CFR 3.73(b) (Form PTO/SB/96) submitted herewith or filed on _____.

### SIGNATURE of Applicant or Assignee of Record

| Signature | | Date | |
|---|---|---|---|
| Name | | Telephone | |
| Title and Company | |

NOTE: Signatures of all the inventors or assignees of record of the entire interest or their representative(s) are required. Submit multiple forms if more than one signature is required, see below*.

☐ *Total of _____ forms are submitted.

This collection of information is required by 37 CFR 1.31, 1.32 and 1.33. The information is required to obtain or retain a benefit by the public which is to file (and by the USPTO to process) an application. Confidentiality is governed by 35 U.S.C. 122 and 37 CFR 1.11 and 1.14. This collection is estimated to take 3 minutes to complete, including gathering, preparing, and submitting the completed application form to the USPTO. Time will vary depending upon the individual case. Any comments on the amount of time you require to complete this form and/or suggestions for reducing this burden, should be sent to the Chief Information Officer, U.S. Patent and Trademark Office, U.S. Department of Commerce, P.O. Box 1450, Alexandria, VA 22313-1450. DO NOT SEND FEES OR COMPLETED FORMS TO THIS ADDRESS. **SEND TO: Commissioner for Patents, P.O. Box 1450, Alexandria, VA 22313-1450.**

*If you need assistance in completing the form, call 1-800-PTO-9199 and select option 2.*

# Privacy Act Statement

**The Privacy Act of 1974 (P.L. 93-579)** requires that you be given certain information in connection with your submission of the attached form related to a patent application or patent. Accordingly, pursuant to the requirements of the Act, please be advised that: (1) the general authority for the collection of this information is 35 U.S.C. 2(b)(2); (2) furnishing of the information solicited is voluntary; and (3) the principal purpose for which the information is used by the U.S. Patent and Trademark Office is to process and/or examine your submission related to a patent application or patent. If you do not furnish the requested information, the U.S. Patent and Trademark Office may not be able to process and/or examine your submission, which may result in termination of proceedings or abandonment of the application or expiration of the patent.

The information provided by you in this form will be subject to the following routine uses:

1. The information on this form will be treated confidentially to the extent allowed under the Freedom of Information Act (5 U.S.C. 552) and the Privacy Act (5 U.S.C. 552a). Records from this system of records may be disclosed to the Department of Justice to determine whether disclosure of these records is required by the Freedom of Information Act.
2. A record from this system of records may be disclosed, as a routine use, in the course of presenting evidence to a court, magistrate, or administrative tribunal, including disclosures to opposing counsel in the course of settlement negotiations.
3. A record in this system of records may be disclosed, as a routine use, to a Member of Congress submitting a request involving an individual, to whom the record pertains, when the individual has requested assistance from the Member with respect to the subject matter of the record.
4. A record in this system of records may be disclosed, as a routine use, to a contractor of the Agency having need for the information in order to perform a contract. Recipients of information shall be required to comply with the requirements of the Privacy Act of 1974, as amended, pursuant to 5 U.S.C. 552a(m).
5. A record related to an International Application filed under the Patent Cooperation Treaty in this system of records may be disclosed, as a routine use, to the International Bureau of the World Intellectual Property Organization, pursuant to the Patent Cooperation Treaty.
6. A record in this system of records may be disclosed, as a routine use, to another federal agency for purposes of National Security review (35 U.S.C. 181) and for review pursuant to the Atomic Energy Act (42 U.S.C. 218(c)).
7. A record from this system of records may be disclosed, as a routine use, to the Administrator, General Services, or his/her designee, during an inspection of records conducted by GSA as part of that agency's responsibility to recommend improvements in records management practices and programs, under authority of 44 U.S.C. 2904 and 2906. Such disclosure shall be made in accordance with the GSA regulations governing inspection of records for this purpose, and any other relevant (i.e., GSA or Commerce) directive. Such disclosure shall not be used to make determinations about individuals.
8. A record from this system of records may be disclosed, as a routine use, to the public after either publication of the application pursuant to 35 U.S.C. 122(b) or issuance of a patent pursuant to 35 U.S.C. 151. Further, a record may be disclosed, subject to the limitations of 37 CFR 1.14, as a routine use, to the public if the record was filed in an application which became abandoned or in which the proceedings were terminated and which application is referenced by either a published application, an application open to public inspection or an issued patent.
9. A record from this system of records may be disclosed, as a routine use, to a Federal, State, or local law enforcement agency, if the USPTO becomes aware of a violation or potential violation of law or regulation.

# APPENDIX 38:
# RIGHT OF PRIORITY

## SECTION 119 OF THE PATENT ACT

(a) An application for patent for an invention filed in this country by any person who has, or whose legal representatives or assigns have, previously regularly filed an application for a patent for the same invention in a foreign country which affords similar privileges in the case of applications filed in the United States or to citizens of the United States, or in a WTO member country, shall have the same effect as the same application would have if filed in this country on the date on which the application for patent for the same invention was first filed in such foreign country, if the application in this country is filed within 12 months from the earliest date on which such foreign application was filed; but no patent shall be granted on any application for patent for an invention which had been patented or described in a printed publication in any country more than one year before the date of the actual filing of the application in this country, or which had been in public use or on sale in this country more than one year prior to such filing.

(b)(1) No application for patent shall be entitled to this right of priority unless a claim is filed in the Patent and Trademark Office, identifying the foreign application by specifying the application number on that foreign application, the intellectual property authority or country in or for which the application was filed, and the date of filing the application, at such time during the pendency of the application as required by the Director.

(2) The Director may consider the failure of the applicant to file a timely claim for priority as a waiver of any such claim. The Director may establish procedures, including the payment of a surcharge, to accept an unintentionally delayed claim under this section.

(3) The Director may require a certified copy of the original foreign application, specification, and drawings upon which it is based, a translation if not in the English language, and such other information as the Director considers necessary. Any such certification shall be made by the foreign intellectual property authority in which the foreign application was filed and show the date of the application and of the filing of the specification and other papers.

(c) In like manner and subject to the same conditions and requirements, the right provided in this section may be based upon a subsequent regularly filed application in the same foreign country instead of the first filed foreign application, provided that any foreign application filed prior to such subsequent application has been withdrawn, abandoned, or otherwise disposed of, without having been laid open to public inspection and without leaving any rights outstanding, and has not served, nor thereafter shall serve, as a basis for claiming a right of priority.

(d) Applications for inventors' certificates filed in a foreign country in which applicants have a right to apply, at their discretion, either for a patent or for an inventor's certificate shall be treated in this country in the same manner and have the same effect for purpose of the right of priority under this section as applications for patents, subject to the same conditions and requirements of this section as apply to applications for patents, provided such applicants are entitled to the benefits of the Stockholm Revision of the Paris Convention at the time of such filing.

(e)(1) An application for patent filed under section 111(a) or section 363 of this title for an invention disclosed in the manner provided by the first paragraph of section 112 of this title in a provisional application filed under section 111(b) of this title, by an inventor or inventors named in the provisional application, shall have the same effect, as to such invention, as though filed on the date of the provisional application filed under section 111(b) of this title, if the application for patent filed under section 111(a) or section 363 of this title is filed not later than 12 months after the date on which the provisional application was filed and if it contains or is amended to contain a specific reference to the provisional application. No application shall be entitled to the benefit of an earlier filed provisional application under this subsection unless an amendment containing the specific reference to the earlier filed provisional application is submitted at such time during the pendency of the application as required by the Director. The Director may consider the failure to submit such an amendment within that time period as a waiver of any benefit under this subsection. The Director may establish procedures, including the payment of a surcharge, to accept an unintentionally delayed submission of an amendment under this subsection during the pendency of the application

(2) A provisional application filed under section 111(b) of this title may not be relied upon in any proceeding in the Patent and Trademark Office unless the fee set forth in subparagraph (A) or (C) of section 41(a)(1) of this title has been paid.

(3) If the day that is 12 months after the filing date of a provisional application falls on a Saturday, Sunday, or Federal holiday within the District of Columbia, the period of pendency of the provisional application shall be extended to the next succeeding secular or business day.

(f) Applications for plant breeder's rights filed in a WTO member country (or in a foreign UPOV Contracting Party) shall have the same effect for the purpose of the right of priority under subsections (a) through (c) of this section as applications for patents, subject to the same conditions and requirements of this section as apply to applications for patents.

(g) As used in this section—

(1) the term "WTO member country" has the same meaning as the term is defined in section 104(b)(2) of this title; and

(2) the term "UPOV Contracting Party" means a member of the International Convention for the Protection of New Varieties of Plants.

### SECTION 365 OF THE PATENT ACT

(a) In accordance with the conditions and requirements of subsections (a) through (d) of section 119 of this title, a national application shall be entitled to the right of priority based on a prior filed international application which designated at least one country other than the United States.

(b) In accordance with the conditions and requirements of section 119(a) of this title and the treaty and the Regulations, an international application designating the United States shall be entitled to the right of priority based on a prior foreign application, or a prior international application designating at least one country other than the United States.

(c) In accordance with the conditions and requirements of section 120 of this title, an international application designating the United States shall be entitled to the benefit of the filing date of a prior national application or a prior international application designating the United States, and a national application shall be entitled to the benefit of the filing date of a prior international application designating the United States. If any claim for the benefit of an earlier filing date is based on a prior international application which designated but did not originate in the United States, the Director may require the filing in the Patent and Trademark Office of a certified copy of such application together with a translation thereof into the English language, if it was filed in another language.

### SECTION 1.78 OF TITLE 37 OF THE CFR

(a)(1) A nonprovisional application or international application designating the United States of America may claim an invention disclosed in one or more prior-filed copending nonprovisional applications or international applications designating the United States of America. In order for an application to claim the benefit of a prior-filed copending nonprovisional application or international application designating the United States of America, each prior-filed application must name as an inventor at least one inventor named in the later-filed application and disclose the named inventor's invention claimed in at least one claim of the later-filed application in the manner provided by the first paragraph of 35 U.S.C. 112. In addition, each prior-filed application must be:

(i) An international application entitled to a filing date in accordance with PCT Article 11 and designating the United States of America; or

(ii) Entitled to a filing date as set forth in § 1.53(b) or § 1.53(d) and have paid therein the basic filing fee set forth in § 1.16 within the pendency of the application.

(2)(i) Except for a continued prosecution application filed under § 1.53(d), any nonprovisional application or international application designating the United States of America claiming the benefit of one or more prior-filed copending nonprovisional applications or international applications designating the United States of America must contain or be amended to contain a reference to each such prior-filed application, identifying it by application number (consisting of the series code and serial number) or international application number and international filing date and indicating the relationship of the applications. Cross references to other related applications may be made when appropriate (see § 1.14).

(ii) This reference must be submitted during the pendency of the later-filed application. If the later-filed application is an application filed under 35 U.S.C. 111(a), this reference must also be submitted within the later of four months from the actual filing date of the later-filed application or sixteen months from the filing date of the prior-filed application. If the later-filed application is a nonprovisional application which entered the national stage from an international application after compliance with 35 U.S.C. 371, this reference must also be submitted within the later of four months from the date on which the national stage commenced under 35 U.S.C. 371 (b) or (f) in the later-filed international application or sixteen months from the filing date of the prior-filed application. These time periods are not extendable. Except as provided in paragraph (a)(3) of this section, the failure to timely submit the reference required by 35 U.S.C. 120 and paragraph (a)(2)(i) of this section is considered a waiver of any benefit under 35 U.S.C. 120, 121, or 365(c) to such prior-filed application. The time periods in this paragraph do not apply if the later-filed application is:

(A) An application for a design patent;

(B) An application filed under 35 U.S.C. 111 (a) before November 29, 2000; or

(C) A nonprovisional application which entered the national stage after compliance with 35 U.S.C. 371 from an international application filed under 35 U.S.C. 363 before November 29, 2000.

(iii) If the later-filed application is a nonprovisional application, the reference required by this paragraph must be included in an application data sheet (§ 1.76), or the specification must contain or be amended to contain such reference in the first sentence(s) following the title.

(iv) The request for a continued prosecution application under § 1.53(d) is the specific reference required by 35 U.S.C. 120 to the prior-filed application. The identification of an application by application number under this section is the identification of every application assigned that application number necessary for a specific reference required by 35 U.S.C. 120 to every such application assigned that application number.

(3) If the reference required by 35 U.S.C. 120 and paragraph (a)(2) of this section is presented after the time period provided by paragraph (a)(2)(ii) of this section, the claim under 35 U.S.C. 120, 121, or 365(c) for the benefit of a prior-filed copending nonprovisional application or international application designating the United States of America may be accepted if the reference identifying the prior-filed application by application number or international application number and international filing date was unintentionally delayed. A petition to accept an unintentionally delayed claim under 35 U.S.C. 120, 121, or 365(c) for the benefit of a prior-filed application must be accompanied by:

(i) The reference required by 35 U.S.C. 120 and paragraph (a)(2) of this section to the prior filed application, unless previously submitted;

(ii) The surcharge set forth in § 1.17(t); and

(iii) A statement that the entire delay between the date the claim was due under paragraph

(a)(2)(ii) of this section and the date the claim was filed was unintentional. The Director may require additional information where there is a question whether the delay was unintentional.

(4) A nonprovisional application, other than for a design patent, or an international application designating the United States of America may claim an invention disclosed in one or more prior-filed provisional applications. In order for an application to claim the benefit of one or more prior-filed provisional applications, each prior-filed provisional application must name as an inventor at least one inventor named in the later-filed application and disclose the named inventor's invention claimed in at least one claim of the later-filed application in the manner provided by the first paragraph of 35 U.S.C. 112. In addition, each prior-filed provisional application must be entitled to a filing date as set forth in § 1.53(c), and the basic filing fee set forth in § 1.16(d) must be paid within the time period set forth in § 1.53(g).

(5)(i) Any nonprovisional application or international application designating the United States of America claiming the benefit of one or more prior filed provisional applications must contain or be amended to contain a reference to each such prior filed provisional application, identifying it by the provisional application number (consisting of series code and serial number).

(ii) This reference must be submitted during the pendency of the later-filed application. If the later-filed application is an application filed under 35 U.S.C. 111(a), this reference must also be submitted within the later of four months from the actual filing date of the later-filed application or sixteen months from the filing date of the prior-filed provisional application. If the later-filed application is a nonprovisional application which entered the national stage from an international patent application after compliance with 35 U.S.C. 371, this reference must also be submitted within the later of four months from the date on which the national stage commenced under 35 U.S.C. 371(b) or (f) in the later-filed international application or sixteen months from the filing date of the prior-filed provisional application. These time periods are not extendable. Except as provided in paragraph(a)(6) of this section, the failure to timely submit the reference is considered a waiver of any benefit under 35 U.S.C. 119(e) to such prior-filed provisional application. The time periods in this paragraph do not apply if the later-filed application is:

(A) An application filed under 35 U.S.C. 111(a) before November 29, 2000; or

(B) A nonprovisional application which entered the national stage after compliance with 35 U.S.C. 371 from an international application filed under 35 U.S.C. 363 before November 29, 2000.

(iii) If the later-filed application is a nonprovisional application, the reference required by this paragraph must be included in an application data sheet (§ 1.76), or the specification must contain or be amended to contain such reference in the first sentence(s) following the title.

(iv) If the prior-filed provisional application was filed in a language other than English and both an English-language translation of the prior-filed provisional application and a statement that the translation is accurate were not previously filed in the prior-filed provisional application, applicant will be notified and given a period of time within which to file, in the prior-filed provisional application, the translation and the statement. If the notice is mailed in a pending nonprovisional application, a timely reply to such a notice must include the filing in the nonprovisional application of either a confirmation that the translation and statement were filed in the provisional application, or an amendment or Supplemental Application Data Sheet withdrawing the benefit claim, or the nonprovisional application will be abandoned. The translation and statement may be filed in the provisional application, even if the provisional application has become abandoned.

(6) If the reference required by 35 U.S.C. 119(e) and paragraph (a)(5) of this section is presented in a nonprovisional application after the time period provided by paragraph (a)(5)(ii) of this section, the claim under 35 U.S.C. 119(e) for the benefit of a prior-filed provisional application may be accepted during the pendency of the later-filed application if the reference identifying the prior-filed application by provisional application number was unintentionally delayed. A petition to accept an unintentionally delayed claim under 35 U.S.C. 119(e) for the benefit of a prior-filed provisional application must be accompanied by:

(i) The reference required by 35 U.S.C. 119(e) and paragraph (a) (5) of this section to the prior-filed provisional application, unless previously submitted;

(ii) The surcharge set forth in § 1.17(t); and

(iii) A statement that the entire delay between the date the claim was due under paragraph

(a)(5)(ii) of this section and the date the claim was filed was unintentional. The Director may require additional information where there is a question whether the delay was unintentional.

(b) Where two or more applications filed by the same applicant contain conflicting claims, elimination of such claims from all but one application may be required in the absence of good and sufficient reason for their retention during pendency in more than one application.

(c) If an application or a patent under reexamination and at least one other application naming different inventors are owned by the same person and contain conflicting claims, and there is no statement of record indicating that the claimed inventions were commonly owned or subject to an obligation of assignment to the same person at the time the later invention was made, the Office may require the assignee to state whether the claimed inventions were commonly owned or subject to an obligation of assignment to the same person at the time the later invention was made, and if not, indicate which named inventor is the prior inventor. Even if the claimed inventions were commonly owned, or subject to an obligation of assignment to the same person, at the time the later invention was made, the conflicting claims may be rejected under the doctrine of double patenting in view of such commonly owned or assigned applications or patents under reexamination.

# APPENDIX 39:
# MAILING AND RECEIPT OF DOCUMENTS

### SECTION 21 OF THE PATENT ACT

(a) The Director may by rule prescribe that any paper or fee required to be filed in the Patent and Trademark Office will be considered filed in the Office on the date on which it was deposited with the United States Postal Service or would have been deposited with the United States Postal Service but for postal service interruptions or emergencies designated by the Director.

(b) When the day, or the last day, for taking any action or paying any fee in the United States Patent and Trademark Office falls on Saturday, Sunday, or a Federal holiday within the District of Columbia, the action may be taken, or fee paid, on the next succeeding secular or business day.

### SECTION 1.6 OF TITLE 37 OF THE CFR

(a) *Date of receipt and Express Mail date of deposit.* Correspondence received in the Patent and Trademark Office is stamped with the date of receipt except as follows:

(1) The Patent and Trademark Office is not open for the filing of correspondence on any day that is a Saturday, Sunday, or Federal holiday within the District of Columbia. Except for correspondence transmitted by facsimile under paragraph (a)(3) of this section, or filed electronically under paragraph (a)(4) of this section, no correspondence is received in the Office on Saturdays, Sundays, or Federal holidays within the District of Columbia.

(2) Correspondence filed in accordance with § 1.10 will be stamped with the date of deposit as "Express Mail" with the United States Postal Service.

(3) Correspondence transmitted by facsimile to the Patent and Trademark Office will be stamped with the date on which the complete transmission is received in the Patent and Trademark Office unless that date is a Saturday, Sunday, or Federal holiday within the District of Columbia, in which case the date stamped will be the next succeeding day which is not a Saturday, Sunday, or Federal holiday within the District of Columbia.

(4) Correspondence may be submitted using the Office electronic filing system only in accordance with the Office electronic filing system requirements. Correspondence submitted to the Office by way of the Office electronic filing system will be accorded a receipt date, which is the date the correspondence is received at the correspondence address for the Office set forth in § 1.1 when it was officially submitted.

(b) [Reserved]

(c) *Correspondence delivered by hand.* In addition to being mailed, correspondence may be delivered by hand during hours the Office is open to receive correspondence.

(d) *Facsimile transmission.* Except in the cases enumerated below, correspondence, including authorizations to charge a deposit account, may be transmitted by facsimile. The receipt date accorded to the correspondence will be the date on which the complete transmission is received in the United States Patent and Trademark Office, unless that date is a Saturday, Sunday, or Federal holiday within the District of Columbia. See § 1.6(a)(3). To facilitate proper processing, each transmission session should be limited to correspondence to be filed in a single application or other proceeding before the United States Patent and Trademark Office. The application number of a patent application, the control number of a reexamination proceeding, the interference number of an interference proceeding, or the patent number of a patent should be entered as a part of the sender's identification on a facsimile cover sheet. Facsimile transmissions are not permitted and, if submitted, will not be accorded a date of receipt in the following situations:

(1) Correspondence as specified in § 1.4(e), requiring an original signature;

(2) Certified documents as specified in § 1.4(f);

(3) Correspondence which cannot receive the benefit of the certificate of mailing or transmission as specified in § 1.8(a)(2)(i)(A) through (D) and (F), and § 1.8(a)(2)(iii)(A), except that a continued

prosecution application under § 1.53(d) may be transmitted to the Office by facsimile;

(4) Color drawings submitted under §§ 1.81, 1.83 through 1.85, 1.152, 1.165, 1.173, or 1.437;

(5) A request for reexamination under § 1.510 or § 1.913;

(6) Correspondence to be filed in a patent application subject to a secrecy order under §§ 5.1 through 5.5 of this chapter and directly related to the secrecy order content of the application;

(7) [Reserved]

(8) [Reserved]

(9) In contested cases before the Board of Patent Appeals and Interferences except as the Board may expressly authorize.

(e) [Reserved]

(f) *Facsimile transmission of a patent application under § 1.53(d).* In the event that the Office has no evidence of receipt of an application under § 1.53(d) (a continued prosecution application) transmitted to the Office by facsimile transmission, the party who transmitted the application under § 1.53(d) may petition the Director to accord the application under § 1.53(d) a filing date as of the date the application under § 1.53(d) is shown to have been transmitted to and received in the Office,

(1) Provided that the party who transmitted such application under § 1.53(d):

(i) Informs the Office of the previous transmission of the application under § 1.53(d) promptly after becoming aware that the Office has no evidence of receipt of the application under § 1.53(d);

(ii) Supplies an additional copy of the previously transmitted application under § 1.53(d); and

(iii) Includes a statement which attests on a personal knowledge basis or to the satisfaction of the Director to the previous transmission of the application under § 1.53(d) and is accompanied by a copy of the sending unit's report confirming transmission of the application under § 1.53(d) or evidence that came into being after the complete transmission and within one business day of the complete transmission of the application under § 1.53(d).

(2) The Office may require additional evidence to determine if the application under § 1.53(d) was transmitted to and received in the Office on the date in question.

(g) *Submission of the national stage correspondence required by § 1.495 via the Office electronic filing system.* In the event that the Office has no evidence of receipt of the national stage correspondence required by § 1.495, which was submitted to the Office by the Office electronic filing system, the party who submitted the correspondence may petition the Director to accord the national stage correspondence a receipt date as of the date the correspondence is shown to have been officially submitted to the Office.

(1) The petition of this paragraph (g) requires that the party who submitted such national stage correspondence:

(i) Informs the Office of the previous submission of the correspondence promptly after becoming aware that the Office has no evidence of receipt of the correspondence under § 1.495;

(ii) Supplies an additional copy of the previously submitted correspondence;

(iii) Includes a statement that attests on a personal knowledge basis, or to the satisfaction of the Director, that the correspondence was previously officially submitted; and

(iv) Supplies a copy of an acknowledgment receipt generated by the Office electronic filing system, or equivalent evidence, confirming the submission to support the statement of paragraph (g)(1)(iii) of this section.

(2) The Office may require additional evidence to determine if the national stage correspondence was submitted to the Office on the date in question.

### SECTION 1.10 OF TITLE 37 OF THE CFR

(a)(1)Any correspondence received by the U.S. Patent and Trademark Office (USPTO) that was delivered by the "Express Mail Post Office to Addressee" service of the United States Postal Service (USPS) will be considered filed with the USPTO on the date of deposit with the USPS.

(2) The date of deposit with USPS is shown by the "date in" on the "Express Mail" label or other official USPS notation. If the USPS deposit date cannot be determined, the correspondence will be accorded the USPTO receipt date as the filing date. See § 1.6(a).

(b) Correspondence should be deposited directly with an employee of the USPS to ensure that the person depositing the correspondence receives a legible copy of the "Express Mail" mailing label with the "date-in" clearly marked. Persons dealing indirectly with the employees of the USPS (such as by deposit in an "Express Mail" drop box) do so at the risk of not receiving a copy of the "Express Mail" mailing label with the desired "date-in" clearly marked. The paper(s) or fee(s) that constitute the correspondence should also include the "Express Mail" mailing label number thereon. See paragraphs (c), (d), and (e) of this section.

(c) Any person filing correspondence under this section that was received by the Office and delivered by the "Express Mail Post Office to Addressee" service of the USPS, who can show that there is a discrepancy between the filing date accorded by the Office to the correspondence and the date of deposit as shown by the "date-in" on the "Express Mail" mailing label or other official USPS notation, may petition the Director to accord the correspondence a filing date as of the "date-in" on the "Express Mail" mailing label or other official USPS notation, provided that:

(1) The petition is filed promptly after the person becomes aware that the Office has accorded, or will accord, a filing date other than the USPS deposit date;

(2) The number of the "Express Mail" mailing label was placed on the paper(s) or fee(s) that constitute the correspondence prior to the original mailing by "Express Mail"; and

(3) The petition includes a true copy of the "Express Mail" mailing label showing the "date-in," and of any other official notation by the USPS relied upon to show the date of deposit.

(d) Any person filing correspondence under this section that was received by the Office and delivered by the "Express Mail Post Office to Addressee" service of the USPS, who can show that the "date-in" on the "Express Mail" mailing label or other official notation entered by the USPS was incorrectly entered or omitted by the USPS, may petition the Director to accord the correspondence a filing date as of the date the correspondence is shown to have been deposited with the USPS, provided that:

(1) The petition is filed promptly after the person becomes aware that the Office has accorded, or will accord, a filing date based upon an incorrect entry by the USPS;

(2) The number of the "Express Mail" mailing label was placed on the paper(s) or fee(s) that constitute the correspondence prior to the original mailing by "Express Mail"; and

(3) The petition includes a showing which establishes, to the satisfaction of the Director, that the requested filing date was the date the correspondence was deposited in the "Express Mail Post Office to Addressee" service prior to the last scheduled pickup for that day. Any showing pursuant to this paragraph must be corroborated by evidence from the USPS or that came into being after deposit and within one business day of the deposit of the correspondence in the "Express Mail Post Office to Addressee" service of the USPS.

(e) Any person mailing correspondence addressed as set out in § 1.1(a) to the Office with sufficient postage utilizing the "Express Mail Post Office to Addressee" service of the USPS but not received by the Office, may petition the Director to consider such correspondence filed in the Office on the USPS deposit date, provided that:

(1) The petition is filed promptly after the person becomes aware that the Office has no evidence of receipt of the correspondence;

(2) The number of the "Express Mail" mailing label was placed on the paper(s) or fee(s) that constitute the correspondence prior to the original mailing by "Express Mail";

(3) The petition includes a copy of the originally deposited paper(s) or fee(s) that constitute the correspondence showing the number of the "Express Mail" mailing label thereon, a copy of any returned postcard receipt, a copy of the "Express Mail" mailing label showing the "date-in," a copy of any other official notation by the USPS relied upon to show the date of deposit, and, if the requested filing date is a date other than the "date-in" on the "Express Mail" mailing label or other official notation entered by the USPS, a showing pursuant to paragraph (d)(3) of this section that the requested filing date was the date the correspondence was deposited in the "Express Mail Post Office to Addressee" service prior to the last scheduled pickup for that day; and

(4) The petition includes a statement which establishes, to the satisfaction of the Director, the original deposit of the correspondence and that the copies of the correspondence, the copy of the "Express Mail" mailing label, the copy of any returned postcard receipt, and any official notation entered by the USPS are true copies of the originally mailed correspondence, original "Express Mail"

mailing label, returned postcard receipt, and official notation entered by the USPS.

(f) The Office may require additional evidence to determine if the correspondence was deposited as "Express Mail" with the USPS on the date in question.

(g) Any person who mails correspondence addressed as set out in § 1.1 (a) to the Office with sufficient postage utilizing the "Express Mail Post Office to Addressee" service of the USPS, but has the correspondence returned by the USPS due to an interruption or emergency in "Express Mail" service, may petition the Director to consider such correspondence as filed on a particular date in the Office, provided that:

(1) The petition is filed promptly after the person becomes aware of the return of the correspondence;

(2) The number of the "Express Mail" mailing label was placed on the paper(s) or fee(s) that constitute the correspondence prior to the original mailing by "Express Mail";

(3) The petition includes the original correspondence or a copy of the original correspondence showing the number of the "Express Mail" mailing label thereon and a copy of the "Express Mail" mailing label showing the "date-in"; and

(4) The petition includes a statement which establishes, to the satisfaction of the Director, the original deposit of the correspondence and that the correspondence or copy of the correspondence is the original correspondence or a true copy of the correspondence originally deposited with the USPS on the requested filing date. The Office may require additional evidence to determine if the correspondence was returned by the USPS due to an interruption or emergency in "Express Mail" service.

(h) Any person who attempts to mail correspondence addressed as set out in § 1.1 (a) to the Office with sufficient postage utilizing the "Express Mail Post Office to Addressee" service of the USPS, but has the correspondence refused by an employee of the USPS due to an interruption or emergency in "Express Mail" service, may petition the Director to consider such correspondence as filed on a particular date in the Office, provided that:

(1) The petition is filed promptly after the person becomes aware of the refusal of the correspondence;

(2) The number of the "Express Mail" mailing label was placed on the paper(s) or fee(s) that constitute the correspondence prior to the attempted mailing by "Express Mail";

(3) The petition includes the original correspondence or a copy of the original correspondence showing the number of the "Express Mail" mailing label thereon; and

(4) The petition includes a statement by the person who originally attempted to deposit the correspondence with the USPS which establishes, to the satisfaction of the Director, the original attempt to deposit the correspondence and that the correspondence or copy of the correspondence is the original correspondence or a true copy of the correspondence originally attempted to be deposited with the USPS on the requested filing date. The Office may require additional evidence to determine if the correspondence was refused by an employee of the USPS due to an interruption or emergency in "Express Mail" service.

(i) Any person attempting to file correspondence under this section that was unable to be deposited with the USPS due to an interruption or emergency in "Express Mail" service which has been so designated by the Director, may petition the Director to consider such correspondence as filed on a particular date in the Office, provided that:

(1) The petition is filed in a manner designated by the Director promptly after the person becomes aware of the designated interruption or emergency in "Express Mail" service;

(2) The petition includes the original correspondence or a copy of the original correspondence; and

(3) The petition includes a statement which establishes, to the satisfaction of the Director, that the correspondence would have been deposited with the USPS but for the designated interruption or emergency in "Express Mail" service, and that the correspondence or copy of the correspondence is the original correspondence or a true copy of the correspondence originally attempted to be deposited with the USPS on the requested filing date.

# APPENDIX 40:
# ASSIGNMENTS

### SECTION 261 OF THE PATENT ACT

Subject to the provisions of this title, patents shall have the attributes of personal property.

Applications for patent, patents, or any interest therein, shall be assignable in law by an instrument in writing. The applicant, patentee, or his assigns or legal representatives may in like manner grant and convey an exclusive right under his application for patent, or patents, to the whole or any specified part of the United States.

A certificate of acknowledgment under the hand and official seal of a person authorized to administer oaths within the United States, or, in a foreign country, of a diplomatic or consular officer of the United States or an officer authorized to administer oaths whose authority is proved by a certificate of a diplomatic or consular officer of the United States, or apostille of an official designated by a foreign country which, by treaty or convention, accords like effect to apostilles of designated officials in the United States, shall be *prima facie* evidence of the execution of an assignment, grant, or conveyance of a patent or application for patent.

An assignment, grant, or conveyance shall be void as against any subsequent purchaser or mortgagee for a valuable consideration, without notice, unless it is recorded in the Patent and Trademark Office within three months from its date or prior to the date of such subsequent purchase or mortgage.

### SECTIONS 3.28 AND 3.31 OF TITLE 37 OF THE CFR

#### Section 3.28:

Each document submitted to the Office for recording must include a single cover sheet (as specified in § 3.31) referring either to those patent applications and patents, or to those trademark applications and registrations, against which the document is to be recorded. If a document to be recorded includes interests in, or transactions involving, both patents and trademarks, then separate patent and trademark cover sheets, each accompanied by a copy of the document to be recorded, must be submitted. If a document to be recorded is not accompanied by a completed cover sheet, the document and the incomplete cover sheet will be returned pursuant to § 3.51 for proper completion, in which case the document and a completed cover sheet should be resubmitted.

**Section 3.31:**

(a) Each patent or trademark cover sheet required by § 3.28 must contain:

(1) The name of the party conveying the interest;

(2) The name and address of the party receiving the interest;

(3) A description of the interest conveyed or transaction to be recorded;

(4) Identification of the interests involved:

(i) For trademark assignments and trademark name changes: Each trademark registration number and each trademark application number, if known, against which the Office is to record the document. If the trademark application number is not known, a copy of the application or a reproduction of the trademark must be submitted, along with an estimate of the date that the Office received the application; or

(ii) For any other document affecting title to a trademark or patent application, registration, or patent: Each trademark or patent application number or each trademark registration number or patent against which the document is to be recorded, or an indication that the document is filed together with a patent application;

(5) The name and address of the party to whom correspondence concerning the request to record the document should be mailed;

(6) The date the document was executed;

(7) The signature of the party submitting the document. For an assignment document or name change filed electronically, the person who signs the cover sheet must either:

(i) Place a symbol comprised of letters, numbers, and/or punctuation marks between forward slash marks (e.g., Thomas O'Malley III) in the signature block on the electronic submission; or

(ii) Sign the cover sheet using some other form of electronic signature specified by the Director.

(8) For trademark assignments, the entity and citizenship of the party receiving the interest. In addition, if the party receiving the interest is a domestic partnership or domestic joint venture, the cover sheet must set forth the names, legal entities, and national citizenship (or the state or country of organization) of all general partners or active members that compose the partnership or joint venture.

(b) A cover sheet should not refer to both patents and trademarks, since any information, including information about pending patent applications, submitted with a request for recordation of a document against a trademark application or trademark registration will become public record upon recordation.

(c) Each patent cover sheet required by § 3.28 seeking to record a governmental interest as provided by § 3.11(b) must:

(1) Indicate that the document relates to a Government interest; and

(2) Indicate, if applicable, that the document to be recorded is not a document affecting title (see § 3.41(b)).

(d) Each trademark cover sheet required by § 3.28 seeking to record a document against a trademark application or registration should include, in addition to the serial number or registration number of the trademark, identification of the trademark or a description of the trademark, against which the Office is to record the document.

(e) Each patent or trademark cover sheet required by § 3.28 should contain the number of applications, patents, or registrations identified in the cover sheet and the total fee.

(f) Each trademark cover sheet should include the citizenship of the party conveying the interest.

(g) The cover sheet required by § 3.28 seeking to record a joint research agreement or an excerpt of a joint research agreement as provided by § 3.11(c) must:

(1) Identify the document as a "joint research agreement" (in the space provided for the description of the interest conveyed or transaction to be recorded if using an Office-provided form);

(2) Indicate the name of the owner of the application or patent (in the space provided for the name and address of the party receiving the interest if using an Office-provided form);

(3) Indicate the name of each other party to the joint research agreement party (in the space provided for the name of the party conveying the interest if using an Office-provided form); and

(4) Indicate the date the joint research agreement was executed.

# APPENDIX 41:
# CHANGE OF CORRESPONDENCE ADDRESS

PTO/SB/122 (11-08)
Approved for use through 11/30/2011. OMB 0651-0035
U.S. Patent and Trademark Office; U.S. DEPARTMENT OF COMMERCE
Under the Paperwork Reduction Act of 1995, no persons are required to respond to a collection of information unless it displays a valid OMB control number.

| CHANGE OF CORRESPONDENCE ADDRESS *Application* | Application Number | |
| | Filing Date | |
| | First Named Inventor | |
| Address to:<br>Commissioner for Patents<br>P.O. Box 1450<br>Alexandria, VA 22313-1450 | Art Unit | |
| | Examiner Name | |
| | Attorney Docket Number | |

Please change the Correspondence Address for the above-identified patent application to:

☐ The address associated with Customer Number:

OR

☐ Firm or Individual Name

Address

| City | State | Zip |
| --- | --- | --- |

Country

| Telephone | Email |
| --- | --- |

This form cannot be used to change the data associated with a Customer Number. To change the data associated with an existing Customer Number use "Request for Customer Number Data Change" (PTO/SB/124).

I am the:

☐ Applicant/Inventor

☐ Assignee of record of the entire interest.
Statement under 37 CFR 3.73(b) is enclosed. (Form PTO/SB/96).

☐ Attorney or agent of record. Registration Number _____.

☐ Registered practitioner named in the application transmittal letter in an application without an executed oath or declaration. See 37 CFR 1.33(a)(1). Registration Number_____.

Signature

Typed or Printed Name

| Date | Telephone |
| --- | --- |

NOTE: Signatures of all the inventors or assignees of record of the entire interest or their representative(s) are required. Submit multiple forms if more than one signature is required, see below*.

☐ *Total of _____ forms are submitted.

This collection of information is required by 37 CFR 1.33. The information is required to obtain or retain a benefit by the public which is to file (and by the USPTO to process) an application. Confidentiality is governed by 35 U.S.C. 122 and 37 CFR 1.11 and 1.14. This collection is estimated to take 3 minutes to complete, including gathering, preparing, and submitting the completed application form to the USPTO. Time will vary depending upon the individual case. Any comments on the amount of time you require to complete this form and/or suggestions for reducing this burden, should be sent to the Chief Information Officer, U.S. Patent and Trademark Office, U.S. Department of Commerce, P.O. Box 1450, Alexandria, VA 22313-1450. DO NOT SEND FEES OR COMPLETED FORMS TO THIS ADDRESS. SEND TO: Commissioner for Patents, P.O. Box 1450, Alexandria, VA 22313-1450.

If you need assistance in completing the form, call 1-800-PTO-9199 and select option 2.

## Privacy Act Statement

The **Privacy Act of 1974 (P.L. 93-579)** requires that you be given certain information in connection with your submission of the attached form related to a patent application or patent. Accordingly, pursuant to the requirements of the Act, please be advised that: (1) the general authority for the collection of this information is 35 U.S.C. 2(b)(2); (2) furnishing of the information solicited is voluntary; and (3) the principal purpose for which the information is used by the U.S. Patent and Trademark Office is to process and/or examine your submission related to a patent application or patent. If you do not furnish the requested information, the U.S. Patent and Trademark Office may not be able to process and/or examine your submission, which may result in termination of proceedings or abandonment of the application or expiration of the patent.

The information provided by you in this form will be subject to the following routine uses:

1. The information on this form will be treated confidentially to the extent allowed under the Freedom of Information Act (5 U.S.C. 552) and the Privacy Act (5 U.S.C 552a). Records from this system of records may be disclosed to the Department of Justice to determine whether disclosure of these records is required by the Freedom of Information Act.
2. A record from this system of records may be disclosed, as a routine use, in the course of presenting evidence to a court, magistrate, or administrative tribunal, including disclosures to opposing counsel in the course of settlement negotiations.
3. A record in this system of records may be disclosed, as a routine use, to a Member of Congress submitting a request involving an individual, to whom the record pertains, when the individual has requested assistance from the Member with respect to the subject matter of the record.
4. A record in this system of records may be disclosed, as a routine use, to a contractor of the Agency having need for the information in order to perform a contract. Recipients of information shall be required to comply with the requirements of the Privacy Act of 1974, as amended, pursuant to 5 U.S.C. 552a(m).
5. A record related to an International Application filed under the Patent Cooperation Treaty in this system of records may be disclosed, as a routine use, to the International Bureau of the World Intellectual Property Organization, pursuant to the Patent Cooperation Treaty.
6. A record in this system of records may be disclosed, as a routine use, to another federal agency for purposes of National Security review (35 U.S.C. 181) and for review pursuant to the Atomic Energy Act (42 U.S.C. 218(c)).
7. A record from this system of records may be disclosed, as a routine use, to the Administrator, General Services, or his/her designee, during an inspection of records conducted by GSA as part of that agency's responsibility to recommend improvements in records management practices and programs, under authority of 44 U.S.C. 2904 and 2906. Such disclosure shall be made in accordance with the GSA regulations governing inspection of records for this purpose, and any other relevant (*i.e.*, GSA or Commerce) directive. Such disclosure shall not be used to make determinations about individuals.
8. A record from this system of records may be disclosed, as a routine use, to the public after either publication of the application pursuant to 35 U.S.C. 122(b) or issuance of a patent pursuant to 35 U.S.C. 151. Further, a record may be disclosed, subject to the limitations of 37 CFR 1.14, as a routine use, to the public if the record was filed in an application which became abandoned or in which the proceedings were terminated and which application is referenced by either a published application, an application open to public inspection or an issued patent.
9. A record from this system of records may be disclosed, as a routine use, to a Federal, State, or local law enforcement agency, if the USPTO becomes aware of a violation or potential violation of law or regulation.

PTO/SB/123 (11-08)
Approved for use through 11/30/2011. OMB 0651-0035
U.S. Patent and Trademark Office; U.S. DEPARTMENT OF COMMERCE
Under the Paperwork Reduction Act of 1995, no persons are required to respond to a collection of information unless it displays a valid OMB control number.

**CHANGE OF CORRESPONDENCE ADDRESS**
*Patent*

Address to:
Mail Stop Post Issue
Commissioner for Patents
P.O. Box 1450
Alexandria, VA 22313-1450

| | |
|---|---|
| Patent Number | |
| Issue Date | |
| Application Number | |
| Filing Date | |
| First Named Inventor | |
| Attorney Docket Number | |

Please change the Correspondence Address for the above-identified patent to:

☐ The address associated with Customer Number:

OR

☐ Firm *or* Individual Name

**Address**

| City | State | ZIP |
|---|---|---|

**Country**

| Telephone | Email |
|---|---|

This form cannot be used to change the data associated with a Customer Number. To change the data associated with an existing Customer Number use "Request for Customer Number Data Change" (PTO/SB/124).

This form will not affect any "fee address" provided for the above-identified patent. To change a "fee address" use the "Fee Address Indication Form" (PTO/SB/47).

I am the:

☐ Patentee.

☐ Assignee of record of the entire interest. See 37 CFR 3.71.
Statement under 37 CFR 3.73(b) is enclosed. (Form PTO/SB/96).

☐ Attorney or agent of record. Registration Number _____.

Signature

Typed or Printed Name

| Date | Telephone |
|---|---|

NOTE: Signatures of all the inventors or assignees of record of the entire interest or their representative(s) are required. Submit multiple forms if more than one signature is required, see below*.

☐ *Total of _____ forms are submitted.

This collection of information is required by 37 CFR 1.33. The information is required to obtain or retain a benefit by the public which is to file (and by the USPTO to process) an application. Confidentiality is governed by 35 U.S.C. 122 and 37 CFR 1.11 and 1.14. This collection is estimated to take 3 minutes to complete, including gathering, preparing, and submitting the completed application form to the USPTO. Time will vary depending upon the individual case. Any comments on the amount of time you require to complete this form and/or suggestions for reducing this burden, should be sent to the Chief Information Officer, U.S. Patent and Trademark Office, U.S. Department of Commerce, P.O. Box 1450, Alexandria, VA 22313-1450. DO NOT SEND FEES OR COMPLETED FORMS TO THIS ADDRESS. **SEND TO: Mail Stop Post Issue, Commissioner for Patents, P.O. Box 1450, Alexandria, VA 22313-1450.**

*If you need assistance in completing the form, call 1-800-PTO-9199 and select option 2.*

## Privacy Act Statement

The **Privacy Act of 1974 (P.L. 93-579)** requires that you be given certain information in connection with your submission of the attached form related to a patent application or patent. Accordingly, pursuant to the requirements of the Act, please be advised that: (1) the general authority for the collection of this information is 35 U.S.C. 2(b)(2); (2) furnishing of the information solicited is voluntary; and (3) the principal purpose for which the information is used by the U.S. Patent and Trademark Office is to process and/or examine your submission related to a patent application or patent. If you do not furnish the requested information, the U.S. Patent and Trademark Office may not be able to process and/or examine your submission, which may result in termination of proceedings or abandonment of the application or expiration of the patent.

The information provided by you in this form will be subject to the following routine uses:

1. The information on this form will be treated confidentially to the extent allowed under the Freedom of Information Act (5 U.S.C. 552) and the Privacy Act (5 U.S.C 552a). Records from this system of records may be disclosed to the Department of Justice to determine whether disclosure of these records is required by the Freedom of Information Act.
2. A record from this system of records may be disclosed, as a routine use, in the course of presenting evidence to a court, magistrate, or administrative tribunal, including disclosures to opposing counsel in the course of settlement negotiations.
3. A record in this system of records may be disclosed, as a routine use, to a Member of Congress submitting a request involving an individual, to whom the record pertains, when the individual has requested assistance from the Member with respect to the subject matter of the record.
4. A record in this system of records may be disclosed, as a routine use, to a contractor of the Agency having need for the information in order to perform a contract. Recipients of information shall be required to comply with the requirements of the Privacy Act of 1974, as amended, pursuant to 5 U.S.C. 552a(m).
5. A record related to an International Application filed under the Patent Cooperation Treaty in this system of records may be disclosed, as a routine use, to the International Bureau of the World Intellectual Property Organization, pursuant to the Patent Cooperation Treaty.
6. A record in this system of records may be disclosed, as a routine use, to another federal agency for purposes of National Security review (35 U.S.C. 181) and for review pursuant to the Atomic Energy Act (42 U.S.C. 218(c)).
7. A record from this system of records may be disclosed, as a routine use, to the Administrator, General Services, or his/her designee, during an inspection of records conducted by GSA as part of that agency's responsibility to recommend improvements in records management practices and programs, under authority of 44 U.S.C. 2904 and 2906. Such disclosure shall be made in accordance with the GSA regulations governing inspection of records for this purpose, and any other relevant (*i.e.*, GSA or Commerce) directive. Such disclosure shall not be used to make determinations about individuals.
8. A record from this system of records may be disclosed, as a routine use, to the public after either publication of the application pursuant to 35 U.S.C. 122(b) or issuance of a patent pursuant to 35 U.S.C. 151. Further, a record may be disclosed, subject to the limitations of 37 CFR 1.14, as a routine use, to the public if the record was filed in an application which became abandoned or in which the proceedings were terminated and which application is referenced by either a published application, an application open to public inspection or an issued patent.
9. A record from this system of records may be disclosed, as a routine use, to a Federal, State, or local law enforcement agency, if the USPTO becomes aware of a violation or potential violation of law or regulation.

# APPENDIX 42:
# EXPRESS ABANDONMENT

Doc Code: EABN

Document Description: Letter Express Abandonment of the application

PTO/SB/24 (07-09)
Approved for use through 07/31/2012. OMB 0651-0031
U.S. Patent and Trademark Office; U.S. DEPARTMENT OF COMMERCE
Under the Paperwork Reduction Act of 1995, no persons are required to respond to a collection of information unless it displays a valid OMB control number.

**EXPRESS ABANDONMENT UNDER
37 CFR 1.138**

**File** the petition electronically using EFS-Web
Or **Mail** the petition to:
**Mail Stop Express Abandonment**
Commissioner for Patents
P.O. Box 1450, Alexandria, VA 22313-1450

| | |
|---|---|
| Application Number | |
| Filing Date | |
| First Named Inventor | |
| Art Unit | |
| Examiner Name | |
| Attorney Docket Number | |

Please **check only one** of boxes 1 or 2 below:
*(If no box is checked, this paper will be treated as a request for express abandonment as if box 1 is checked.)*

1. ☐ **Express Abandonment**
   I request that the above-identified application be expressly abandoned as of the filing date of this paper.

2. ☐ **Express Abandonment in Favor of a Continuing Application**
   I request that the above-identified application be expressly abandoned as of the filing date accorded the continuing application filed previously or herewith.

NOTE: A paper requesting express abandonment of an application is not effective unless and until an appropriate USPTO official recognizes and acts on the paper. See the Manual of Patent Examining Procedure (MPEP), section 711.01.

---

**TO AVOID PUBLICATION, USE FORM PTO/SB/24A INSTEAD OF THIS FORM.**

**TO REQUEST A REFUND OF SEARCH FEE AND EXCESS CLAIMS FEE (IF ELIGIBLE), USE FORM PTO/SB/24B INSTEAD OF THIS FORM.**

---

I am the: ☐ applicant.

☐ assignee of record of the entire interest. See 37 CFR 3.71.
Statement under 37 CFR 3.73(b) is enclosed. (Form PTO/SB/96)

☐ attorney or agent of record. Attorney or agent registration number is _____

☐ attorney or agent acting under 37 CFR 1.34, who is authorized under 37 CFR 1.138(b) because the application is expressly abandoned in favor of a continuing application (box 2 above must be checked). Attorney or agent registration number is _____

| | |
|---|---|
| _____ | _____ |
| Signature | Date |
| _____ | _____ |
| Typed or printed name | Telephone Number |

Note: Signature of all the inventors or assignees of record of the entire interest or their representative(s) are required. Submit multiple forms if more than one signature is required, see below.

☐ Total of _____ forms are submitted.

This collection of information is required by 37 CFR 1.138. The information is required to obtain or retain a benefit by the public which is to file (and by the USPTO to process an application). Confidentiality is governed by 35 U.S.C. 122 and 37 CFR 1.11 and 1.14. This collection is estimated to take 12 minutes to complete, including gathering, preparing, and submitting the completed application form to the USPTO. Time will vary depending upon the individual case. Any comments on the amount of time you require to complete this form and/or suggestions for reducing this burden, should be sent to the Chief Information Officer, U.S. Patent and Trademark Office, U.S. Department of Commerce, P.O. Box 1450, Alexandria, VA 22313-1450. DO NOT SEND FEES OR COMPLETED FORMS TO THIS ADDRESS. SEND TO: Mail Stop Express Abandonment, Commissioner for Patents, P.O. Box 1450, Alexandria, VA 22313-1450.

*If you need assistance in completing the form, call 1-800-PTO-9199 and select option 2*

## Privacy Act Statement

The **Privacy Act of 1974 (P.L. 93-579)** requires that you be given certain information in connection with your submission of the attached form related to a patent application or patent. Accordingly, pursuant to the requirements of the Act, please be advised that: (1) the general authority for the collection of this information is 35 U.S.C. 2(b)(2); (2) furnishing of the information solicited is voluntary; and (3) the principal purpose for which the information is used by the U.S. Patent and Trademark Office is to process and/or examine your submission related to a patent application or patent. If you do not furnish the requested information, the U.S. Patent and Trademark Office may not be able to process and/or examine your submission, which may result in termination of proceedings or abandonment of the application or expiration of the patent.

The information provided by you in this form will be subject to the following routine uses:

1. The information on this form will be treated confidentially to the extent allowed under the Freedom of Information Act (5 U.S.C. 552) and the Privacy Act (5 U.S.C 552a). Records from this system of records may be disclosed to the Department of Justice to determine whether disclosure of these records is required by the Freedom of Information Act.
2. A record from this system of records may be disclosed, as a routine use, in the course of presenting evidence to a court, magistrate, or administrative tribunal, including disclosures to opposing counsel in the course of settlement negotiations.
3. A record in this system of records may be disclosed, as a routine use, to a Member of Congress submitting a request involving an individual, to whom the record pertains, when the individual has requested assistance from the Member with respect to the subject matter of the record.
4. A record in this system of records may be disclosed, as a routine use, to a contractor of the Agency having need for the information in order to perform a contract. Recipients of information shall be required to comply with the requirements of the Privacy Act of 1974, as amended, pursuant to 5 U.S.C. 552a(m).
5. A record related to an International Application filed under the Patent Cooperation Treaty in this system of records may be disclosed, as a routine use, to the International Bureau of the World Intellectual Property Organization, pursuant to the Patent Cooperation Treaty.
6. A record in this system of records may be disclosed, as a routine use, to another federal agency for purposes of National Security review (35 U.S.C. 181) and for review pursuant to the Atomic Energy Act (42 U.S.C. 218(c)).
7. A record from this system of records may be disclosed, as a routine use, to the Administrator, General Services, or his/her designee, during an inspection of records conducted by GSA as part of that agency's responsibility to recommend improvements in records management practices and programs, under authority of 44 U.S.C. 2904 and 2906. Such disclosure shall be made in accordance with the GSA regulations governing inspection of records for this purpose, and any other relevant (*i.e.*, GSA or Commerce) directive. Such disclosure shall not be used to make determinations about individuals.
8. A record from this system of records may be disclosed, as a routine use, to the public after either publication of the application pursuant to 35 U.S.C. 122(b) or issuance of a patent pursuant to 35 U.S.C. 151. Further, a record may be disclosed, subject to the limitations of 37 CFR 1.14, as a routine use, to the public if the record was filed in an application which became abandoned or in which the proceedings were terminated and which application is referenced by either a published application, an application open to public inspection or an issued patent.
9. A record from this system of records may be disclosed, as a routine use, to a Federal, State, or local law enforcement agency, if the USPTO becomes aware of a violation or potential violation of law or regulation.

Doc Code: PGEA
Document Description: Request for Exp Aband for refund or to avoid pub

PTO/SB/24A (07-09)
Approved for use through 07/31/2012. OMB 0651-0031
U.S. Patent and Trademark Office; U.S. DEPARTMENT OF COMMERCE
Under the Paperwork Reduction Act of 1995, no persons are required to respond to a collection of information unless it displays a valid OMB control number.

| PETITION FOR EXPRESS ABANDONMENT TO AVOID PUBLICATION UNDER 37 CFR 1.138(c) | Application Number | |
|---|---|---|
| | Filing Date | |
| | First Named Inventor | |
| **File** the petition electronically using EFS-Web Or **Mail** the petition to: | Art Unit | |
| **Mail Stop Express Abandonment** Commissioner for Patents | Examiner Name | |
| P.O. Box 1450, Alexandria, VA 22313-1450 | Attorney Docket Number | |

**Petition for Express Abandonment to Avoid Publication under 37 CFR 1.138(c)**

I hereby petition to expressly abandon the above-identified application to avoid publication.

Petition Fee – must be filed with petition to avoid delays in recognizing the petition.

a. ☐ The Director is hereby authorized to charge the petition fee under 37 CFR 1.17(h) to Deposit Account No. _____.

b. ☐ Check in the amount of $ _____ is enclosed.

c. ☐ Payment by credit card (Form PTO-2038 is enclosed).

**NOTE:** A paper requesting express abandonment of an application is not effective unless and until an appropriate USPTO official recognizes and acts on the paper. See the Manual of Patent Examining Procedure (MPEP), section 711.01. In addition, the paper will not stop publication of the application unless a petition under 37 CFR 1.138(c) is recognized and acted on by the Pre-Grant Publication Division in sufficient time to avoid publication (e.g., more than four (4) weeks prior to the projected publication date).

---

**TO REQUEST A REFUND OF SEARCH FEE AND EXCESS CLAIMS FEE (IF ELIGIBLE), PLEASE ALSO INCLUDE FORM PTO/SB/24B WITH THIS FORM.**

---

I am the:

☐ applicant.

☐ assignee of record of the entire interest. See 37 CFR 3.71. Statement under 37 CFR 3.73(b) is enclosed. (Form PTO/SB/96)

☐ attorney or agent of record. Attorney or agent registration number is _____

☐ attorney or agent acting under 37 CFR 1.34, who is authorized under 37 CFR 1.138(b) because the application is expressly abandoned in favor of a continuing application. Attorney or agent registration number is _____.

| _____ | _____ |
|---|---|
| Signature | Date |
| _____ | _____ |
| Typed or printed name | Telephone Number |

Note: Signatures of all the inventors or assignees of record of the entire interest or their representative(s) are required. Submit multiple forms if more than one signature is required, see below.

☐ Total of _____ forms are submitted.

This collection of information is required by 37 CFR 1.138(c). The information is required to obtain or retain a benefit by the public which is to file (and by the USPTO to process) an application. Confidentiality is governed by 35 U.S.C. 122 and 37 CFR 1.11 and 1.14. This collection is estimated to take 12 minutes to complete, including gathering, preparing, and submitting the completed application form to the USPTO. Time will vary depending upon the individual case. Any comments on the amount of time you require to complete this form and/or suggestions for reducing this burden, should be sent to the Chief Information Officer, U.S. Patent and Trademark Office, U.S. Department of Commerce, **P.O. Box 1450, Alexandria, VA 22313-1450.** DO NOT SEND FEES OR COMPLETED FORMS TO THIS ADDRESS. **SEND TO: Mail Stop Express Abandonment, Commissioner for Patents, P.O. Box 1450, Alexandria, VA 22313-1450.**

*If you need assistance in completing the form, call 1-800-PTO 9199 and select option 2.*

## Privacy Act Statement

The **Privacy Act of 1974 (P.L. 93-579)** requires that you be given certain information in connection with your submission of the attached form related to a patent application or patent. Accordingly, pursuant to the requirements of the Act, please be advised that: (1) the general authority for the collection of this information is 35 U.S.C. 2(b)(2); (2) furnishing of the information solicited is voluntary; and (3) the principal purpose for which the information is used by the U.S. Patent and Trademark Office is to process and/or examine your submission related to a patent application or patent. If you do not furnish the requested information, the U.S. Patent and Trademark Office may not be able to process and/or examine your submission, which may result in termination of proceedings or abandonment of the application or expiration of the patent.

The information provided by you in this form will be subject to the following routine uses:

1. The information on this form will be treated confidentially to the extent allowed under the Freedom of Information Act (5 U.S.C. 552) and the Privacy Act (5 U.S.C 552a). Records from this system of records may be disclosed to the Department of Justice to determine whether disclosure of these records is required by the Freedom of Information Act.
2. A record from this system of records may be disclosed, as a routine use, in the course of presenting evidence to a court, magistrate, or administrative tribunal, including disclosures to opposing counsel in the course of settlement negotiations.
3. A record in this system of records may be disclosed, as a routine use, to a Member of Congress submitting a request involving an individual, to whom the record pertains, when the individual has requested assistance from the Member with respect to the subject matter of the record.
4. A record in this system of records may be disclosed, as a routine use, to a contractor of the Agency having need for the information in order to perform a contract. Recipients of information shall be required to comply with the requirements of the Privacy Act of 1974, as amended, pursuant to 5 U.S.C. 552a(m).
5. A record related to an International Application filed under the Patent Cooperation Treaty in this system of records may be disclosed, as a routine use, to the International Bureau of the World Intellectual Property Organization, pursuant to the Patent Cooperation Treaty.
6. A record in this system of records may be disclosed, as a routine use, to another federal agency for purposes of National Security review (35 U.S.C. 181) and for review pursuant to the Atomic Energy Act (42 U.S.C. 218(c)).
7. A record from this system of records may be disclosed, as a routine use, to the Administrator, General Services, or his/her designee, during an inspection of records conducted by GSA as part of that agency's responsibility to recommend improvements in records management practices and programs, under authority of 44 U.S.C. 2904 and 2906. Such disclosure shall be made in accordance with the GSA regulations governing inspection of records for this purpose, and any other relevant (*i.e.*, GSA or Commerce) directive. Such disclosure shall not be used to make determinations about individuals.
8. A record from this system of records may be disclosed, as a routine use, to the public after either publication of the application pursuant to 35 U.S.C. 122(b) or issuance of a patent pursuant to 35 U.S.C. 151. Further, a record may be disclosed, subject to the limitations of 37 CFR 1.14, as a routine use, to the public if the record was filed in an application which became abandoned or in which the proceedings were terminated and which application is referenced by either a published application, an application open to public inspection or an issued patent.
9. A record from this system of records may be disclosed, as a routine use, to a Federal, State, or local law enforcement agency, if the USPTO becomes aware of a violation or potential violation of law or regulation.

**Understanding Patent Law: A Beginner's Guide**

Doc Code: PGEA
Document Description: Request for Exp Aband for refund or to avoid pub

PTO/SB/24B (07-09)
Approved for use through 07/31/2012. OMB 0651-0031
U.S. Patent and Trademark Office; U.S. DEPARTMENT OF COMMERCE
Under the Paperwork Reduction Act of 1995, no persons are required to respond to a collection of information unless it displays a valid OMB control number.

| PETITION FOR EXPRESS ABANDONMENT TO OBTAIN A REFUND | Application Number | |
| --- | --- | --- |
| | Filing Date | |
| | First Named Inventor | |
| **File** the petition electronically using EFS-Web Or **Mail** the petition to: | Art Unit | |
| **Mail Stop Express Abandonment** Commissioner for Patents | Examiner Name | |
| P.O. Box 1450, Alexandria, VA 22313-**1450** | Attorney Docket Number | |

**Petition for Express Abandonment Under 37 CFR 1.138(d) to Obtain a Refund**

I hereby petition to expressly abandon the above-identified application to obtain a refund of any previously paid search fee and excess claims fee in the application. Please refund any search fee and excess claims fee paid in this application.

☐ The Director is hereby authorized to credit the fee(s) to Deposit Account No. _____

**NOTE**: The provisions of 37 CFR 1.138(d) only apply to applications filed under 35 U.S.C. 111(a) on or after December 8, 2004. A paper requesting express abandonment of an application is not effective unless and until an appropriate USPTO official recognizes and acts on the paper. See the Manual of Patent Examining Procedure (MPEP), section 711.01.

---

**TO AVOID PUBLICATION, INCLUDE FORM PTO/SB/24A AND PETITION FEE WITH THIS FORM.**

---

I am the:

☐ Applicant

☐ Assignee of record of the entire interest. See 37 CFR 3.71.
Statement under 37 CFR 3.73(b) is enclosed. (Form PTO/SB/96)

☐ Attorney or agent of record. Attorney or agent registration number is _____

☐ Attorney or agent acting under 37 CFR 1.34, who is authorized under 37 CFR 1.138(b) because the application is expressly abandoned in favor of a continuing application.

Attorney or agent registration number is _____

_____          _____
Signature                                                              Date

_____          _____
Typed or printed name                                        Telephone Number

---

Note: Signatures of all the inventors or assignees of record of the entire interest or their representative(s) are required. Submit multiple forms if more than one signature is required, see below.

☐ Total of _____ forms are submitted

---

This collection of information is required by 37 CFR 1.138(c). The information is required to obtain or retain a benefit by the public which is to file (and by the USPTO to process an application). Confidentiality is governed by 35 U.S.C. 122 and 37 CFR 1.11 and 1.14. This collection is estimated to take 12 minutes to complete, including gathering, preparing, and submitting the completed application form to the USPTO. Time will vary depending upon the individual case. Any comments on the amount of time you require to complete this form and/or suggestions for reducing this burden, should be sent to the Chief Information Officer, U.S. Patent and Trademark Office, U.S. Department of Commerce, P.O. Box 1450, Alexandria, VA 22313-1450. DO NOT SEND FEES OR COMPLETED FORMS TO THIS ADDRESS. **SEND TO: Mail Stop Express Abandonment, Commissioner for Patents, P.O. Box 1450, Alexandria, VA 22313-1450.**

*If you need assistance in completing the form, call 1-800-PTO-9199 and select option 2.*

# Privacy Act Statement

**The Privacy Act of 1974 (P.L. 93-579)** requires that you be given certain information in connection with your submission of the attached form related to a patent application or patent. Accordingly, pursuant to the requirements of the Act, please be advised that: (1) the general authority for the collection of this information is 35 U.S.C. 2(b)(2); (2) furnishing of the information solicited is voluntary; and (3) the principal purpose for which the information is used by the U.S. Patent and Trademark Office is to process and/or examine your submission related to a patent application or patent. If you do not furnish the requested information, the U.S. Patent and Trademark Office may not be able to process and/or examine your submission, which may result in termination of proceedings or abandonment of the application or expiration of the patent.

The information provided by you in this form will be subject to the following routine uses:

1. The information on this form will be treated confidentially to the extent allowed under the Freedom of Information Act (5 U.S.C. 552) and the Privacy Act (5 U.S.C 552a). Records from this system of records may be disclosed to the Department of Justice to determine whether disclosure of these records is required by the Freedom of Information Act.
2. A record from this system of records may be disclosed, as a routine use, in the course of presenting evidence to a court, magistrate, or administrative tribunal, including disclosures to opposing counsel in the course of settlement negotiations.
3. A record in this system of records may be disclosed, as a routine use, to a Member of Congress submitting a request involving an individual, to whom the record pertains, when the individual has requested assistance from the Member with respect to the subject matter of the record.
4. A record in this system of records may be disclosed, as a routine use, to a contractor of the Agency having need for the information in order to perform a contract. Recipients of information shall be required to comply with the requirements of the Privacy Act of 1974, as amended, pursuant to 5 U.S.C. 552a(m).
5. A record related to an International Application filed under the Patent Cooperation Treaty in this system of records may be disclosed, as a routine use, to the International Bureau of the World Intellectual Property Organization, pursuant to the Patent Cooperation Treaty.
6. A record in this system of records may be disclosed, as a routine use, to another federal agency for purposes of National Security review (35 U.S.C. 181) and for review pursuant to the Atomic Energy Act (42 U.S.C. 218(c)).
7. A record from this system of records may be disclosed, as a routine use, to the Administrator, General Services, or his/her designee, during an inspection of records conducted by GSA as part of that agency's responsibility to recommend improvements in records management practices and programs, under authority of 44 U.S.C. 2904 and 2906. Such disclosure shall be made in accordance with the GSA regulations governing inspection of records for this purpose, and any other relevant (i.e., GSA or Commerce) directive. Such disclosure shall not be used to make determinations about individuals.
8. A record from this system of records may be disclosed, as a routine use, to the public after either publication of the application pursuant to 35 U.S.C. 122(b) or issuance of a patent pursuant to 35 U.S.C. 151. Further, a record may be disclosed, subject to the limitations of 37 CFR 1.14, as a routine use, to the public if the record was filed in an application which became abandoned or in which the proceedings were terminated and which application is referenced by either a published application, an application open to public inspection or an issued patent.
9. A record from this system of records may be disclosed, as a routine use, to a Federal, State, or local law enforcement agency, if the USPTO becomes aware of a violation or potential violation of law or regulation.

# APPENDIX 43:
# NOTICE OF APPEAL

PTO/SB/31 (07-09)
Approved for use through 07/31/2012. OMB 0651-0031
U.S. Patent and Trademark Office; U.S. DEPARTMENT OF COMMERCE
Under the Paperwork Reduction Act of 1995, no persons are required to respond to a collection of information unless it displays a valid OMB control number.

**NOTICE OF APPEAL** FROM THE EXAMINER TO
THE BOARD OF PATENT APPEALS AND INTERFERENCES

Docket Number (Optional)

I hereby certify that this correspondence is being facsimile transmitted to the USPTO or deposited with the United States Postal Service with sufficient postage as first class mail in an envelope addressed to "Commissioner for Patents, P.O. Box 1450, Alexandria, VA 22313-1450" [37 CFR 1.8(a)]

on _____

Signature_____

Typed or printed name _____

In re Application of

| Application Number | Filed |
|---|---|
| | |

For

| Art Unit | Examiner |
|---|---|
| | |

Applicant hereby **appeals** to the Board of Patent Appeals and Interferences from the last decision of the examiner.

The fee for this Notice of Appeal is (37 CFR 41.20(b)(1))          $ _____

☐ Applicant claims small entity status. See 37 CFR 1.27. Therefore, the fee shown above is reduced by half, and the resulting fee is:          $ _____

☐ A check in the amount of the fee is enclosed.

☐ Payment by credit card. Form PTO-2038 is attached.

☐ The Director has already been authorized to charge fees in this application to a Deposit Account.

☐ The Director is hereby authorized to charge any fees which may be required, or credit any overpayment to Deposit Account No. _____ .

☐ A petition for an extension of time under 37 CFR 1.136(a) (PTO/SB/22) is enclosed.

**WARNING: Information on this form may become public. Credit card information should not be included on this form. Provide credit card information and authorization on PTO-2038.**

I am the

☐ applicant/inventor.

_____
Signature

☐ assignee of record of the entire interest.
See 37 CFR 3.71. Statement under 37 CFR 3.73(b) is enclosed.
(Form PTO/SB/96)

_____
Typed or printed name

☐ attorney or agent of record.
Registration number _____ .

_____
Telephone number

☐ attorney or agent acting under 37 CFR 1.34.
Registration number if acting under 37 CFR 1.34. _____

_____
Date

NOTE: Signatures of all the inventors or assignees of record of the entire interest or their representative(s) are required. Submit multiple forms if more than one signature is required, see below*.

☐ *Total of _____ forms are submitted.

This collection of information is required by 37 CFR 41.31. The information is required to obtain or retain a benefit by the public which is to file (and by the USPTO to process) an application. Confidentiality is governed by 35 U.S.C. 122 and 37 CFR 1.11, 1.14 and 41.6. This collection is estimated to take 12 minutes to complete, including gathering, preparing, and submitting the completed application form to the USPTO. Time will vary depending upon the individual case. Any comments on the amount of time you require to complete this form and/or suggestions for reducing this burden, should be sent to the Chief Information Officer, U.S. Patent and Trademark Office, U.S. Department of Commerce, P.O. Box 1450, Alexandria, VA 22313-1450. DO NOT SEND FEES OR COMPLETED FORMS TO THIS ADDRESS. **SEND TO: Commissioner for Patents, P.O. Box 1450, Alexandria, VA 22313-1450.**

If you need assistance in completing the form, call 1-800-PTO-9199 and select option 2.

# Privacy Act Statement

The **Privacy Act of 1974 (P.L. 93-579)** requires that you be given certain information in connection with your submission of the attached form related to a patent application or patent. Accordingly, pursuant to the requirements of the Act, please be advised that: (1) the general authority for the collection of this information is 35 U.S.C. 2(b)(2); (2) furnishing of the information solicited is voluntary; and (3) the principal purpose for which the information is used by the U.S. Patent and Trademark Office is to process and/or examine your submission related to a patent application or patent. If you do not furnish the requested information, the U.S. Patent and Trademark Office may not be able to process and/or examine your submission, which may result in termination of proceedings or abandonment of the application or expiration of the patent.

The information provided by you in this form will be subject to the following routine uses:

1.  The information on this form will be treated confidentially to the extent allowed under the Freedom of Information Act (5 U.S.C. 552) and the Privacy Act (5 U.S.C 552a). Records from this system of records may be disclosed to the Department of Justice to determine whether disclosure of these records is required by the Freedom of Information Act.
2.  A record from this system of records may be disclosed, as a routine use, in the course of presenting evidence to a court, magistrate, or administrative tribunal, including disclosures to opposing counsel in the course of settlement negotiations.
3.  A record in this system of records may be disclosed, as a routine use, to a Member of Congress submitting a request involving an individual, to whom the record pertains, when the individual has requested assistance from the Member with respect to the subject matter of the record.
4.  A record in this system of records may be disclosed, as a routine use, to a contractor of the Agency having need for the information in order to perform a contract. Recipients of information shall be required to comply with the requirements of the Privacy Act of 1974, as amended, pursuant to 5 U.S.C. 552a(m).
5.  A record related to an International Application filed under the Patent Cooperation Treaty in this system of records may be disclosed, as a routine use, to the International Bureau of the World Intellectual Property Organization, pursuant to the Patent Cooperation Treaty.
6.  A record in this system of records may be disclosed, as a routine use, to another federal agency for purposes of National Security review (35 U.S.C. 181) and for review pursuant to the Atomic Energy Act (42 U.S.C. 218(c)).
7.  A record from this system of records may be disclosed, as a routine use, to the Administrator, General Services, or his/her designee, during an inspection of records conducted by GSA as part of that agency's responsibility to recommend improvements in records management practices and programs, under authority of 44 U.S.C. 2904 and 2906. Such disclosure shall be made in accordance with the GSA regulations governing inspection of records for this purpose, and any other relevant (*i.e.*, GSA or Commerce) directive. Such disclosure shall not be used to make determinations about individuals.
8.  A record from this system of records may be disclosed, as a routine use, to the public after either publication of the application pursuant to 35 U.S.C. 122(b) or issuance of a patent pursuant to 35 U.S.C. 151. Further, a record may be disclosed, subject to the limitations of 37 CFR 1.14, as a routine use, to the public if the record was filed in an application which became abandoned or in which the proceedings were terminated and which application is referenced by either a published application, an application open to public inspection or an issued patent.
9.  A record from this system of records may be disclosed, as a routine use, to a Federal, State, or local law enforcement agency, if the USPTO becomes aware of a violation or potential violation of law or regulation.

# APPENDIX 44:
# MAINTENANCE FEE TRANSMITTAL FORM

PTO/SB/45 (03-09)
Approved for use through 03/31/2012. OMB 0651-0016
U.S. Patent and Trademark Office; U.S. DEPARTMENT OF COMMERCE
Under the Paperwork Reduction Act of 1995, no persons are required to respond to a collection of information unless it displays a valid OMB control number.

## MAINTENANCE FEE TRANSMITTAL FORM
### (Do not submit this form electronically via EFS-Web)

**Address to:**
**Director of the United States**
**Patent and Trademark Office**
**Attn: Maintenance Fee**
**2051 Jamieson Avenue, Suite 300**
**Alexandria, VA 22314**

- OR -

**Fax to: 571-273-6500**

I hereby certify that this correspondence is being deposited with the United States Postal Service with sufficient postage as first class mail in an envelope addressed to "Director of the United States Patent and Trademark Office, Attn: Maintenance Fee, 2051 Jamieson Avenue, Suite 300, Alexandria, VA 22314" on _____.

Signature _____

Typed or printed name _____

Enclosed herewith is the payment of the maintenance fee(s) for the listed patent(s).

1. ☐ A check for the amount of $_____ for the full payment of the maintenance fee(s) and any necessary surcharge is enclosed.

2. ☐ Payment by credit card. Form PTO-2038 is enclosed.

3. ☐ The Director is hereby authorized to charge $_____ to cover the payment of the fee(s) indicated below to Deposit Account No. _____.

4. ☐ The Director is hereby authorized to charge any deficiency in the payment of the required fee(s) or credit any overpayment to Deposite Account No. _____.

\* Information required by 37 CFR 1.366(c) (columns 1 & 2). Information requested under 37 CFR 1.366(d) (columns 3, 4, & 5).

| Item | Patent Number* | U.S. Application Number* [e.g., 06/555,555] | Maintenance Fee Amount (37 CFR 1.20(e)-(g)) | Surcharge Amount (37 CFR 1.20(h)) | Payment Year (select one below) Column 5 | | |
|---|---|---|---|---|---|---|---|
| | Column 1 | Column 2 | Column 3 | Column 4 | 3.5 yrs | 7.5 yrs | 11.5 yrs |
| 1 | | | | | | | |
| 2 | | | | | | | |
| 3 | | | | | | | |
| 4 | | | | | | | |
| 5 | | | | | | | |

Subtotals: Columns 3 & 4 _____

Total Payment _____

☐ ____ additional sheets attached for listing additional patents.

**WARNING:** Information on this form may become public. Credit card information should not be included on this form. Provide credit card information and authorization on Form PTO-2038.

Respectfully submitted, \*\*

Customer's Signature _____

Customer's Name _____   Registration Number, if applicable: _____

Telephone: _____   Fax: _____

Note: All correspondence will be forwarded to the "Fee Address" or to the "Correspondence Address" if no "Fee Address" has been provided. See 37 CFR 1.363.

Payment of small entity fee is appropriate if small entity status still exists, see 37 CFR 1.27(g). To establish small entity status or to change status from small to large entity, a written assertion is required. See 37 CFR 1.27 and 1.33(b).

\*\* WHERE MAINTENANCE FEE PAYMENTS ARE TO BE MADE BY AUTHORIZATION TO CHARGE A DEPOSIT ACCOUNT, BOTH THE NAME AND SIGNATURE OF AN AUTHORIZED USER ARE REQUIRED.

This collection of information is required by 37 CFR 1.366. The information is required to obtain or retain a benefit by the public which is to file (and by the USPTO to process) an application. Confidentiality is governed by 35 U.S.C. 122 and 37 CFR 1.11 and 1.14. This collection is estimated to take 5 minutes to complete, including gathering, preparing, and submitting the completed application form to the USPTO. Time will vary depending upon the individual case. Any comments on the amount of time you require to complete this form and/or suggestions for reducing this burden, should be sent to the Chief Information Officer, U.S. Patent and Trademark Office, U.S. Department of Commerce, P.O. Box 1450, Alexandria, VA. 22313-1450. DO NOT SEND FEES OR COMPLETED FORMS TO THIS ADDRESS. SEND TO: Director of the United States Patent and Trademark Office, Attn: Maintenance Fee, 2051 Jamieson Avenue, Suite 300, Alexandria, VA 22314.

*If you need assistance in completing the form, call 1-800-PTO-9199 and select option 2.*

## Privacy Act Statement

The **Privacy Act of 1974 (P.L. 93-579)** requires that you be given certain information in connection with your submission of the attached form related to a patent application or patent. Accordingly, pursuant to the requirements of the Act, please be advised that: (1) the general authority for the collection of this information is 35 U.S.C. 2(b)(2); (2) furnishing of the information solicited is voluntary; and (3) the principal purpose for which the information is used by the U.S. Patent and Trademark Office is to process and/or examine your submission related to a patent application or patent. If you do not furnish the requested information, the U.S. Patent and Trademark Office may not be able to process and/or examine your submission, which may result in termination of proceedings or abandonment of the application or expiration of the patent.

The information provided by you in this form will be subject to the following routine uses:

1. The information on this form will be treated confidentially to the extent allowed under the Freedom of Information Act (5 U.S.C. 552) and the Privacy Act (5 U.S.C 552a). Records from this system of records may be disclosed to the Department of Justice to determine whether disclosure of these records is required by the Freedom of Information Act.
2. A record from this system of records may be disclosed, as a routine use, in the course of presenting evidence to a court, magistrate, or administrative tribunal, including disclosures to opposing counsel in the course of settlement negotiations.
3. A record in this system of records may be disclosed, as a routine use, to a Member of Congress submitting a request involving an individual, to whom the record pertains, when the individual has requested assistance from the Member with respect to the subject matter of the record.
4. A record in this system of records may be disclosed, as a routine use, to a contractor of the Agency having need for the information in order to perform a contract. Recipients of information shall be required to comply with the requirements of the Privacy Act of 1974, as amended, pursuant to 5 U.S.C. 552a(m).
5. A record related to an International Application filed under the Patent Cooperation Treaty in this system of records may be disclosed, as a routine use, to the International Bureau of the World Intellectual Property Organization, pursuant to the Patent Cooperation Treaty.
6. A record in this system of records may be disclosed, as a routine use, to another federal agency for purposes of National Security review (35 U.S.C. 181) and for review pursuant to the Atomic Energy Act (42 U.S.C. 218(c)).
7. A record from this system of records may be disclosed, as a routine use, to the Administrator, General Services, or his/her designee, during an inspection of records conducted by GSA as part of that agency's responsibility to recommend improvements in records management practices and programs, under authority of 44 U.S.C. 2904 and 2906. Such disclosure shall be made in accordance with the GSA regulations governing inspection of records for this purpose, and any other relevant (*i.e.*, GSA or Commerce) directive. Such disclosure shall not be used to make determinations about individuals.
8. A record from this system of records may be disclosed, as a routine use, to the public after either publication of the application pursuant to 35 U.S.C. 122(b) or issuance of a patent pursuant to 35 U.S.C. 151. Further, a record may be disclosed, subject to the limitations of 37 CFR 1.14, as a routine use, to the public if the record was filed in an application which became abandoned or in which the proceedings were terminated and which application is referenced by either a published application, an application open to public inspection or an issued patent.
9. A record from this system of records may be disclosed, as a routine use, to a Federal, State, or local law enforcement agency, if the USPTO becomes aware of a violation or potential violation of law or regulation.

# APPENDIX 45:
# ADHERENTS TO TREATIES

| States Party to the PCT and the Paris Convention and Members of the World Trade Organization (status on 13 October 2009) | | | | | | | |
|---|---|---|---|---|---|---|---|
| States/Members | PCT (141) | Paris (173) | WTO (153) | States/Members | PCT | Paris | WTO |
| Albania (AL) | X | X | X | Cape Verde (CV) | – | – | X |
| Algeria (DZ) | X | X | – | Central African Republic (CF) | X | X | X |
| Andorra (AD) | – | X | – | Chad (TD) | X | X | X |
| Angola (AO) | X | X | X | Chile (CL) | X | X | X |
| Antigua and Barbuda (AG) | X | X | X | China (CN) | X[1] | X[1,2] | X |
| Argentina (AR) | – | X | X | Colombia (CO) | X | X | X |
| Armenia (AM) | X | X | X | Comoros (KM) | X | X | – |
| Australia (AU) | X | X | X | Congo (CG) | X | X | X |
| Austria (AT) | X | X | X | Costa Rica (CR) | X | X | X |
| Azerbaijan (AZ) | X | X | – | Côte d'Ivoire (CI) | X | X | X |
| Bahamas (BS) | – | X | – | Croatia (HR) | X | X | X |
| Bahrain (BH) | X | X | X | Cuba (CU) | X | X | X |
| Bangladesh (BD) | – | X | X | Cyprus (CY) | X | X | X |
| Barbados (BB) | X | X | X | Czech Republic (CZ) | X | X | X |
| Belarus (BY) | X | X | – | Democratic People's Republic of Korea (KP) | X | X | – |
| Belgium (BE) | X | X | X | Democratic Republic of the Congo (CD) | – | X | X |
| Belize (BZ) | X | X | X | Denmark (DK) | X | X | X |
| Benin (BJ) | X | X | X | Djibouti (DJ) | – | X | X |
| Bhutan (BT) | – | X | – | Dominica (DM) | X | X | X |
| Bolivia (Plurinational State of) (BO) | – | X | X | Dominican Republic (DO) | X | X | X |
| Bosnia and Herzegovina (BA) | X | X | – | Ecuador (EC) | X | X | X |
| Botswana (BW) | X | X | X | Egypt (EG) | X | X | X |
| Brazil (BR) | X | X | X | El Salvador (SV) | X | X | X |
| Brunei Darussalam (BN) | – | – | X | Equatorial Guinea (GQ) | X | X | – |
| Bulgaria (BG) | X | X | X | Estonia (EE) | X | X | X |
| Burkina Faso (BF) | X | X | X | European Communities | – | – | X |
| Burundi (BI) | – | X | X | Fiji (FJ) | – | – | X |
| Cambodia (KH) | – | X | X | Finland (FI) | X | X | X |
| Cameroon (CM) | X | X | X | France (FR) | X | X | X |
| Canada (CA) | X | X | X | Gabon (GA) | X | X | X |

[continued on next page]

| States Party to the PCT and the Paris Convention and Members of the World Trade Organization (status on 13 October 2009) | | | | | | | |
|---|---|---|---|---|---|---|---|
| States/Members | PCT | Paris | WTO | States/Members | PCT | Paris | WTO |
| Gambia (GM) | X | X | X | Lebanon (LB) | – | X | – |
| Georgia (GE) | X | X | X | Lesotho (LS) | X | X | X |
| Germany (DE) | X | X | X | Liberia (LR) | X | X | – |
| Ghana (GH) | X | X | X | Libyan Arab Jamahiriya (LY) | X | X | – |
| Greece (GR) | X | X | X | Liechtenstein (LI) | X | X | X |
| Grenada (GD) | X | X | X | Lithuania (LT) | X | X | X |
| Guatemala (GT) | X | X | X | Luxembourg (LU) | X | X | X |
| Guinea (GN) | X | X | X | Macao, China (MO) | – | $-^2$ | X |
| Guinea–Bissau (GW) | X | X | X | Madagascar (MG) | X | X | X |
| Guyana (GY) | – | X | X | Malawi (MW) | X | X | X |
| Haiti (HT) | – | X | X | Malaysia (MY) | X | X | X |
| Holy See (VA) | – | X | – | Maldives (MV) | – | – | X |
| Honduras (HN) | X | X | X | Mali (ML) | X | X | X |
| Hong Kong, China (HK) | $-^1$ | $-^1$ | X | Malta (MT) | X | X | X |
| Hungary (HU) | X | X | X | Mauritania (MR) | X | X | X |
| Iceland (IS) | X | X | X | Mauritius (MU) | – | X | X |
| India (IN) | X | X | X | Mexico (MX) | X | X | X |
| Indonesia (ID) | X | X | X | Monaco (MC) | X | X | – |
| Iran (Islamic Republic of) (IR) | – | X | – | Mongolia (MN) | X | X | X |
| Iraq (IQ) | – | X | – | Montenegro (ME) | X | X | – |
| Ireland (IE) | X | X | X | Morocco (MA) | X | X | X |
| Israel (IL) | X | X | X | Mozambique (MZ) | X | X | X |
| Italy (IT) | X | X | X | Myanmar (MM) | – | – | X |
| Jamaica (JM) | – | X | X | Namibia (NA) | X | X | X |
| Japan (JP) | X | X | X | Nepal (NP) | – | X | X |
| Jordan (JO) | – | X | X | Netherlands (NL) | X | X | X |
| Kazakhstan (KZ) | X | X | – | New Zealand (NZ) | X | X | X |
| Kenya (KE) | X | X | X | Nicaragua (NI) | X | X | X |
| Kuwait (KW) | – | – | X | Niger (NE) | X | X | X |
| Kyrgyzstan (KG) | X | X | X | Nigeria (NG) | X | X | X |
| Lao People's Democratic Republic (LA) | X | X | – | Norway (NO) | X | X | X |
| Latvia (LV) | X | X | X | Oman (OM) | X | X | X |

[continued on next page]

| States Party to the PCT and the Paris Convention and Members of the World Trade Organization (status on 13 October 2009) | | | | | | | |
|---|---|---|---|---|---|---|---|
| States/Members | PCT | Paris | WTO | States/Members | PCT | Paris | WTO |
| Pakistan (PK) | – | X | X | Sri Lanka (LK) | X | X | X |
| Panama (PA) | – | X | X | Sudan (SD) | X | X | – |
| Papua New Guinea (PG) | X | X | X | Suriname (SR) | – | X | X |
| Paraguay (PY) | – | X | X | Swaziland (SZ) | X | X | X |
| Peru (PE) | X | X | X | Sweden (SE) | X | X | X |
| Philippines (PH) | X | X | X | Switzerland (CH) | X | X | X |
| Poland (PL) | X | X | X | Syrian Arab Republic (SY) | X | X | – |
| Portugal (PT) | X | X | X | Taiwan, Province of China (TW)[3] | – | – | X |
| Qatar (QA) | – | X | X | Tajikistan (TJ) | X | X | – |
| Republic of Korea (KR) | X | X | X | Thailand (TH) | X[4] | X | X |
| Republic of Moldova (MD) | X | X | X | The former Yugoslav Republic of Macedonia (MK) | X | X | X |
| Romania (RO) | X | X | X | Togo (TG) | X | X | X |
| Russian Federation (RU) | X | X | – | Tonga (TO) | – | X | X |
| Rwanda (RW) | – | X | X | Trinidad and Tobago (TT) | X | X | X |
| Saint Kitts and Nevis (KN) | X | X | X | Tunisia (TN) | X | X | X |
| Saint Lucia (LC) | X | X | X | Turkey (TR) | X | X | X |
| Saint Vincent and the Grenadines (VC) | X | X | X | Turkmenistan (TM) | X | X | – |
| San Marino (SM) | X | X | – | Uganda (UG) | X | X | X |
| Sao Tome and Principe (ST) | X | X | – | Ukraine (UA) | X | X | X |
| Saudi Arabia (SA) | – | X | X | United Arab Emirates (AE) | X | X | X |
| Senegal (SN) | X | X | X | United Kingdom (GB) | X | X | X |
| Serbia (RS) | X | X | – | United Republic of Tanzania (TZ) | X | X | X |
| Seychelles (SC) | X | X | – | United States of America (US) | X | X | X |
| Sierra Leone (SL) | X | X | X | Uruguay (UY) | – | X | X |
| Singapore (SG) | X | X | X | Uzbekistan (UZ) | X | X | – |
| Slovakia (SK) | X | X | X | Venezuela (Bolivarian Republic of) (VE) | – | X | X |
| Slovenia (SI) | X | X | X | Viet Nam (VN) | X | X | X |
| Solomon Islands (SB) | – | – | X | Yemen (YE) | – | X | – |
| South Africa (ZA) | X | X | X | Zambia (ZM) | X | X | X |
| Spain (ES) | X | X | X | Zimbabwe (ZW) | X | X | X |

1. China has notified the Director General of WIPO that the PCT and the Paris Convention apply also to the Hong Kong Special Administrative Region.
2. China has notified the Director General of WIPO that the Paris Convention applies also to the Macao Special Administrative Region.
3. Also referred to as "Chinese Taipei" or, within the context of the WTO, as "Separate Customs Territory of Taiwan, Penghu, Kinmen and Matsu."
4. Will become bound by the PCT on 24 December 2009.

Source: http://www.wipo.int

# APPENDIX 46:
# INVENTION PROMOTION COMPLAINT

PTO/SB/2048A
Approved for use through 12/31/09. OMB 0651-0044
Patent and Trademark Office; U.S. DEPARTMENT OF COMMERCE
Under the Paperwork Reduction Act of 1995, no persons are required to respond to a collection of information unless it displays a valid OMB control number.

## COMPLAINT REGARDING INVENTION PROMOTER

Instructions: Read the reverse side of this form before completing and submitting the form. Complete as much of the form as possible and return it to the **U.S. Patent and Trademark Office, Mail Stop 24, Commissioner for Patents, P.O. Box 1450, Alexandria, VA 22313-1450** or fax to (571) 273-0170. Please type or write clearly.

Name of the Invention Promotion Company:

Invention Promoter's Address:

City                                State                        Zip Code

Complainant's Name:

Complainant's Address:

City                                State                        Zip Code

Customer's Name:

### WHAT IS YOUR COMPLAINT?

Please be as specific as possible within the space provided

Name of mass media invention promoter advertised in: (i.e., TV, Radio, Newspaper, Magazine, Other)

Invention promotion services offered to be performed:

Explanation of complaint between customer and invention promoter:

Signed: _____ Date: _____

Burden Hour Statement: This collection of information is provided for by 35 U.S.C. § 297(d). The information regarding invention promoters will be released to the public. This form is estimated to take 15 minutes to complete. This time will vary depending upon the needs of the individual case. Any comments on the amount of time you are required to complete this form should be sent to the U.S. Patent and Trademark Office, Mail Stop Chief Information Officer, P.O. Box 1450, Alexandria, VA 22313-1450. DO NOT SEND FEES OR COMPLETED FORMS TO THIS ADDRESS.

PRIVACY ACT STATEMENT

Section 297 of Title 35, United States Code, authorizes collection of this information. The primary use of this information is to make complaints publicly available. Additional disclosures will be made to (i) persons or entities identified in the complaint, and (ii) a Federal, State, and local law enforcement agency.

Furnishing the information on this form is voluntary, but failure to submit the information may prevent the communication from being a publicly available complaint.

Carefully read the following:

An "Invention Promoter" is defined in 35 U.S.C. § 297(c)(3) as "any person, firm, partnership, corporation, or other entity who offers to perform or performs invention promotion services for, or on behalf of, a customer, and who holds out itself through advertising in any mass media as providing such services, but does not include
 (A) any department or agency of the Federal Government or of a State or local government;
 (B) any nonprofit, charitable, scientific, or educational organization, qualified under applicable State law or described under section 170(b)(1)(A) of the Internal Revenue Code;
 (C) any person or entity involved in the evaluation to determine commercial potential of, or offering to license or sell, a utility patent or a previously filed nonprovisional utility patent application;
 (D) any party participating in a transaction involving the sale of the stock or assets of a business; or
 (E) any party who directly engages in the business of retail sales of products or the distribution of products."

"Invention Promotion Services" is defined in 35 U.S.C. § 297(c)(4) as "the procurement or attempted procurement for a customer of a firm, corporation, or other entity to develop and market products or services that include the invention of the customer."

"Customer" is defined in 35 U.S.C. § 297(c)(2) as "any individual who enters into a contract with an invention promoter for invention promotion services."

"Contract for invention promotion services" is defined in 35 U.S.C. § 297(c)(1) as "a contract by which an invention promoter undertakes invention promotion services for a customer."

Any individual completing and filing the complaint form should understand the following.

 1. No action will be taken by the U.S. Patent and Trademark Office on behalf of the individual against the invention promoter based on the complaint. The U.S. Patent and Trademark Office has no authority to pursue a cause of action on behalf of any individual against an invention promoter or provide the individual with any personal remedy. If an individual believes that he or she has an actionable case, the individual should consult with an attorney about the possible legal options which may be available.
 2. The complaint will be published.
 3. The U.S. Patent and Trademark Office will provide the invention promoter with a reasonable opportunity to respond.
 4. The response by the invention promoter will be published.

Submit your complaint form by mail to:

U. S. Patent and Trademark Office
Mail Stop 24
Commissioner for Patents
P.O. Box 1450
Alexandria, VA 22313-1450

# GLOSSARY

**Accelerated examination**—a means of fast-track examination of an application for those qualifying by reason of such factors as age or health or those meeting the requirements of the PTO's accelerated examination program. See also **Patent Prosecution Highway**.

**Best mode**—the preferred mode or method of carrying out an invention (not necessarily a production specimen) that enables one skilled in the art of the invention to practice it.

**BPAI**—acronym for Board of Patent Appeals and Interferences. BPAI is a tribunal within the PTO that hears appeals of adverse decisions of patent examiners and retains jurisdiction over interference proceedings.

**CFR**—acronym for Code of Federal Regulations, title 37 of which includes the rules of practice governing patents.

**Claim**—a characteristic of an invention that is purported to be useful, novel and nonobvious. A claim may be dependent or independent.

**Continuation** (or **continuation in part**)—relates to an application that continues, or follows on in some manner, an earlier application, referred to as the "parent" application. See **Parent application**.

**Contributory infringement**—a form of indirect infringement provided for in section 271(c) of the Patent Act involving the offer, sale or importation of a material component of a patented invention, especially made or especially adapted for use in infringement of the patent rather than for a substantial, non-infringing use. See **Indirect infringement**.

**Court of Appeals for the Federal Circuit**—the federal appellate court hearing, among other things, appeals related to PTO proceedings.

**Design patent**—a type of patent protection covering an invention's ornamentality rather than its functionality.

**Direct (or literal) infringement**—an event wherein the claim(s) of the defendant's patent match the claim(s) in the plaintiff's patent.

**Disclaimer**—a statement filed by a patent owner or assignee in which certain legal rights to the patent are relinquished. See also **Statutory disclaimer** and **Terminal disclaimer**.

**Divisional application**—an application resulting from matter carved out of a parent application, typically arising when a parent application claims more than one distinct invention. See **Parent application**.

**Doctrine of equivalents**—a principle providing for a finding of infringement notwithstanding a lack of identicality in the patent claims of a plaintiff and a defendant if both parties' devices do the same work in substantially the same way and accomplish the same result.

**Double patenting**—a rejection of a patent, either statutory or nonstatutory in nature, related to matters of term or scope. See **Statutory double patenting rejection** and **Nonstatutory double patenting rejection**.

**Enabling disclosure**—a specification of an invention rendered in sufficient detail so as to enable one skilled in the art of the invention to make and use it.

**Equivalents infringement**—a type of infringement based on application of the doctrine of equivalents. See **Doctrine of equivalents**.

**EFS-Web**—the PTO's online filing system for certain patent applications and other documents related to the patent filing process.

**eOG:P**—the PTO's electronic edition of the *Official Gazette* for patents. See also *Official Gazette*.

**File wrapper (prosecution history) estoppel**—a doctrine limiting the applicability of the doctrine of equivalents with respect to claims that have been surrendered during the course of prosecution of a patent.

**Indirect infringement**—a cause of action for infringement by way of inducement or contributory infringement. See also **Inducement of infringement** and **Contributory infringement**.

**Inducement of infringement**—a form of indirect infringement provided for in section 271(b) of the Patent Act. See **Indirect infringement**.

**Inequitable conduct**—a defense against infringement claiming an act of bad faith with intent to deceive on the part of a patentee or its agent.

**Interference**—refers to a proceeding conducted at the BPAI to resolve priority between different inventors regarding the same invention.

**International application**—a centralized application filed under the Patent Cooperation Treaty wherein one application filed in a home patent office may be acknowledged as a national filing in as many other nations as the applicant designates. See **Patent Cooperation Treaty**.

**International Bureau**—known as the IB, the agency within WIPO acting as the central coordinating body for all applications filed under the Patent Cooperation Treaty.

**International Searching Authority**—also referred to as an ISA, a patent office granted authority under the Patent Cooperation Treaty to prepare search reports and written opinions with respect to claims identified in an international application.

**Invalidity**—a defense often used in infringement proceedings wherein the defendant rebuts the presumption of validity of the plaintiff's patent.

**Invention promoter**—an individual or entity engaged in the business of procuring for a patentee or inventor a third party to develop and market products or services that include the invention.

**Inventor's notebook**—a series of documentation often embodied in a notebook showing concepts, experiments, results, drawings and other information related to the invention.

**Maintenance**—a term referring to the fees payable during the life of an issued utility patent to avoid its abandonment.

**March-in right**—a form of compulsory licensing entitling a funding agency to issue its own license for the commercialization of an invention.

**Markman hearing**—a non-jury hearing often invoked in infringement proceedings for the resolution of claims construction disputes.

**MPEP**—acronym for Manual of Patent Examining Procedure, a guide used by examiners in addressing issues related to patent applications and post-issuance matters.

**National stage**—refers to the submission of an international application to national procedures for granting of patents in each country designated by the international application.

**Nonobvious**—a requirement for patentability related to the inventiveness of the subject matter, taking into account whether a purported invention is contemplated in the prior art. See **Prior art**.

**Nonprovisional application**—a patent application containing all the required elements for subsequent examination by a patent examiner. See also **Provisional application**.

**Nonstatutory double patenting rejection**—a judicially created doctrine intended to prevent prolongation of a patent term by prohibiting claims in a second patent that are not materially distinguishable from claims in a first patent.

**Notice of abandonment**—a written notice issued by the PTO stating that an application is no longer pending and therefore cannot mature into an issued patent.

**Notice of allowance**—a written notice issued by the PTO allowing an application to proceed to the grant of a patent.

**Notice of publication**—a written notice issued by the PTO notifying an applicant that its patent application has been published.

**Novel (novelty)**—a requirement for patentability, conditions for which are set forth in section 102 of the Patent Act.

**Office action**—a written communication from an examiner at the PTO requesting a response from the patent applicant concerning a matter related to the application.

**Official Gazette**—a weekly publication of the PTO containing data on such matters as issued, expired and reinstated patents, certificates of correction and PTO notices. See also **eOG:P**.

**Parent application**—an earlier application from which a subsequent application continues in some manner. See also **Continuation** and **Divisional application**.

**Paris Convention (Convention)**—refers to the Paris Convention for the Protection of Industrial Property, an international treaty offering reciprocal rights of intellectual property protection to nations that adhere to the treaty.

**Patent**—a U.S. patent constitutes a property right granted by the United States, giving a patent holder the right for a term of years to exclude others from commercializing its patented invention throughout the United States.

**Patent Act**—the law governing patents as codified in title 35 of the United States Code.

**Patent agent**—a nonlawyer qualified through technical expertise to represent an inventor in the prosecution of a patent application at the PTO.

**Patent aggregator**—a business that buys and sells patents.

**Patent Cooperation Treaty**—referred to frequently as PCT, an international agreement allowing patent applicants to file one application covering several countries with a single filing authority.

**Patentee**—the holder of a patent.

**Patent exhaustion**—a doctrine holding that the authorized sale of an article that substantially embodies a patent exhausts the patent holder's rights and prevents the patent holder from invoking the patent law to control post-sale use of the article.

**Patent misuse**—a defense against infringement alleging a form of anticompetitive behavior by the patent owner, including acting outside the patent's scope.

**Patent Pending (Patent Applied For)**—a notice commonly used to indicate the filing of a patent application for an invention.

**Patent Prosecution Highway**—a method of fast tracking examination of an application in a second office of filing based on a ruling from a first office of filing that at least one claim is patentable. See also **Accelerated examination**.

**Patent watch**—a term frequently used to describe the monitoring of applications and issued patents of competitors or those in a field of interest.

**PHOSITA**—popular acronym meaning "person having ordinary skill in the art," a hypothetical standard referring to a person having average skills and knowledge in a certain technical field.

**Plant patent**—a type of patent protection for a new and distinct variety of an asexually reproducing plant.

**Power of attorney**—an applicant's grant of authorization to a third party to act on its behalf.

**Prior art**—any information related to the scope or field of an invention that has been previously disclosed to the public, including issued patents and publications.

**Prosecution**—a term encompassing the full range of tasks involved in pursuing the issuance of a patent by the PTO.

**Provisional application**—a preliminary patent application, remaining in effect for 12 months following its filing date. A provisional application is not examined by a patent examiner. See also **Nonprovisional application**.

PTO—the United States Patent and Trademark Office.

**Reduction (reduced) to practice**—refers in the alternative to (i) the actual construction of an invention in such a manner as to enable one who is skilled in the art of the invention to practice it or (ii) the filing of an application completely disclosing the invention, resulting in constructive reduction to practice.

**Reexamination**—a proceeding conducted by the PTO at the request of a third party claiming that prior art affects one or more of the claims cited in a patent.

**Reissue**—refers to a patent issued in replacement of an original patent as a means by which to cure errors made by an applicant in the pursuit of the original patent that are not subject to the issuance of a certificate of correction.

**Right of priority (priority)**—the ability to use a first filing date in a previous application as the effective filing date in a subsequent application.

**Shop right**—an employer's non-exclusive right to use an employee's invention.

**Specification**—the principal part of a patent application, setting forth such elements as an enabling disclosure, best mode for carrying out the invention and at least one claim.

**Statutory bar**—refers to a bar against patentability arising from an event set out in section 102 of the Patent Act.

**Statutory disclaimer**—a surrender of one or more claims in a patent. See also **Disclaimer** and **Terminal disclaimer**.

**Statutory double patenting rejection**—arising from an application containing more than one distinct invention in violation of section 101 of the Patent Act, thus requiring a restriction of the application to a single invention.

**Terminal disclaimer**—a dedication to the public of the term or any portion of the term of a patent or patent to be granted. See also **Disclaimer** and **Statutory disclaimer**.

**Trade secret**—confidential business information that may or may not be patentable.

**TRIPS**—acronym for the Agreement on Trade-Related Aspects of Intellectual Property, a treaty designed to bring global harmonization to patent protection and enforcement.

**Utility**—a requirement for patentability relating to an invention's usefulness.

**Utility patent**—a type of patent protection generally covering inventions related to a process, machine, manufacture, composition of matter or any improvements of the foregoing.

**WIPO**—World Intellectual Property Organization.

**WTO**—World Trade Organization.

# BIBLIOGRAPHY AND RECOMMENDED READING

Chisum, Donald S., *Chisum on Patents* (Matthew Bender, 1978–)

The European Union Online, http://europa.eu

The United States Patent and Trademark Office, http://www.uspto.gov

The World Intellectual Property Organization, http://www.wipo.int

The World Trade Organization, http://www.wto.org